JULIAN GRENFELL

JULI

1900

NICHOLAS MOSLEY

JULIAN GRENFELL

His life and the times of his death
1888~1915

HOLT, RINEHART AND WINSTON
NEW YORK

Library of Congress Cataloging in Publication Data

Mosley, Nicholas, (date)
Julian Grenfell, his life and the times of his death,
1888-1915.

1. Grenfell, Julian Henry Francis, 1888-1915.
DA574.G8M6   1976   941.082'092'4 [B] 76-4720
ISBN 0-03-017596-8

Printed in the United States of America
10 9 8 7 6 5 4 3 2 1

To
Shaun, Ivo, Robert and Clare
Julian's great-nephews and great-niece

❧ CONTENTS ❧

The information for this book comes mainly from the Grenfell family papers, which, after the death of Julian's last surviving sister, were lent to me, for which I am grateful.

I am grateful to Sir Alan Lascelles for his help: also to the Marquess of Anglesey, for letting me quote from Julian's letters to Marjorie Manners.

The people mentioned in this book are called for the most part by the names by which they were known familiarly. More details are given in the index.

The illustrations come from the Grenfell family papers.

N.M.

❧ ILLUSTRATIONS ❧

Frontispiece
Julian, drawing by Violet Rutland, 1909

between pp 86 and 87
Ettie Grenfell
Katie Cowper and Ettie, 1880s
Willy Grenfell, 1880s
Ettie and Julian, 1888
Willy and Julian, 1890
The Grenfell family, 1900
Julian and Billy, 1897
Ettie, Julian and Billy, 1900
House party, 1890s
John Baring with Monica
Maurice Baring, Ettie, Evan Charteris and Julian
Bron Herbert, Winston Churchill and Henry Wilson
Monica and Archie Gordon
The Grenfell family, 1904
Julian and Ivo, 1901
Julian and Lord Kitchener, 1902

between pp 182 and 183
Taplow Court
Julian, Billy and Monica, 1903
Eton: editorial staff of *The Outsider*
Julian's illustration of the upbringing of Imogen
Julian, 1906
The family in 1905

PART I

Mother and Childhood
1888–1901

In this book I try not just to describe life in an aristocratic family before the First World War, but to suggest states of mind that drove many families to embrace such a war: because there is evidence that behind the machinations and confusions of politicians in 1914 people had been brought up to feel that war was desirable and so, simply, wanted it. The Grenfell family seemed to possess everything – intelligence, talent, charm, good looks, money; yet when war came they and their friends entered into it eagerly and most of the young men were killed as if death was their justification.

The hero of this book, Julian Grenfell, saw as a very young man some of the patterns that were driving his grandiose world to destruction; he tried to step aside – not just to rebel, but to form different attitudes within himself and towards society. He saw the society around him based on ideals of competitiveness and self-sacrifice; that these were contradictory, and led to fantasy and disaster. He thought there might be a form of individualism free from both competitiveness and guilt; that this might be truly sociable.

In the event, the values of the world in which he had been brought up defeated him: he accepted the war and even enjoyed it. He killed, and was soon killed himself. But there is the impression that he, more than others, knew what he was doing. One of the insights he had retained was that, by standing back, a fate that could not be prevented need not seem desolating. In a world which rejected patterns of liveliness there could still be a point, and some irony, in this old world's self-destruction.

N.M.

❦ ONE ❦

William Henry Grenfell courted Ethel Priscilla Fane in the summer of 1885. He was twenty-nine. She was just eighteen. Willy Grenfell had been Liberal MP for Salisbury in the early eighties and, briefly, private secretary to the Chancellor of the Exchequer, William Harcourt: but what he was chiefly renowned for was every kind of sport – he had played cricket for Harrow, rowed for Oxford, held the schools' record in the mile; had climbed the Matterhorn, fenced for Oxford, won the amateur punting championship, and had swum across the pool at the bottom of Niagara. He was famous not for being uniquely proficient at any one sport, but for being able to deal with any challenge that was presented to him.

Ettie Fane was a granddaughter of the 11th Earl of Westmorland on her father's side and of the 6th Earl Cowper on her mother's: she had been orphaned at the age of two – her mother Adine dying just after the birth of her second child, Johnnie, and her father, Julian Fane, First Secretary at the Embassy in Paris, surviving her for not much more than a year. Ettie and Johnnie were brought up by their grandmothers and by an aunt and an uncle from each side of the family; affection was lavished on them as orphans, but Johnnie died when Ettie was eight and her best-loved grandmother, Lady Cowper, died when she was thirteen; so Ettie grew up in the presence of death – she never wore anything but black, she wrote later, until she was five. One of her earliest memories was of 'sitting in a rather dark room in Portman Square and all the people around us were crying; but the fact that remains vivid in memory is that we were tasting chocolate for the first time'.

The Cowpers owned vast possessions and there was a lack of direct male heirs in the family: this meant that daughters and granddaughters were potential heiresses. Ettie grew up in a world of riches; also – through her uncle Francis Cowper who was Lord Lieutenant of Ireland and her uncle Henry Cowper who was a Liberal MP – into a world of politics and men of letters. While still in the schoolroom she became friends with Arthur Balfour, Alfred Lyttelton, John Morley. She grew accustomed to being charming to older men; she nearly became engaged, at seventeen, to a brother of her aunt-by-marriage Katie Cowper. When she started to go to parties in London she became the centre of a host of younger admirers. This was an age when girls, if rich and fashionable, were treated like goddesses.

Willy Grenfell did not come from a family quite so rich or so aristocratic as the Cowpers; but he was the owner of a large house with three thousand acres at Taplow in Buckinghamshire – his father having died when he was five – and he was thus an eligible suitor. He decided to try to marry Ettie: and his talent for getting what he wanted was matched against what seemed to be Ettie's feeling that there was safety in numbers.

> 24 Upper Brook St. W.
> 16/6/85

My dear Miss Fane,

I have, at last, succeeded in getting an invitation to the Caledonian Ball on Monday. Now, as you know, I am going for the sole purpose of meeting you, so I shall expect you to be very nice to me for once, and not snub me quite so severely as usual!

We had beautiful weather at Taplow, and a pleasant party but somehow I did not enjoy it much – I wonder if you can guess why?

Goodbye, my dear Miss Fane; it seems such a weary time until Monday – nearly a whole week. Why, oh why, are you not coming to Ascot?

> Goodbye –
> Yours ever
> Willy Grenfell

Ettie had two other suitors whom she took seriously; one was Lord Skelmersdale, an officer in the Guards; and another was referred to in letters to and from her girl-friends as Berger. Ettie had four great girl-friends at the time – Betty and Maggie Ponsonby, daughters of Sir Henry Ponsonby the private secretary to Queen Victoria; and Mabell and Alice Gore, daughters of the 5th Earl of Arran, and Ettie's cousins. These girls were jealous of Ettie's success with men – 'You know how envious and horrid I sometimes feel about you' (Alice); 'I am so often green-eyed

about you my darling though you know how I love you all the time; it is
so nice and comforting to feel how we all love one another' (Mabell). The
girls wrote to each other about their suitors and their flirtations. Betty
was on the side of Berger – 'You see, darling, you *do* feel just now that
feeling for Berger which is real L – – –, and it seems such a wicked pity
to stifle it'. Alice was sorry for Lord Skelmersdale – 'He was quite ill and
upset at the excitement of seeing you at Carlisle station; I think he must
have taken a Cockles Anti-Bilious Pill.' Maggie was in favour of as many
goings-on as possible – 'Do warn me Ettie who is uppermost in your
four-in-hand: I don't want to be surprised'. However Willy seemed to be
too serious a contender for such treatment. 'Just wait a little longer, a
month or two, don't accept Wilhelmji at once': for all this was 'like the
most exciting novel, except that one cares so much more when one's
greatest friend is the heroine' (Betty).

Ettie herself made notes for a journal describing her life at the age of
eighteen, while staying with her Aunt Katie Cowper in London and at
Panshanger, her house in Hertfordshire.

Panshanger 1885

Monday Nov 1st. A lot of people came. Lyttons, de Greys, da Vescis, Lord
Skelmersdale, Lord Wiltshire, Katie and Laurence Drummond. Sat by Laurence
who is just back from Africa. After, talked to Lord Wilty – chiefly politics.

Tuesday Nov 2nd. Bowls after tea. De Lana came. Wore new pink gown. De L
sang in evening. Lord Skel would talk politics to me all the time sitting on the
little sofa close to the piano.

Wed Nov 3rd. A pouring wet day. We played about all morn as they couldn't
shoot. Wore red gown. We played our banjos, and Lord Skel tried to teach me the
bones. They call him 'Bootles Baby' in his regiment. Afternoon, we drove to
Hertford; some on the cart, and I in pony carriage with Lord Wilty: and bought
masks, and put them on. Lord Skel took me into dinner. Evening, we danced a
little.

Thurs Nov 4th. They shot at Brocket and we went over to lunch. I sat next
Bootles. I like him rather. After tea we played bowls. Laurence took me in, and
said something which made me glow – though why? Afterwards we played Old
Maid, and Skel wrote me a list of books to read on my fan. They are of a sporting
nature. By the way, he isn't going tomorrow . . .

London 1886

Fri March 5th. Ball at Lady Suffield's. Skel there: only danced with him once,
the first. I think he went away. A *lovely* perfect ripping ball!

Tues March 9th. Dinner here and party after. Skel dined, but we sat at opposite ends of the table. Talked to me afterwards, but there were lots of other people – Willy G, Arthur Balfour, Horace West, etc. So perfect, seeing all one's friends again.

Tues March 16th. Auntie K in bed with cold. Dull dinner here but charming party after. *Berger!!!* Just back. Heart-leap! Sat on sofa in white room between W.G. and Skel, and went to supper with latter, but treated him badly, hardly speaking, having someone other side!

Mon May 31st. Came up v. early and sold all day at Bazaar at Knightsbridge Barracks. The first person I see there is Skel, looking rather well in his uniform! He was about all day, and made us go and have lunch and tea in Barracks – great fun!

Tues June 1st. Again all day at Bazaar. He is really so nice, and v. cross at not sitting next to me at lunch, having to take Princess Mary. Princess of Wales there too. (Mem. Queer *mental attack* in Alice's room!!! Surely it can't be – ?)

Wed June 2nd. All day at Bazaar. He perhaps not quite so nice, till afternoon when W.G. appeared which fanned him to fury, and then he never left me. Such fun! We did penny raffles – a great success; and then we all went round the stables. Alas, last day! (No, *it isn't!*)

Tues June 22nd. Niddry Lodge Bazaar. Mother of Moses! Christopher Columbus!

Whatever happened at the Niddry Lodge Bazaar (the account ends here: there is just one more entry, crossed out, for 22 June which can be deciphered as 'Oh Lord, it came off walking . . .') it was evident that in the battle for Ettie, Willy or Wilhelmji (also known as 'Bullfrog') was coming off better than Lord Skel or Bootles Baby (his family name was Bootle-Wilbraham). Nothing more was said of Berger. Towards the end of the summer Willy sent Ettie a present –

24 Upper Brook St. W.
Saturday

Dear Miss Fane,

I send you a small acknowledgement of my mounting debt. I am told these little watches go well. If not, they make capital things to throw at anybody . . .

Believe me,
yours sincerely,
W.H. Grenfell.

This was reported to Mabell, who was slightly older than Ettie, and who herself had recently married David, Earl of Airlie. Willy's gift called for serious comment –

August 4th 1886

My darling Puppy,

    . . . Do send me Bullfrog's letter. I must tell you that I did not quote your name or his, but I simply asked David that if a man did that, what it meant, and he said 'It means marriage': and that the decision only rested with the girl. So you see you must let me know if you have seen anything more of him . . .

    Poor Ettie you have had such a tiresome worrying time of it this season, but still think of what a success you have had and what heaps of men have wanted to marry you! . . .

    One thing darling, if you don't mean to marry Bullfrog do send him back the watch.

God bless you my own darling.
Your *very very* loving
Mabell

But Ettie did mean to marry Bullfrog: and Mabell had in fact advised her to do this in an earlier letter –

March 6th 1886

My *darling* Puppy,

    First and foremost about W.G. . . . . If you do not absolutely hate him I should marry him, I think; first everyone says he is an absolute angel; and he may be a little dull, but after all what a comfort it is to be cleverer than one's husband! Then he has got such awfully nice relatives, and he is altogether so sweet, and if you care for that sort of thing you could get him made a peer any time. My goodness me, you could do anything you liked! But if you make up your mind for him I should go at him hammer and tongs and not *look* at another man till you had finished him off – because when a man really wants to marry a girl he is so awfully particular. You don't mind my saying this do you? . . .

Ettie had not taken Mabel's advice then and she continued not to do so for a time; she kept Willy's watch, and let Lord Skelmersdale propose to her. But in December Willy was writing again –

Taplow Court
Taplow
Dec 7th 1866

Dear Miss Fane,

I meant to try to find out on Sunday whether you cared for me at all, but somehow I couldn't as I felt like an owl. But I hope you will not mind my writing to you now. If you do, could you get Lady Rose to drop me a line to Hothfield Place, Ashford, Kent, and I could come up on Sunday – and if you don't (– !) will you drop me a line to say the house is full or that they have all got scarlet fever or mumps.

Yours,
W.H. Grenfell.

This time Ettie, who was staying with her aunt Rose Weigal in London, did make up her mind: for two days later Willy was writing –

Hothfield Place
Ashford Kent
December 9th 1886

I cannot say how delighted I was to get your letter today – I can get out of this place tomorrow if I can see you – if you will send me a telegram 'most important, come at once' – there is a telegraph in the house – you can sign it Snooks or Tomkins or Dr Jeykel and I can make up something – though I am rather a bad hand at it. There are trains up at 10.30, 12.55, 1.5, 2.45, 5.35, and I should have to get a fly at Ashford about 3 miles off – they shoot tomorrow but there are plenty of guns without me – could I come to dinner I wonder?

What do you think your respected relatives will say? Mine will be delighted, and with good reason, and surprised, as I am by way of going to Cashmere and Thibet; but perhaps yours will think I am not nearly good enough, in which case they will be quite right. I wonder what you thought when you got my letter. I suppose you *laughed*.

Yours aff.
William G.

Willy and Ettie were married at St George's, Hanover Square, on 17 February 1887, and all their relatives seemed to be delighted. The Prince of Wales was one of the witnesses. The Grenfells went for their honeymoon to Cannes, Rome and Venice: for part of the time they travelled, adventurously, without any servants. They returned in the

spring to Taplow Court, Willy's tall red turreted house high above the
banks of the Thames. Willy's mother and unmarried sister had moved out,
and a suite of rooms had been newly furnished for Ettie.

During the summer Ettie became pregnant; the unborn baby came to
be known as Maximilian, or Maxima, or Max. In September Willy spent
some time in Scotland; Ettie went to stay with her favourite uncle
Henry Cowper. It had been Henry Cowper who had largely brought Ettie
up after the death of her grandmother. Now, after Ettie's marriage and
after the death shortly before of his favourite sister Dolly, he himself
was dying: he seemed to be wasting away, apparently of melancholy.
Willy wrote to Ettie 'I loathe being away from you' and 'I will come
down whenever you like'; but 'shooting sets one up for the winter and
keeps one fit'. He felt he would be in the way of the family gathering
round Uncle Henry. When he wrote to Ettie now he called her 'My Tiny
Catts' or 'My darling Cats-doodle-Flaps'; he signed himself 'Your ever
loving W'. Ettie wrote to him as 'Darling Gent' or 'My dearest Wicks'.
They corresponded almost daily. Uncle Henry died in November. The
day of his death, and the day of his funeral, Ettie kept the pages of her
engagement diary blank.

Ettie and Willy remained at Taplow throughout the winter, waiting
for the baby. Ettie's young-girl's world of dinner parties, teas, balls,
bazaars and amateur dramatics was temporarily suspended; but a mass
of people came to see her – Taplow was only half an hour by train from
London – and now, being married, she was more free to see people than
when she had had to be chaperoned. Her girl-friends kept up their
correspondence: Betty wrote 'How very nice your "manflash" must have
been after the "womanstodge" (by the way I hope "manflash" is not a
bad word is it?).' By 'manflash' she referred to married women being able
to be with men on their own.

Willy and Ettie became known as a very devoted and respectful
couple. This was rare in this age and in this society, even just after
marriage. Mabell Airlie had written to Ettie shortly after her own
marriage – 'Don't be afraid about David seeing your letters – *certainly not!*
He is well trained already and quite meek on the subject. I however see
all his, as he is too young to have letters which I don't know about.'
(She had added 'One's honeymoon is chiefly passed in feeling dreadfully
ill. I, who never feel ill as a rule, did nothing but faint . . . I was nearly
frightened to death and suffered *tortures!*') Women were expected to
exercise their domineering energies in the home: they had no entry into

business or into politics. And men, with their quiet sides, were often glad at home to be treated like babies; they reserved their masculine authority for the world outside. Everyone, with these transpositions, suffered or enjoyed some torture; and women's femininity went into fantasy, or on to their sons.

✲ TWO ✲

Julian Grenfell was born on 30 March 1888 at 4 St James's Square, his great-aunt Katie Cowper's house in London. Ettie had a six-hour labour, and was given chloroform at the end. Willy had had very bad toothache and had a wisdom tooth out the day before. Ettie and the baby flourished. She was allowed no visitors except Willy and her closest family for two weeks as was the custom; she was allowed downstairs after three weeks, and was taken for a drive in a carriage after four. She received the congratulations of her women friends at having produced a boy ('It's such a horrible disappointment when one opens one's second parcel and finds the same contents – that is, if it's a girl') though she and Willy had made it clear that they did not mind about this. The baby was christened Julian Henry Francis, but his parents and their friends continued to call him Max. Mabell Airlie wrote – 'I do not believe that Max is ugly but I think one always thinks one's own baby is monstrous'. Ettie and Willy thought him beautiful. The manager of the Taplow estate wrote – 'His dear little winsome face warms one's heart like golden sunshine'.

Julian had a wet nurse: it was not considered proper that ladies should feed their babies. He also had a nanny, Mrs Wake, who had been Ettie's nanny. Mrs Wake was, in Ettie's words, 'a north-country woman, small, with a very fine face and pink and white colouring and silver hair'. The world of the nursery was established on the second floor at Taplow above the main bedrooms on the first floor and below the servants' bedrooms at the top of the house. There were a housekeeper and a cook and six maids at Taplow, in addition to the butler and footman and valet and various menservants connected with the horses and carriages and garden.

Ettie and Willy went away to America in the summer of 1888 – he to shoot big game in the Rockies, and she to travel across the country sightseeing with friends and to join him on the west coast in October. Willy stopped off at the scene of his old triumph at Niagara; there he found that people would not believe he had swum across the bottom of the falls, so he did it again. He wrote to Ettie – 'it was an awful day and blowing half a gale which made it worse for swimming but I had to do it . . . I hope you will not think me a beast for doing it, but I don't call it *risky* really'. His shooting trip ran into difficulties and he was late in meeting her at Vancouver. Ettie wrote – 'My darling Gent, I am rather in despair at your being so much longer than you thought, but I believe you would have come out sooner if you could. You were *very* good about writing – I have had nine letters from you – I only hope you have had *real* good sport and have enjoyed yourself'.

From Taplow, Ettie and Willy were kept informed by Willy's mother about Julian's progress with his wet nurse and with Mrs Wake:

I am glad that Julian has at last consented to take his bottle, as I am sure that such a vigorous child wanted a little more than what Mrs B could give. He seemed determined for a time not to take any other form of nourishment, but Dr Moore said it must be fought out, the sooner the better, and now Mrs Wake has triumphed, and says he seems to like it. He is a little person with a very strong will of his own!

After Ettie's return in the winter of 1888 she began to keep a record of Julian's sayings and doings: this turned into the Children's Journal which she kept about all her children:

May 1st 1889: Julian said 'Go up' – his first two words together.
June 9th: If anything goes wrong he says 'Oh dear dear dear!' Sometimes when he sees strangers he makes such faces that Nannie has to tell them his mother taught him.
August 17th: There was a garden party here yesterday and a lot of children. We had performing dogs and monkeys for them, and Max enjoyed it all hugely. He insisted on running into the arena and trying to join in the performance, and when restrained by Nannie Wake he stood on a table stamping and clapping his hands and shouting with joy.
Dec 31st: When Nannie was scolding him he looked up at her and said 'Poor little fellow.'
Jan 17th 1890: He was much excited over a little mouse that got into the nursery today: he ran after it with a shovel saying 'Determined to kill a mouse. Hammer it with a hammer!'

Ettie became pregnant again in the summer of 1889. She noted that Julian became unhappy.

He is cutting his two-year-old teeth which makes him rather sad and unsociable: he says – 'Don't like people – 'ate cumpany'. When Mrs Boyle came to see him and asked him what he was called he said 'A peeg, a wretch!'. When old Mr Clifford came he would only say in a clear little voice – 'Like him to go away: like to see him *start!*' When we ask him if he is a good boy he says 'No, a dirty disagreeable fellow!'. The only punishments we can think of for Max when he is in a 'passion' he now likes better than anything – he is always saying 'Go in a dark room!' 'Put me on the chimney-beast!'. The other day when we asked him what he was doing he said 'Making an awful filthy mess.' When I said 'Are you little Max?' he said 'I'm Julian Grenfell.'

A second son was born on 29 March 1890 and was christened Gerald William. When Julian saw him, Ettie recorded, he said 'A little live thing, what a queer little thing, call him Billy.' When Billy was weaned from his wet nurse and joined Julian in the nursery Julian was again sad: he bit Nanny's finger in one of his 'passons' and when told not to do it again he said 'No, I've done biting Nanny'. Ettie took him away to Swanage to be on her own with him for a few days and she slept in the same room and he got better. He said 'Don't you think Dada's such a nice woman?'

Billy grew quickly so that he was soon almost as big as Julian; once, after hearing a painter talk about shortening a portrait of his mother, Julian said 'I will take an inch and a half off that boy'. Ettie recorded that Billy was Nanny Wake's favourite child; Julian was too independent. One day before Julian could even speak Ettie found him sitting on the floor with Nanny Wake standing over him and she was saying 'That child has broken his word to me, he gave me his solemn promise that he would go to bed if he had a biscuit.' Ettie recorded of Nanny Wake 'there can never have been a character of greater integrity and truth'.

Julian continued to dislike his mother's· friends. He said 'I think company is beastible'. Also – 'I should not like to be king, because then I should be dead and should not have myself'. When his mother said to him 'Be good and be my Julian Grenfell' he said 'No, I won't lend myself to you'.

The friends of his mother whom Julian found so unpleasant were part of the most scintillating group in the country; this was the beginning of the circles of friends known as the 'Souls' – men and women for the most part in their twenties and early thirties but the men already prominent in public life and the women renowned for intelligence as well as beauty. These friends had been nick-named by Lord Charles Beresford at a dinner party in 1888 – 'You all sit and talk about each other's souls, I shall call you the Souls' – a moderate joke, as Ettie remarked, and one which was in any case misleading; because it suggested seriousness and intensity whereas what the Souls wanted to be above everything was witty. Ettie and Willy were original members of the Souls: others were people whose names crop up throughout this book – Arthur Balfour, George Curzon, George Wyndham, Evan Charteris, Margot Tennant, Hugo and Mary Elcho, Tommy and Charty Ribblesdale. There were also some Souls of an older generation such as Lord and Lady Cowper and Lord and Lady Pembroke who entertained the young in their large country houses. The men were hardworking, usually in politics; Arthur Balfour was Irish Secretary in 1891, George Wyndham was his private secretary, George Curzon was Under Secretary of State for India. The women were illustrious in their homes around which the men fluttered like moths. Ettie was only in her early twenties but she already shone in this world: she had a house, and could entertain in it. Willy was appreciated for his kindliness and goodness. The Souls met at dinners and parties in London; but their main centres of activity were country house weekends. Here they assembled and talked – mainly about ideas, books, personalities. Lord Pembroke wrote 'There is a good deal of personal talk in our set but it is hard to avoid: the proper study of mankind is man and the improper of woman'. They did not refer to themselves as the Souls but sometimes as 'the gang': and a true criticism of them might be, as Ettie remarked, 'an extreme lightness of touch'. Their speciality was the games they played in the evenings – pencil-and-paper games, acting games, guessing games – Literary Consequences, Acrostics, Telegrams; Clumps, Charades, Dumb-crambo; Qualities, Analogies. The point of these games was to show off not just erudition but, as always, wit. There were card games for those not quite up to all this – Poker, Piquet, Vingt-et-un, Whist: with music and singing for the more serious. And in the afternoons – before the days of golf and tennis – there were Rounders and Prisoner's Base.

Another game of the Souls was flirtation. Ettie was young and clever and she had an air of warmth and yet of untouchability that had been captivating men since she was fifteen. She was also becoming known as one of the most sought-after hostesses in the country. In the flirtation game, men saw themselves as counters on Ettie's board of snakes-and-ladders:

Carlton Club
Pall Mall S.W.
Monday

My dear Ettie,

Glad you will have me and that I have not been voted too risqué, too licentious or too inveterate a bore.

Off to Paris tomorrow, Ettie, so shall not see you again yet awhile.

Keep me in Class II even though I be low down in that proud category; and believe that few hearts beat with fonder affection for Ettie

old Ettie

incomparable Ettie

than the dilapidated organ of her affectionate

George C.

Ettie accepted this picture of herself as holding her admirers in categories. George Curzon, by his own account, soon graduated to Class I; but as he was usually off on some trip abroad he did not stay there long. 'Duty, desire to learn, contempt for idleness and a mission for *The Times* drive me from England ... In my absence I shall fall from Ettie's Class I to Class IV ... but Ettie's image will grace the bivouac of the distant traveller as he tosses in Persian hovels and plods on jaded steeds over Persian wilds ...' Other admirers were content to elaborate on their lowly status: enjoyment, as with many keen games-players, seemed to derive less from winning than from the game itself. Hugo Elcho was the husband of one of Ettie's best friends, Mary –

Auchnashellach
Ross-shire
August 23rd

My dear Mrs Willy,

Heaven knows why I am sitting down (an operation which through an un-accustomed indulgence in the art of deerstalking has in itself become most difficult) to write to you, since judged from the standpoint of the probable appreciation of my efforts there is none less worthy of them. This painful fact, obvious as you have made it to me, in no wise deters me; it only makes me moralise on my perversity in preferring to be trampled on by you to being caressed by anyone else ...

I have now wrapped myself up in my cloak of humility, and abandoning all fond hopes of figuring prominently in your alphabet, am sadly resigned to regarding you as more than my Alpha and myself as less than your Omega ...

The seriousness (or lack of it) of such letters could be judged by the style: but the pattern was the same – whether from Hugo Elcho, who spent much of his life writing such letters and following them up; or from George Curzon, who from his journey around Persia produced a scholarly book; or from more serious adorers, whose attentions will be described later. It was the men who played the parts of humble and unworthy petitioners, and the women who assumed the status of cornucopias from whom all bounties either did, or did not, come. Of those who were steady in Ettie's Class I at this time – Arthur Balfour, George Wyndham, Evan Charteris (Ettie kept a list, by their initials, of those in Class I, in her engagement diaries every year) – it was only Arthur Balfour, the doyen of the Souls, who did not conform to this pattern. This was perhaps because he himself cultivated an almost feminine air of aloofness and untouchability. For the rest – whether frivolous, ecstatic, or seriously smitten – it seemed to be the custom for men to appear as hungry children, to gain the favours of life-giving mothers.

Reading through the lists of Ettie's social engagements during these years it is difficult to believe that she had any time for her real children at all: but she did, and as well as becoming renowned as an accomplished hostess, a bewitching siren, and a dutiful wife, she gained the reputation of a loved and loving mother. A fashionable mother in the 1890s was expected to spend only specific times with her children: some mothers spent more time and some less. Ettie spent much more than most – when she was at Taplow she went out with the children in the afternoons and she played and read to them in the evenings – but she was often away, and perhaps her very closeness to the children while at home gave her partings from them an extra painfulness. And fashionable mothers in any case saw only the clean and pretty side of their children; they handed over the messes and the rages to professionals. And it was accepted professionally that mess and rage were met by punishment – children when in 'passons' were put in dark rooms or set on chimney-pieces – and it was the test of a good family just whether such punishments were inflicted and suffered cheerfully. For together with the parents who came and went, and the separation of prettiness from dirt, there was this insistence on cheerfulness – cheerfulness as something that could be achieved and held by will – and if it could not, then this was reprehensible. Children had not only to be good but to publicize themselves as good. Even before Julian could write, Nanny Wake was holding and guiding his hand in writing letters to Ettie – 'I am quite well and such a good little boy, I love you and my dear Dad so much, I have only been in one passion it was a very short one. All my eczema is gone . . .' And to this sort of thing Nanny Wake would add in her own hand – 'I don't know if you can make out his little letter, but he has not the patience to hold the pencil for long'. This was when Ettie and Willy were away visiting their friends. And then there would be a scrawl at the bottom of a letter as if from Julian again – 'I do want you and my own dear Dada to come back to your little son, Julian Grenfell'.

❧ THREE ❧

In 1891 there was some crisis in Ettie's life: she moved for a time beyond the boundaries of her exclusive and somewhat intellectual world and was taken up by a more flashy crowd, the racing set, people who paraded around Newmarket or surrounded the Prince of Wales. This was a time when fashionable society moved strictly according to seasons: people spent the winter in the country hunting and shooting, in the spring they came to London for the Season of parties and balls until August; in the autumn they migrated to Scotland to prey again on other animal species or play golf. Even the politicians could fit in to some extent with these seasons, since Parliament usually got through its work in the early part of the year and did not sit between August and December. The height of the London Season was in June and July; it was then, in 1891, that Ettie expanded.

She went to Ascot and Newmarket with Lady Randolph Churchill ('great rows going on; lost my money but enjoyed the day very much!'); was driven round the town by Lord Londonderry in his coach ('the greatest fun; terrific bear-fight; Lord L in my bed!'); was pursued by young Guards officers to London, and then to Taplow from the barracks at Windsor. (There was a joke – that if you hired a horse at Windsor, it automatically turned its head towards Taplow.) She became involved in some more-or-less serious affairs – young Guards officers and men at Newmarket did not quite play the flirtation game within the same literary conventions of the Souls. Amongst her more ardent admirers were Charles Edward 'Tops' Hartopp, to whom Ettie gave the present of a pin and whom his friends advised to leave the country for a while; Lord Dunraven, who tried to get her on his yacht at Cowes and when he failed went to Carlsbad to take the cure; Charles Lister Kaye, who haunted the gardens in front of Ettie's aunt's house in St James's Square to see who went in and out of the front door. With all these the patterns Ettie had established round herself were repeated: 'Tops' Hartopp wrote – 'I have been so weak, I do like you so much, and fear that my own folly has lost a friend that cannot be replaced'; Lord Dunraven lamented from Carlsbad, 'Oh dear Mrs Grenfell, is not this shocking, and do you suffer from remorse? I fear not, but you ought . . . you will understand the abomination of desolation in which I am existing'; and Charles Lister Kaye 'wondered whether the agony of mind which was rending my soul in twain was gracefully depicted on the flagstones outside where I said Goodbye with a frozen smile on my face and anger, rage, jealousy, fury tearing at my mental vitals . . .'. There is evidence that Ettie herself was emotionally involved with at least one – probably Hartopp – since her friend Betty wrote to her 'Darling, I think you have been so good and brave about it, and are trying so hard to get over it'. But it was the glamour and the excitement that Ettie loved: she referred to 1891 as her 'golden year' and kept a record of references to herself in the press and personal compliments paid to her. 'Ettie has been the loveliest lady wherever she has been this year' (Lady Granby). She made new friends in the political and literary worlds of the Souls: Herbert Asquith became an admirer – 'wherever you appeared on the horizon you were surrounded by such a dense and imposing escort that I had not the courage to approach you' – but he soon did, for it was his appearance that drove Charles Lister Kaye to such jealous transports in St James's Square. She was taken up by Oscar Wilde:

> 16 Tite Street
> Chelsea S.W.
> May 23rd 1891

Dear Mrs Grenfell,

I am afraid that by June 3rd poor Hedda will have given up looking for scarlet sensations in a drab-coloured existence. I went there on Thursday night and the house was dreary – the pit full of sad vegetarians and the stalls occupied by men in mackintoshes and women in knitted shawls of red wool. So at least it seemed to me. However we might go to L'Enfant Prodigue or The Dancing Girl – but is it necessary to go anywhere? Why not a little dinner? you, Lady Elcho, Arthur Balfour and myself. It would be entrancing and delightful. But of course, I would go anywhere with pleasure, and June 3rd is set aside for a delightful evening.

How nice of you to ask us to Taplow. I look forward to a charming Sunday.

> Believe
> very truly yours
> Oscar Wilde

Oscar Wilde came to Taplow during two weekends that summer; and when _A House of Pomegranates_ was published later in the year he dedicated his story of the Infanta to Ettie.

Ettie called forth passionate admiration not only from men but from women; or, as Betty Ponsonby put it – 'What a quantity of both flash and stodge are devoted to you!' The attentions of the stodge seemed sometimes as extravagant as those of the flash – 'You won me from the first; I was afraid to let you see how much!'; 'I sometimes think in heaven everyone must be like you!' Ettie's response was the same – gratitude, gracious attention, and then for the most part withdrawal; leaving the adorer inflamed and unassuaged. She became known as someone who indeed caused trouble: but again, this did not cool affection. Lord Pembroke wrote – 'Oh you wicked little lady! I found you out! Can't I see you gravely inciting poor Lady Randolph at Newmarket to make play with me in order to pay Nellie out for the way she treated you about A.J.B. and then assuring me that Dusky Jane's feelings were most friendly! . . .'. And A. J. Balfour – 'My dear Mrs Ettie, You certainly are the most untrustworthy of mortals, the slipperiest, the least to be depended upon! All the same your letter gave me so much pleasure that I was almost tempted for one short moment to forgive you your treachery . . . I do forgive _you_'. Ettie's special accomplishment seemed to be the making of conquests wtihout making enemies. How she did this, and its consequences, is one of the themes of this book.

She was not a great beauty according to the spectacular conventions of the time: yet in addition to her charm and cleverness there was something about her physical presence – the way she walked, stood, cast down her eyes – that was at once commanding and called forth the desire to protect her. She had a tiny waist, a straight back, soft hair; her eyes were mysteriously lidded. Her admirers tried to put this into words – 'You remind me of one of Fra Angelico's dancing angels' (Constance Wenlock); 'Ettie riding on top of her wave of spirituelle and graceful pre-eminence; always gentle, always thoughtful of others, always well equipped for any call either of brain or heart; always incomparably dressed and an epicure's feast for the eye' (George Curzon). There was the courteous absorption with which she received confidences and gave sympathy; the way she would offer advice or gently intervene in the troubles of her friends. She and they would praise each other extravagantly – 'My blessed sweet, what can I say to you? you make me cover my face with my hands and thank God I have such a friend!' (Margot Tennant). Sometimes they passed the same compliment round and round – 'It really is a privilege to have lived in the same century with you' (Edgar D'Abernon); 'I am thankful to have lived in the Mary Elcho epoch' (Ettie). There was her way of flattering people with the very praises that they were about to sing of her: 'You say it must make me happy to be able to give so much happiness; but you must know that is exactly what everyone says about you'. But above all there was her ability to seem everything to any one person at a time; and then suddenly, in the nature of time, not to be there any more – which is the technique by which the images of goddesses are implanted in the minds of children.

It was fashionable in 1891 for a young married woman to have lovers: what is ambiguous was just what this word implied. To unmarried girls even the word was taboo – in 1886 Betty was referring to Ettie's 'l----s' and even after marriage another name was preferred; Betty now spoke of a 'culte' or a 'spangle'. And even when the word was used, a 'lover' was someone who professed his devotion in words and demonstrated it in his attitudes: the word did not refer to sexuality. There were some groups, such as those around the Prince of Wales, in which the sexual relations of lovers were taken for granted – bedrooms were arranged in country houses with this in mind – but there were equally those families in which they were not. In neither case was the matter of sexuality much mentioned; so it is difficult, now, to assess exactly what went on; though guesses can be made from the context.

Before the end of 1891 it seems unlikely that Ettie had sexual lovers; she was too happy in being loved by crowds, in being carried adored from scene to scene, in having her refuge perhaps in Willy. And she would have learned that adoration is won not so much by favours granted, as by what is left to brew in the imagination. But towards the end of 1891 it is likely that one of her involvements became briefly sexual; this is implied both in her diary and in the gentle warnings of her friends. As well as referring to her 'golden year' she wrote that she was 'so tired, and choked with Hell's delights'. The anxiety of her friends seemed to be stirred by her own bad conscience:

You make me anxious. Why do you seem unhappy? So much as this I am safe to assume – you feel the difficulty of being a belle and not being spoiled. I doubt if I ever knew one who was not . . .

(Oliver Wendell Holmes)

Were you tired at the end of the season? Your success has been so brilliant that all nice ambitious women who are young look to your career to imitate it . . . It is rather a serious thing to be made a model of . . .

(Alfred Lyttelton)

God bless you you delightful girl. Don't drive too big a team. It will knock your hands (and their mouths) about in the long run: and always keep a stall in a subsidiary but comfortable stable for your loving G.

(George Curzon)

At the end of 1891 Willy took Ettie off to India, perhaps to get her away from London and Newmarket; but still without appearing to think there was much cause for alarm. He went off to shoot tigers and elephants and Ettie stayed at the Governor's house in Madras. There she continued to touch the hearts of those who came in contact with her. The young ADCs fell in love (George Curzon wrote – 'You are probably pursuing some wild animal or rather Willy is and someone is pursuing you') and the Governor's wife, Constance Wenlock, loved her too. ('You were such a dream of freshness and youthful beauty as had never been seen in Madras.') But Ettie was trying now to get over 'hell's delights'; to build an image that would be more god-like. Constance Wenlock wrote:

I am so enjoying Ettie Grenfell's visit . . . She seems too wonderful and delicious with her marvellous power of diffusing mirth and making everybody happy. She has such spirits and such prodigious intention of pleasing, and all the time she is exquisitely 'grande dame' . . . She really is the most perfect type of womanhood that has been evolved out of modern times. She combines all charms, ancient and modern. I doubt if she could have existed precisely as she is 30 years ago, when it was distinctly not allowed as the metier of a woman to be charming after marriage. Still, she owes very little of her perfection to modern emancipation – freedom from restraint in intercourse with men – and nearly all of it to merits that have always been recognized and appreciated in all ages.

While Ettie and Willy were away they were kept in touch with the children as before by letters to and from Nanny Wake. Willy wrote to the boys – 'It is great fun seeing the elephants crashing through the jungle; they look very big and it is a fine thing to see them fighting; one of them would have squashed your dear dad the other day but he had a big gun which went bang and knocked it over or rather both of them over'. And while Ettie was knocking over the ADCs (George Curzon

wrote 'Poor fellows, I am sorry for them: inflammable material at any
time, and in the East trembling on the verge of perpetual combustion')
Nanny Wake wrote of the progress of Julian and Billy. They were staying
with Katie and Francis Cowper at Panshanger:

Dec 10th 1891. The day you left us the little Julian said to me Nanna, don't
you think it is unkind of my Dada and Mama to go and leave us for so long? They
soon forgot again . . .
We went on the Hertford road, the dogs with us, and Julian delighted to have
leave from her ladyship to use a whip to them if they ever barked too much. She
gave him the whip which has to be left at the bottom of the stairs when we come
in so that he may not lash Billy.
      Dec 17th. Dear little Julian is really a changed child, he never cries about any-
thing and they both sleep so well . . . Lady Cowper is so good and dear and kind,
she has them down every evening . . . Julian could not play the organ as his legs
were not long enough and I said – Did they laugh at you? and he said – No no, I
laughed at them . . .
One day I told Julian to do something and he took no notice so I said Do you hear
Sir what I say? and he turned his little head on one side and said Oh yes, I heard,
but I was thinking of something else.
I got your portrait out and Julian looked at it for some time and at last he said
'Dear Mama, make her speak . . .'
One day he looked in the glass and said What a very disagreeable face I have got
. . . I told him I was going to write to you today and would tell you he was still
unkind to Billy, and he said – Oh don't tell them that it will make them so
comfortable. He meant uncomfortable . . .
Billy is so fond of Julian, and wants to do everything his brother does . . . He
asked Julian the other day to dance and sing to him and Julian said No, Billy, my
dancing and singing days are over. I said to Ada one day Oh, we must have his hair
cut; and his face got so red he left off his play, and said No no, don't cut my hair
or my strength will go out of me . . .
One day Billy said to him Don't hurt me Max, and he said Hurt you, no, I
should think not, it would go to my back to hurt you . . .
This morning I was talking to Master Julian about being good, and he put out his
little finger and said – Well you see, Nanna, whenever I am very good great big
tears run down my cheeks, and that is why I am not always good.

❧ FOUR ❧

The patterns that Ettie set up with her admirers seemed to provide some solace for them – it is striking how many of her male correspondents at this time wrote that they were depressed – so that they were satisfied for a while and even ecstatic; but they then woke to the impression that their provider had abandoned them. This feeling of loss was to some extent inevitable in the comings-and-goings of social life: but when to do with Ettie there seemed to be a panic about it, and it was this that was like the relationship between a mother and a child. Children, especially babies, are desolate when their mother disappears because she is all the world to them. And they feel it is their fault, because to feel otherwise would be to risk the whole framework of their lives – it is easier to feel guilt than non-existence. So, in their minds at least, lovers humble themselves in front of a mother who can do no wrong to gain her return to them. There was this pattern around Ettie and all her grown-up lovers; there was also something of it with her children. But a real child is in a real relationship with its mother – not just in the mind – and there is the chance for it to grow up and to distinguish between reality and fantasy. But with grown-ups, what are operative in the parts of them that are still children are old fantasies and terrors and these do not easily change.

Ettie's own needs in these relationships were partly primitive: as a child she had suffered repeatedly from the loss of loved ones; for her there might be safety in numbers. But when grown up, this attitude led to remorse. She wrote of her guilt in 1891 to Betty Ponsonby who replied 'You who are so beautifully, sweetly sanely well ought never to have the fin-de-siècle remords and horrors – what Maggie calls "morbidezza".' Ettie also talked to an old childhood friend, Douglas Compton, the brother of her aunt Katie Cowper and of Alwyne Compton to whom at seventeen she had almost been engaged. But Douglas Compton too was in love with her, and had remorse. He wrote – 'I had a severe attack of the morals last night; my talk with you made me feel what brutes men are – myself especially. You have always influenced me on the right side of duty and right. I suppose if I had seen a great deal of you I might have become upright and good, a slave to duty'. But with duty – 'alas, people often become dull at the same time; and who can say whether in that case I should have made more happiness in the world for myself and other people or not?' He concluded – 'I suppose, after all, happiness is the final object'.

Ettie used her correspondence with Douglas Compton as a sounding board for her own doubts and convictions. She had been brought up to honour truth, fidelity, duty; but she also had needs, passions, hungers. The year 1891 had exhausted her; duty could seem desirable but needs and panics went on. Ettie was a person of great energy and appetite, and in the 1890s there were not many satisfactions available to women. In the winter of 1891–2 she seems to have come to some decision; if the love-games of the social world were hellish, there might yet be some private behaviour by which needs might not remain unsatisfied.

Ettie came back to England in the summer of 1892 and she seemed to look round for a lover. She did not want to appear to be too unfaithful to Willy; but Willy was a conventional man, and lovers were conventionally acceptable if not too much about them was known. Husbands were away a lot of the time; and lovers, if fantastical, were anyway less to do with love than with security and power. But it was characteristic of Ettie that she took on not one lover but three. At the end of 1891 she copied into her diary a quotation from an 'Indian Pilgrim's song' – 'Oh woman, lock up thine heart three times; and when he who holds the key shall have opened it, say thou to him – "Mine heart is locked up six times"; so shall thou have and retain power'.

George Wyndham was four years older than Ettie; he was the brother of Mary Elcho and the brother-in-law of Hugo; he had been a Guards officer when young, had fought briefly in Egypt in 1885, had left the army and had entered Parliament as Conservative member for Dover and had become private secretary to Arthur Balfour, the Irish Secretary. He had married a few weeks before Ettie in 1887, and lived for the most part in Cheshire with his wife and son and step-children. He came to London for the Season, and for Parliamentary business. He had been a member of the Souls from the beginning; he was a noted sportsman, and very good looking. He was also a poet.

Saighton Grange
Chester
September 25th 1892

Dear Lady,

I dreamt of you last night. We are told that our savage ancestors built up from their dreams a belief in ghosts; and from their belief in ghosts a religion and a complete philosophy of life. I throw back to primitive man more perhaps than most people and retain enough of his reverence for all mental experience, whether waking or sleeping, to welcome in all seriousness any dear ghost who visits me in sleep. So I thank you for coming and for playing the same pleasant part in the inextricable confusion of a long and weary nightmare full of travel and tiresome persons as you have already filled in the still longer and wearier experience we have to put up with by daylight . . .

In my life, since I knew you, you have always appeared on the scene and said something memorable at every important emotional crisis. You take no part in the crisis and as yet your connection with the plot is by no means clear. Still your persistent reappearance on all these occasions makes me sometimes hope that I guess the author's intention; that you are the mysterious character who for no obvious cause haunts Vols I and II in order to seize on the reins of the story and direct its course to the happy consummation of Vol. III. If you are to do this (and please don't tell me you are to drop out of the tale like the interesting stranger at the beginning of 'An African Farm') it is necessary you should know where the scene will be laid. During the next few pages it will shift from Saighton to Wynyard on Oct 17, to Panshanger on Nov 28, and to Welbeck on Dec 19. I am not much of a novel reader, but unless I know nothing of construction, or the story is to be insufferably dull, the characters ought to be brought together again at least at Panshanger in order that the action may be a little further developed . . .

From George Wyndham, Ettie learned how, if one wants to succeed both with fantasies and with facts, it is necessary to do so in style: the fantasies have to be embodied; the facts dressed. George Wyndham's conceits had a practical value: by pretending that he and Ettie were characters in a novel, they could both write to each other in an extravagant way that might otherwise be dangerous and they could make practical arrangements where to meet – at Wynyard or Panshanger or Welbeck. For a time it was George Wyndham who seemed to be in control of the story; it was he who was writing it and was hard to pin down as a character. But this was before Ettie had had time to establish her own patterns of power.

Saighton Grange
Chester
Nov 7th 1892

Dear Lady,

I rarely write unless I have something to say and time to say it. Both conditions are unhappily hardly ever fulfilled; or at any rate, to excuse my idleness I like to think so . . .

This is only to thank you again and again for a dear delightful letter and for the little signal of friendship you sent fluttering from Wynyard a week ago. Yes, you have often been in my thoughts, and the projected vision of your company beacons me across the winds and waves of political controversy. I have been nearly immersed in an article and a speech or two and the arrangements for an organised visit to Dover . . . Rational communication is in these circumstances out of the question . . . I am going to ask you to write to me all the same. Will you? As I have absolutely no right to expect this I hope you will accord it: for with the kindness of women, as with the 'Garter', there is, thank God, no 'nonsense about merit' . . .

They did meet at Panshanger on 28 November, and there something happened more or less than fantasy for a year later George Wyndham was writing 'Such an anniversary!!!! I shall not tell you what of!' At the time, Ettie recorded in her diary 'George W read to me in drawing room after tea'. He was soon sending her poetry:

House of Commons
Jan 31 1893

Dearest Primavera, here is the little thaw-song of which I spoke last night.

> Though yesterday I knew
>   That spring should come
> It did not then seem true:
>   The woods were dumb;
> The fields were blind with snow.
>   I knew, and did not know.
>   My soul was numb . . .
>
> Today, look up on high.
>   The heavens are drowned!

> Blue oceans flood the sky,
>   Green lakes the ground!
> As by a miracle
> Clear springs of colour well
>   Up all around. . . .

and so on, for ten verses.

But then Ettie became ill with 'flu and could not see him. And perhaps with George Wyndham now committed, she felt safe to stay aloof.

> House of Commons
> Monday 20.3.93

Dear Mrs Grenfell,

I wrote you a little line today in doubt whether you were ill or not. Someone said you were, others had not heard of it. I really did feel anxious, all the more since at Dudley House I thought you seemed stricken through with a venomous chill . . .

I should not have ventured to write had you not reminded me of the novel we tried to imagine. Do let us continue our collaboration! Your few words recall the incidents we discussed so vividly to my mind that I feel as if I had actually lived through them all myself. I am *so* sorry we left off at a sad division. I suppose with the selfish sympathy of my sex it is the man whom I pity most. The woman would of course know, as you all do, that she is and must still be over and above everything. But think of the poor man! not knowing what had happened! suddenly cut off from all solace of companionship and all ease of service to the woman he adores! I wonder whether it is artistic to make him quite broken hearted and miserable, feeling he had better go away and attend to other duties, say in the country, but still utterly unable to leave the neighbourhood of the woman he loves though he cannot see her. That seems a fine situation, but one which to my mind should not be prolonged. Can you invent any alternative? Do you think he ought forsaking all else to obey the dictates of his heart and pass her door three times a day throwing his whole soul into prayer and desire for her recovery? I believe indeed that would be more natural. How I wish I could see her to talk about the book!

George Wyndham himself became ill: the Parliamentary session of 1893 was a particularly arduous one – men fought with fists in the House of Commons over Gladstone's Irish Home Rule Bill – George Wyndham 'shambled through a speech on Uganda' and lamented the 'heavy price he had to pay' for being successful in a ballot to allow him to introduce a

private member's bill. He retired to bed and dreamed of the 'flower-like
lady passing among the flowers and under the arcades of budding boughs –
Primavera in very truth'. His wife Sibell came up to London: he asked
Ettie to write to him in a stricter code, telling her a story of two lovers for
whom 'Don't forget the guinea-pig' had stood for 'My dearest love how I
long to see you!' He added – 'I am thinking of advertising for some
animal that lives to a great age, say an elephant'.

Ettie recovered from 'flu and George Wyndham returned to the House
of Commons but still she would not see him; he wrote:

I try to reconcile myself to your new dispensation by remembering that my
health and high spirits were the things you found least unworthy of me. And
now being abject in mind and body I ought to welcome the chance you give me
of staying away and not disclosing to your critical eye the great falling-off in all
that ever recommended me to your kindness. But lying awake last night I could
think of nothing but the ghastly waste of life: ours was so fair a Friendship; and
yet it seems I am never to see you . . . I am telegraphing a humble request that
you will write to me. If you can find a kind word to say *please* say it. I am too
dispirited to care for speaking in this debate. If I can get out I will call on you
at 11 o'clock tomorrow morning.

For a while Ettie did see him again; he had been abject, and enthralment
could be maintained by a dazzling re-appearance like the sun –

Clouds
Salisbury
May 8th 1893

Dear 'April'

For so I must be allowed to call you – April you have been and must ever be!
An April of sunshine and no rain; of laughter and no tears; all radiant and
dazzling blossoms robbed from May. Please remember always to be April,
and to refuse to all anything but flowers; for fruits are born of sorrow and lost
delight . . .

And now let me say that I hope, perhaps, to see you between 3.30 and 4.30:
perhaps after dinner in the House. Either will be a fairer flower than I have
deserved . . .

– but after this the sun went in again, as is apt to happen in April –

Dear but invisible and bewildering Lady, what crime have I committed?
Murder itself could not deserve such punishment. I had so counted on seeing
you for a min. on the river or at the Springs. But no, you would not appear.

Are you angry because then I dared at last in desperation to trespass on your lawn in the hope of finding you absorbed in Tennis? Was that very wrong? Else why do you refuse me one little line in answer to my letter? I did most humbly beg for a word if you could not see me yesterday.

I planned the whole of this Whitsuntide to be free yesterday and suppose the manner in which I spent my day walking and rowing past your house was supremely ridiculous. Yet why should I not wish to see you before settling down to months of Home Rule? And though ridiculous I am not at all ashamed of my day. I travelled down early on various pretexts and listened to the singing of 'Holy Holy Holy' in Church and waited in the hope of catching a glimpse; but was unfortunate, or perhaps you were not there? Then went round and stalked the gate into Taplow, but did not see you return. In the afternoon rowed from the Springs past your landing stage (1) in the Canadian canoe (2) in the English canoe (3) in a skiff. I hoped the change of craft would make the operation less conspicuous! But the waterman, I fear, has no illusions and quite understood my fervour for aquatics. He even buoyed up my courage by telling me at about 5 that Mr Grenfell was coming directly. At 6.30 I had the hardihood to land and walk up to your tennis courts: of course, to see the tennis. But they were quite deserted, and I realised that my day was done and all my planning and scheming to reach the river utterly frustrated.

But why no letter? Why? Are you angry with me?

Yours ever

G. W.

There was another brief respite when 'suddenly in place of the image, within the frame of our love, is the face, the real face, real eyes and hair, the living voice speaking to our ears that have been mocked with echoes; and the nature of the joy is *Rest*, Infinite Relief . . .' but then, a fortnight later, Ettie went to help Willy in his constituency in Hereford and George Wyndham went to a dinner party given by Margot Tennant in London; and there –

House of Commons

June 9th 1893

My dear Mrs Grenfell,

. . . Well, on Wed. I sat between Lady Helen and Lady Randolph: the one too cold, the other too hot, for the wounded. The tepid bath of kindly companionship was my need, but denied. Lady Helen was beautiful to look at and so fulfilled her mission; Lady R played vigorously with the 'coup de massue' on my emotions and feelings. She is too full of life and empty of perception to escape bruising the patient. With the soup she opened her gambit with a bald allusion to one whom rightly or wrongly she believes I hold or held dear, and informed me as a fact that her affections were bestowed elsewhere. The rest of the conversation cannot be repeated. Its effect was as though she had thrown a bloodstained surgical saw before me on the table. After dinner I talked to Miss Margot. She was more human but equally indiscreet, saying that were she a man she could not tolerate anyone she cared for at all being wholly occupied with frivolity. Tra-la-la. I brush these midges away, but at the moment they were fatiguing . . .

George Wyndham did not again quite expose himself to Ettie, though their friendship continued and she remained for him something of an exemplar – 'Dear invisible loadstar and inapproachable star of my soul's magnetic needle'. He went on to other loves: to a brief triumph in Parliament in 1903 when, himself as Irish Secretary, he carried through reforms in his Irish Land Bill; then to illness again, and an early death in 1913. He was perhaps too much like Ettie for their love to have been deep; Ettie liked to be the one to blow hot and cold, while others were constant. But in her relationship with George Wyndham she had learned the possibility of a game within rules; the patterns of adoration and bewitchment that were played out with other lovers over the years. Romance and passion, if they were to co-exist with ideas of fidelity and duty, had to remain largely in the mind: like this they could be controlled – or rather there was the illusion they could be controlled, for consequences were not recognized. And the stress of feelings could be kept for poetry. George Wyndham wrote Ettie a farewell poem:

> A lady left her lover
>   And bade him like a queen
> That he should straight recover
>   The gladness of his mien.
>   She knew not that we borrow
>   All sunny days from sorrow
>   And find not one tomorrow
>   As yesterdays have been.
>
> Gone days of April weather
>   Without the April rain;
> Lost days of love together
>   Of Love without the pain;

Of tenderness and laughter
No weeping followed after:
What wind of love may waft her
Such April days again?

Blind love, for all his blindness
Sees this thing cannot be;
Kind love for all his kindness
Denies it even *Thee*;
Strong love, for all his powers
May grow no lasting flowers
Unwatered by the showers
Of weak Love's misery.

❧ FIVE ❧

What went on in the grown-up world in London and in other country houses was not of course seen by children and not much of what went on in their own homes. At Taplow the world of the children revolved around Nanny Wake and Ada and Harriet the nursery-maids; the other familiar inhabitants of this world were Mr Barrett Good the butler, Mrs Hurton the housekeeper, Mrs Neave the cook, Mr Williams the groom and Mr Joel the boatman. These servants stayed for great lengths of time at Taplow – Mr Barrett Good for over forty years and Mrs Neave for over thirty and Mr Williams was transformed into a chauffeur in 1906. The lesser inhabitants of the nursery world – the six maids, the valet, the coachmen, the gardeners – came and went from time to time but while they were there they were the residents and it was the parents and their friends who had lives that went on largely elsewhere. The world of the nursery was something that the grown-ups from time to time graciously descended to; at weekends, often with hordes of what must have seemed like angels or devils. They were preceded by their outriders – the valets and ladies' maids, many of whom were themselves notable characters and friends. All this would have inculcated into the minds of children impressions of divinities.

It is difficult to get a true idea of the nursery world; it was centred on servants, but servants were hardly ever mentioned; the world of parents who came and went still seemed more real. Ettie and Willy looked after their servants and were loved by them – there are letters to Ettie from servants who were ill, or in trouble, thanking her for her help and assuring her of their devotion – but while servants were around they existed as a sort of ghostly sub-world like that of atomic particles; their existence was recognized, but easily ignored. Ettie for instance would have seldom dressed or travelled without her lady's maid; she would probably have spent more time, morning and evening, with her than anyone else; yet in all Ettie's extant letters there is only one mention of her lady's maid – Martins – when Ettie was planning a bicycling holiday in 1895. It was an age of many confusions between reality and what was worth talking about.

A third child was born to Ettie and Willy in August 1893 – a girl, Monica Margaret. She arrived after only half an hour of labour and before the doctor or nurse could come; she weighed only 3 lb 15 oz and had to be dressed in doll's clothes and put in a drawer. (It might have been Ettie's pregnancy that had cooled her and George Wyndham's relationship in the spring – George Wyndham made no mention of it in his letters – but it did not cool Ettie's other admirers). When Julian saw the baby he said 'Oh she is pretty, the living image of I, only she hasn't got no eyes'. He called her 'Mama's bottle-baby'.

Julian had scarlet fever in 1893; Ettie wished to nurse him herself, but was kept away by Willy and the doctor. She wrote to Arthur Balfour – 'That wretched Dr Moore told him every *idiocy* about the dangers of being with Max . . . It is too bad, he was in my arms the whole of Sunday and Monday'. Ettie was good about wanting to be with her children when they were ill physically: it was any form of mental stress that frightened her away.

Julian and Billy often fought. Ettie recorded in her journal –

Once when they went to tea with an old lady they rolled down her entire staircase locked together fighting; and once when their mother was in a bedroom next door she noticed a curious silence and a sound of deep breathing and on going in found them grappling each other's throats and both very black in the face.

They began doing lessons with a governess in 1894, reading and writing and history and geography and dictation. In the afternoons they would play in the garden or in the woods. Taplow Woods were very beautiful, high on slopes above the river. In the evenings the boys were dressed in their best clothes: 'in the summer they generally wore white, with bright green or scarlet stockings and shoes; and in the winter red or dark blue jerseys with breeches to match and velvet shoes on Sundays, with frilled shirts'.

Julian said about Taplow Woods – 'No one can have ever loved these woods more than I!' And one night – 'I wish the moon would tumble down and I could kiss her!'

Monica remembered the family governess, Miss Poulson, as being very strict – 'turning everything I did with her into rather a fatigue'. When Ettie was away, Miss Poulson or Nanny would keep a day-to-day account of the children's moral behaviour: 'Miss Monica very cross after Mrs Grenfell left – lashed me with her whip and called me "cat's eyes" in earnest – but *very* good the rest part of the day'. Miss Poulson's strictness and the children's rebelliousness was in contrast to the atmosphere in their mother's sitting room where they went each morning and evening when their mother was at home. There, because of the formality and the rarity of such a treat, the feeling was magical.

In 1895 Billy, aged four, began to dictate a History of the Family. When he came down to his mother's room after tea he would talk almost faster than she could write. This is an authentic child's view of the children's world: Ettie would have taken it down faithfully. It gives a better view than anything else can of the world they felt at home in.

BILLY'S HISTORY OF THE FAMILY

Billy is a thin boy, but a good boy, but his Dada will never in the winter stop at home. He is a tall man. But his wife is a good mother. She reads to her boys every evening and plays with the little baby. Sometimes she is a cross baby, and what makes us laugh is when Mama calls her back and she will not come. And she is very fond of her brother named Billy – fonder than of her brother called Julian. Billy is kind to her and lies on the cushions and cuddles with her, and at night he hides behind the curtains and when she comes after him he gallops down the passage and makes her laugh. Her hair is a yellowish golden colour, and her size is about a yard.

And Dad, sometimes when he is not away, he reads to us the book called Gulliver's Travels . . . And very seldom in the summer they go away. 'They' means Mama and Dada. Dada is thirty-nine years old and looks very young for that age and his mother is twenty-seven. I mean Billy's mother . . .

Billy is a very funny boy, he says very funny things which make his nurses laugh. He is nearly five years old and his brother Julian is nearly seven. And Julian, when they are in bed, comes and reads to his brother Billy. We have read twice times through a book called The Little Duke – Mama read us that – and the Heroes. Perseus was one of them, Theseus another, and the Argonauts the next . . .

Nanny is the nurse and Harriet is the other. Nanny has always taken care of us; and our Mama she tooken care of when she was a baby too.

Monica is a very good baby. She roared today when Billy was out of her sight.

Harriet is a good nurse, she takes us out sometimes, and other times Nanny does and Mama . . . Julian is 4 ft 4 ins high and he likes the gardener's boy called Alfred Williams. And Mr Barrett's little boy Willie. And he likes his little brother Billy very much, and plays with him just as well. Julian can ride very well on his little pony Taffy, but he cannot go out without Tommy the stableboy. Billy rides Taffy too but he cannot gallop yet. Billy can do tables up to 12 times 12 and Julian is just going to learn French.

Miss Poulson is very kind, she comes at half past nine, and does not leave off till lunch time. Then holidays we have Saturday and Sunday. We have luncheon with Mama, and Billy's favourite meat is mutton.

Mama is very kind, every week she gives us pennies for our marks. Billy's highest marks for one day is fifty-four. Mama is very dear and when she can she takes us out. Billy does not go skating because I do get so cold, and I stop with Nanny and the baby.

We live at Taplow Court, that is the name of the place. Taplow is a very big house, it looks red outside, and the flower beds are some in the shape of stars and others round-pieces. Taplow has also very kind gardeners. The woods are very dear, they end at the river Thames. The river Thames runs into the North Sea through Taplow and London.

We have tea out in the summer, but in the winter up in the nursery and in the middle Mama and Dada comes in. Sometimes at night when Dada comes up to say goodnight Billy sees the shadow and thinks it is Mama. Sometimes they come up together.

Max and Billy and the little baby Mon come down to Mama's room at six and the little baby goes to bed at half past six. It is a very nice room, it has got a lot of pictures. It has a piano, Max and Billy make an awful din on it, one is called the Iceland Chills and another the Iceland Wings. They light their candles on their own table, and when they go to bed each blows out one. Mon comes in to say good night and comes into their beds, and when she used to be taken away from Billy's bed she used to squall. Mon has her room at the end of the nursery passage, the nursery door leads into the passage. The nursery has got two little chairs of Billy's own, one which Nanny gave him and another which his mother gave. Billy very often sits upon them, he rocks upon his Mama's chair to pretend to go yachting . . .

This is a letter to Mr Moser – Mr Moser is Billy's friend. He teaches him songs, and some of them are awful dins what their mother cannot bear. Mr Moser is not a real person, Billy makes up about him. He tells a lot to Miss Poulson and Mama: he whispers in his sleep and sometimes has funny dreams. I think I will not write a letter to Mr Moser . . .

They went to Scotland last autumn and there was the gillies and the sea and they used to go out and see the deers getting skinned which Dada shot. One day Billy and Maxie had a fig instead of their sweeties, it was poor Dada's figs. Full stop Mama. It takes a day and a night to get to Stack, they went right up into the Highlands, they had to drive from Lairg to Stack that is thirty-four miles. They often went fishing, nearly every day . . . They used to go to the burns at Stack, and those were very long walks, they used to pick up nice stones and there was some very high rocks. They used sometimes to ride on the deer-pony from the Atlantic sea, both on the same pony; and Johnnie, the little gillie-boy, used to lead them. They used to go pearl fishing. Pearl fishing is wading in the river to get shell fish. Johnnie used to rip them open and they used to find inside the fish-flesh real pearls.

The company who often comes here, we like George Curzon best, what gives us fruit under the table. We like him very much, he gives us more than we ought to have of fruit. He is merry and very fond of travelling. He writes books.

Billy and Maxie are going to have birthdays soon, that is at the end of March, they are in the month of March now. It has been a very cold winter, and we have swept their hands along and caught hold of all the icicles they knocked off. Max has got a little place under a pair of bushes in the shape of a hut, and Billy in the shape of a long little passage, and at the end there is a little path into the church-yard where all the graves are: and there is a mount in the middle where they often scramble up. It is a grave too, of a great Sea King; and there is a lot of archways as you go out of the west door of Taplow Court each leading into the churchyard, and a gate at the end. There is some trees in the churchyard – in the summer it is near where we scramble up and Billy digs in his bushes. There is a path near to the dairy, and as you come out of the other side of the house you see a lot of cedar trees; we all play under them and miles and miles in the woods.

We play at Enemies, and tonight before we came down to Mama we had an enemy fight . . .

Spring Adventures

Billy and Max like nothing better than bird's-nesting. They make poor Mama climb the trees, and when they are not very big trees we climb them, and then we take only one egg from each nest in turns – one nest Max and one nest Bill. Last year we watched a little robin's nest in the ivy on a big elm near the cedar-walk where all the cedar-trees are and the Avenue which leads down to the river way; at the end there are some steps and then comes the boat-house, and past the boathouse our dear river . . .

We do look forward to going out after tea now, because Winter is nearly passing off and then Spring time will come – soon we will have tea out too, and play about till bed-time comes and then go in for the night. And in the morning wait till breakfast is over, then out for a run before lessons – and then all the afternoon playing. And an hour walk with Miss Poulson in the morning . . . and a biscuit . . . and the dinner time a quarter to two.

And Mr Balfour came here for Sunday, he is in Parliament. And Evan came too. And the 'babies', as Mum calls them, came down to luncheon. I cannot tell any more about that thing.

Maxie is writing a family history, but he just wrote a line or two and then left off.

We all went to Reading last week to see the biscuits made, Billy and Julian and Mama – and we eat a great quantity of biscuits, and seen a line and a brass rail where the boxes are sent shooting down, and Billy and Maxie pushed off some of the boxes. And they seen the 'Maries' made too, and the cracknels, and how they were put in boiling water the cracknels till they were done, and then men took them out with great sieves and put them into cold water and then bake them: we all took one hot-baked one, so there were three biscuits gone.

Billy and Maxie, it is their birthday evening. They were going to the Zoo, but the rain stopped them, and they had to go to the Aquarium, where they saw flying people, and a juggler, and the strong people, and the strong woman put a pole over her shoulders and two men hung on it and she whirled them round; and the woman lifted a platform with seven men and Dada on it. And how a little girl sang she can't and she won't and two and two make three but of course it doesn't. And then how the little dando came dressed up like a real man and then like a Scotchman and sang. He was a dwarf-man. And then the flying girl blindfolded her eyes and caught hold of the rope and swung herself across the Aquarium and through a paper hoop and smashed it to bits, and caught the other flying lady. And Billy's present from Nanny was a horn and drum . . . and Harriet's present was a Racing game, and Monica's a compass. And Mama's present was real field glasses, and a box of writing paper and envelopes for Billy's very own.

Billy is very fond of writing secret letters to Mr Moser; he has got two letters now what he dictated to Max.

Mama and Dada have gone to London now, but always comes back and stops to them for Sundays. Billy sent Mama a nice letter but Maxie wouldn't. We plays hide-and-seek and Deer-hunt – Mum and Dad played yesterday – it has two horses, three deer and a driver and three hounds. It is a new game and very hot and our favourite game. Sometimes we play in the hay-loft, but then it is only rats or rabbits and not deer – and we have to jump the bundles. We have nearly finished Pilgrim's Progress.

September 15th 1895. Now we have come to Freshwater, we bathe, and one day Mr Rogers came in with us and ducked my head for me and he gave me a little lesson of swimming and floating on my back – I don't think he gave me much. One Sunday we went down on the rocks with Mama with bare legs and I got such a lot of periwinkles. There are slimy things on the rocks made of seaweed and you pinch them and water comes out of them like a fountain. We found some sea-snails too and whelks. Today we went to see the house Farringford where Lord Tennyson lived what wrote Charge of the Light Brigade and went into the garden, and I found a chestnut and cracked it and there was only two little tiny broken things inside. Then we went on to the downs and had tea there and read Treasure Island . . .

We went over to Cowes, and we saw a picture of the Crimea in Osborne, the Queen's house; and we saw a picture of them all going up a hill in Scotland, and two figures of Prince Eddy and Prince George when they was little made of marble. One day we went over to the 'Gabrielle' Yacht, and we each caught a herring, Maxie caught one before Billy when the tide was high. It was a very nice yacht, and the sailors went up the masts for us.

We have gone from Freshwater now a long time, and when we came back we went to Aunt Katie's house and we shot a duck. We did not do it ourselves, Auntie Katie done it. And Uncle Francis was there too, only he went home before we shot the duck. And we had four aims at a bald-coot and didn't hit one. And a pheasant and a partridge we aimed at too, and knocked a feather out of each of their breasts.

❦ SIX ❦

The lover to whom Lady Randolph Churchill referred in 1893 when she told George Wyndham that Ettie's affections were bestowed elsewhere was probably John Baring – a young man of twenty-nine, more down-to-earth and less poetic than George Wyndham. His father was Lord Revelstoke, head of the bank of Baring Brothers in the City. John Baring was not considered a member of the Souls but his family was rich, cosmopolitan, artistic; his mother entertained people from more varied backgrounds than that of the Souls. John was the eldest son and in the course of time succeeded his father in the peerage (1897) and as senior partner in the bank. He met Ettie in her 'golden summer' of 1891; and although she does not seem to have had much time for him at first, he seems to have adored her from the moment he saw her till the day he died nearly forty years later.

> 37 Charles St, Berkeley Square, W.
> 2 June 1891

My Dear Mrs Grenfell,
  I meant to ask you last night (but simply didn't dare) if you thought you would be passing this house today about 5 o'clock. The reason I ask is that Margaret and Lady William are coming to play the organ, violin and piano, and as I know you like music I thought you might be persuaded to look in –
  Your humble and very persistent admirer,

> John Baring.

Ettie in fact loathed music, but she came to appreciate her persistent admirer; for by 1892 they were intimate – their intimacy being demonstrated by the fact that they had to write to each other in code. The purpose of this was the same as that of George Wyndham's pretence that he and Ettie were writing a novel – to be able to say things to each other that they could not say otherwise, and to make practical arrangements. Ettie's and John Baring's pretence was that in his protestations of love for her he was speaking of someone else. This went on at the same time as George Wyndham's 'novel'. Two days after Ettie's meeting with George Wyndham at Panshanger about which he wrote, a year later, 'Such an anniversary!!!' John Baring was writing:

30 November 1892

My dear Mrs Grenfell,

E. (who tells me that you know the address of the enclosed and will not mind forwarding it for me) wants me to write and tell you that she goes to Devon on Friday week 9th; but could you see C. that week. She thinks that you go away the week of the twelfth, but that you are going to be at home *next* week.

If this is so, I wonder if you will be able, and willing, and disposed, to grant *two* days? You see – what C. says is that her friend will be away for a whole dreary fortnight, and then Xmas! so that really next week is the last glimpse for so long.

Monday or Tuesday next week, any place or any time, would suit C.: and on Friday 'la famille' go away so that Rue C would be quite empty; and that afternoon or still better, if equally convenient, Saturday afternoon – would be so heavenly.

E. says that she knows you understand that all this is only written and proposed in the belief that you will only say if you have anything else in the world to do?

Yours sincerely,

J.B.

'E' stood for John Baring; but at first 'C' did too: they seemed to be both women. For a time the code was confused: perhaps this was on purpose, as an added precaution: the message to Ettie was still plain. Then it became established that 'C' stood for Ettie and was the friend of Ettie's with whom 'E' or John Baring was in love and to whom Ettie could pass on messages. And the messages were always of love, whatever happened; never of complaint –

London 19 December 1892

My dear Mrs Ettie,

I was so very glad to get your telegram today saying that you would use the brougham as it is bad for you to drive about in hansoms with your throat. I want you very particularly to write to Greenfield to order him at the station when you come up on Friday next . . .

Will you be amused to hear that I *have* got a sore throat, *such* a sore throat, I am *quite* delighted with it!

I do hope that yours is better? and that you will take care of it and that it will not get worse?

I think that I am going down to Devon by the 10.15 train on Wednesday, but if you have any news of C. and *did* by any chance write by tomorrow's post, a line to Charles St would catch me before my departure.

Dear Mrs Ettie, would you also be very kind and ask C. if ever you are writing whether there would be any chance of seeing her on the *31st* in London? Because I *know* that I *cannot* be a fortnight without seeing her darling face, for which I yearn so sadly when I am away.

Goodbye my dear Mrs Ettie, please believe your ever sincerely

J.B.

This was a different style from that of George Wyndham and the other young men who were apt to talk of love in terms of flowers and enslavement but who would not have thought of sending a carriage to Paddington if one had a sore throat. John Baring's courteous, attentive letters after a time became more passionate –

... E. writes such a thankful letter of gratitude to her for having allowed her to spend such hours of absolute paradise. She tells me she has never felt the absolute sense of rest and happiness conveyed to her by the presence – the dear *dear* presence of her own beloved: or ever been more aware how entirely she loves her with her *whole* heart and soul. From what she tells me I can feel how grateful she is; and she adds that since she left she has thought over every happy minute, and recalled every expression in that beautiful heavenly face, with such a feeling of happiness and with *such* a yearning that it may be a very short time before she has the precious *heaven* of seeing her dear beloved again.

But even when the passion became painful, the letters were without self-pity. At the time when Ettie had 'flu and George Wyndham was complaining about not being able to see her, John Baring showed his anxiety about her though at these times the code was almost dropped.

... I can assure you dear Mrs Ettie that I am perfectly *terrified* at the thought of her getting worse: for when one exists solely and entirely for one dear person, you can fancy how the thought distracts one that perhaps the beloved one is suffering, in pain, and I can do *nothing* to help or comfort her; nothing except pray with my whole heart that my own precious darling girl may soon be as radiantly well as ever. When I am separated from her and I know that she is somewhere where she is happy and enjoying herself I always try to comfort myself by the thought that she is safe, well and happy. But when, as now, I am separated and know besides that she is ill I pass my days in absolute misery . . .

There is something almost too good to be true about John Baring's love for Ettie: he must have known about her friendships with other men; he would have seen for himself; he would not have had to be informed by gossips. But he was never jealous. There is evidence that at times he had other flirtations and mistresses; perhaps he just knew the style in which to win and keep Ettie. But in an age when emotion (or the lack of it) was so often expressed in hyperbole, he had the gift of making his words seem true. And he continued to insist, year after year, that his whole life depended on Ettie; that without her he would die; that for him, whatever she did, she could do no wrong. It was this sort of protestation that she wanted; and because he gave it, he probably got what he wanted in return.

. . . It was such heavenly rest laying my head on her shoulder and her dear cool hand on my forehead – I loved her *much* more than ever before – will you tell her please? and that I thought of her so much *all night*, and *so much so* in fact that I woke up perfectly well. I feel I can never tell her one bit enough *how* I love her or how I hang on, worship, every word that comes from her, every little play of thought that comes over her most lovely face. Even if I did not love her *so*, I should think her so most incomparably more beautiful than any other created being; and when I have my arm round her dear waist, supporting that poor *dear* little *achy* back, I feel that heaven has indeed been good in giving me the most perfect of women for my own angel girl . . .

What happened at these moments beyond an arm round the waist and a head on the shoulder cannot be known: this was the area of life about which, like that of the servants, not much was said – which could be best enjoyed, perhaps, if nothing was said. Thus, pleasure could be separated from guilt. Almost certainly Ettie's and John Baring's love was sexual; just as almost certainly hers and George Wyndham's was for the most part not. But Ettie was never a wife whose lover was automatically expected to come to her at night in country houses at weekends; whose husband would be with his own mistress; for all of whom a bell would be rung half-an-hour before breakfast time in order that moves could be made back towards propriety. (This scene is a perfect model of the fashionable world in which the right eye didn't see what the left might notice; what signs

would lovers and husbands have made to each other as they passed
exhausted in the corridors?) And even at the times that apparently
respectable married women could allot to admirers – between, say, 4.30
and 6.30 in the afternoon – how far could a fashionable lady go, without
a lady's maid if not to undress at least to dress her? In later years, when
Ettie used to stay abroad with John Baring and Evan Charteris – her other
life-long admirer – conventions were probably more permissive; but
still, it is unlikely that sexuality in these relationships was the main point.
What both Ettie and her lovers required was worship – they to give it and
she to receive it – it was by this that her fear of loss was reassured and
substance was provided for their otherwise empty lives. Within this
process there was sometimes sexuality and sometimes not; but probably
always more as a means to worship than as an end. And in fact, if worship-
pers are to be kept as such they can never quite be satisfied; dispensations
have to come and go, to maintain appetite. This was a pattern that was
not only accepted by Ettie and her lovers, it was accepted for the most
part even by those whose sexuality was open: for throughout this age
what was of primary importance was the fancy rather than the fact, the
pursuit of the ideal rather than the experience. This was the point of the
dinners, the balls, the games, the weekends; even the hunting and shooting;
for without the pursuit, the game would be over. It was accepted among
some such families that after the first one or two children others might be
illegitimate; contraception was difficult, and how should anyone know?
But Ettie's children all seemed demonstrably Willy's. It was here she was
different. Her ties with Willy seemed to be sexual, and those with her
lovers were for security.

There is a novel by John Baring's brother Maurice written years later
but describing life in the 1890s in which the heroine and hero are like
Ettie and John Baring – or perhaps like Maurice himself, for he too was in
love with Ettie. The novel is called, curiously or significantly, *C* ('C'
being one of the code names in Ettie's and John Baring's letters), and is
about a young man, 'C', who falls in love with a beautiful married woman
called Leila. Leila has several lovers, but keeps each one thinking he is
unique. Her technique is to blow hot and then cold inexplicably – so
that each lover does not think she can be responsible, but the fault must
be his. In the novel the young man 'C' dies out of love of Leila; he
discovers that her true love is – his brother! But what is of interest here
in the novel is that for all the passion and romanticism the hero and heroine
make sexual love only once or twice; and then at moments of near

fantasy – on a moonlit night, or in a garden redolent with jasmine. This was probably representative of Ettie's world in the 1890s. John Baring, unlike George Wyndham, was down-to-earth in his concern; but not in such a way as to make sexuality easy.

John Baring (or John Revelstoke as he became) lived until 1929; he never married; he continued always to be attentive and adoring towards Ettie. There are photographs of him in Ettie's family albums which show him paternal, upright; his hand on the shoulder of a child. He looks straight into the camera; unlike so many of Ettie's friends who seem to be striking poses. He saw himself, and Ettie saw him, as her protector. When Monica was born in 1893 he wrote – 'Such stories I hear that make me aghast! No nurse! No doctor! A strange doctor that refused to intefere!' He never turned against her when she was inconstant to him, as her other lovers were apt to do. Only once in their long love did he cry out in pain; but this was in 1915, just after Ettie's two sons had been killed and she herself was beyond consolation. Then, when in horror she tried to reject him, he wrote – 'How can you ask me to put you out of my life? It is a life which you have formed and for which you are responsible!' But apart from this – from 1891 to 1929 – 'What an unbroken record of blessed tolerance and unswerving goodness she has had with me!'

❦ SEVEN ❦

The questions remain – what did Willy make of Ettie's relationships with her lovers? And what did Julian make of them? For children learn more from the way that their parents behave – from their attitudes in daily life – than from what is told to them.

It was the convention for a beautiful wife in the fashionable world to have lovers even if these were in fact just admirers. Willy was a conventional man; it was expected of husbands that, if formalities were observed, they should not ask too many questions about what went on in private. And even if husbands did not have mistresses themselves, they would be expected at least to be away from home a great deal. In 1892 Willy was again briefly an MP (he had been defeated in 1886 at Salisbury when he had been backing Gladstone's Home Rule Bill); but in 1893 he found he could not support the new Home Rule Bill and resigned. He spent his time in running the Taplow estate, in championing the cause of bimetallism (a financial system based on the use of both gold and silver currencies), in being chairman of committees (it was estimated that in later life he was a member of 117 committees), in being Mayor of Maidenhead, a JP, and in his innumerable sports. As well as hunting and shooting, he was Amateur Punting Champion for three years, he rowed with two others from London to Oxford in a day, and stroked a racing eight across the Channel.

Willy was a much more attentive husband and father than most men in the fashionable world: he seemed to be faithful to Ettie; he played with and read to the children in the evening. Ettie appreciated this, and appeared to give him genuine devotion. In India in 1892 while he was shooting elephants and she was being worshipped by ADCs she wrote to him: 'I miss my darling Gent *dreadfully* and do long to get him back safe and soon. Nothing is nice when you are away, even the things that would be are half spoiled without you to relever them – and what would be the fun of a "spangle" without Gent to talk him over with?' Like this, flirtation could be made to seem a game in which Willy was on her side; he, she and the children were her reality, however much she enjoyed the fantasies of social life.

I am such a bereaved Catts without either you or babies or any of the things that make up the beautiful happy background of one's life. If one has a nice background how little other things matter, or rather everything looks lovely against it like the sunset skies here which transform every dirty pink native hut into a wonderful scarlet thing . . .

She could only seem all things to many people if Willy and her family were the pivot on which she could turn. She made no secret to Willy of her friendship with John Baring: she just assumed that other people would assume it was respectable if she herself showed enough confidence that it was. They would assume this because they would want to: then no one need feel guilt, and all concerned could go on getting what they wanted.

And it was true that in some such love-relationships nothing much occurred. Ettie's old friend Betty Ponsonby married in 1893; some years later she wrote to Ettie that she was in the middle of '*the* great love-friendship of my life'. This was with 'a young poet'. She wrote – 'I have never seen him, but that is immaterial'.

The idea of sexual relationships, not spoken about directly, could be made to seem harmless by jokes. This was the technique of the Souls. Lord Pembroke wrote to Ettie of – 'Old Lady Windsor working what she called a coverlet and saying in her slow way "It's for a little single bed, and I'm working in it the family motto, 'Jamais jamais jamais': and then we found all our family mottoes were most appropriate; mine – 'Un je servirai'." '

The conventional view of Ettie's behaviour and predicament was put to her by her old childhood friend and confidant, Douglas Compton – he who claimed, after a talk with her, 'I am only giving you back your own thoughts after they have been sifted through my mind' –

. . . Let us take an ordinary case. A girl of complex nature (if her nature was entirely simple none of this would perhaps happen) marries, let us suppose, a man who to a large extent is able to fill her life. He is a 'good fellow', devoted to her, more than kind. But his nature is of a simpler mould: moreover he has a profession that occupies him much, and thus though she fills every gap in his life leaving him nothing to be desired as far as affections of all sorts are concerned, still he does not fill every gap in her life. There are still mental and cultural and spiritual capacities and needs in her of whose very existence he is ignorant. She has children, we will suppose, and they also fill gaps in her heart; but still there are needs and capabilities lying fallow. What happens? Nature, who rightly abhors a vacuum, and always uses any surplus energy in one way or another, causes these needs to be filled by, these capabilities to be expended on, another individual; who must almost certainly be a man because his wants are her capabilities, his capabilities fit in with her needs. It is as when a stone lying at the bottom of a stream has other stones continually rolled over it by the running water, one stone after another rolling over it is arrested for a moment in its course, and then carried on again by the force of the water. After a time, one stone comes by that fits sufficiently well on to it to stick there; and the longer it stays – the more the two get ground and welded together – the less likely they are ever to separate. But one stone of the two is almost certainly larger than the other, or perhaps they both overlap each other on different sides. What happens? The running stream rolls other stones by until one happening to fit on the overlapping edge lodges there and in its turn is ground and welded faster with every second of time probably in its turn leaving an overlapping edge – and so on, ad infinitum . . .

In this graphic description the existence of children is recognized: but what would children have learned? Julian and Billy as they grew up would have asked even fewer questions about Ettie's admirers than Willy: but they would have picked up something from the atmosphere, the style. They would have learned that grown-up relationships are never quite what they seem: there is something unspoken, covered over, in demonstrations of affection.

Julian in fact grew up distrusting people; looking around, he could not make out what they were about. It was this that he said in his later quarrels with his mother. He could not make out what she herself was about – there was her way of being all things to all people; when she was with him of being all things to him; and so he loved her. But what was it that he loved? She always moved on. An admirer wrote to her at this time – 'You escape me like one of your graceful smiles'. Where was the reality? For Julian, it seemed to be in the woods and streams which he loved; which did not have the power of people to be many things at once. But there might be other justifications for lives that were thus bewildering. Douglas Compton had continued his description of Ettie's predicament:

Now in a case such as I have taken a woman cannot be certain of keeping her *cher ami* unless she is prepared to sacrifice everything for him – duty, principles, other affections, etc. This we will take for granted she is not prepared to do . . . So she sacrifices her love, and for a time life seems all grey to her, the sunshine has been taken out of it and in her misery she blames herself. Now *is* she to blame? *Has* she acted wrongly? Not necessarily. There can be no harm in the fact of loving. She has only acted wrongly in so far as she has allowed her attachment to interfere with her duty and her principles . . . She is a better woman probably in every way, more able and anxious to sympathize with others, with a clearer conception of her mission in life, a firmer determination to accomplish it . . . What then is the moral of the whole?

The moral, according to Douglas Compton, was that duty and sacrifice came first, for by this a person could get away with anything. He did not quite say this, but this is what he implied: by talking of duty, stones could go on piling up on one another *ad infinitum* in the stream. Duty, principles, were words by which the practitioners of the craft of power could explain, when it suited them, why, after having blown hot, they suddenly and apparently reasonably blew cold; and then could be ready to appear again in glorious trappings like the sun. For in spite of talk of renunciation Ettie and her lovers always did seem to reappear; there was no question of duty taking them out of the whole routine. Duty was the mechanism by which, in idleness, people could have the illusion of lacing themselves into shape; like polo for young men in India. But then, with all this insubstantiality, young men were apt to long for a more real laceration.

Julian, looking round, would have seen this pattern – the quiet adoring men at the beck and call of his mother; most women hoping to be like her; husbands going off as if furiously to kill animals and birds. Each year they shot thousands and thousands of birds; birds were driven to them in hordes as it were over the tops of trenches; they crawled on their stomachs through the mud shooting stags; they fished, standing up to their thighs in water; they hunted, crashing through hedges as if through barbed wire. And then they came home again to women who were supposed to be everything in the world to them: but this was not quite true; and so they went out again. This is how Willy would have appeared to Julian. One day in Norfolk, with five others, Willy shot thirteen hundred pheasants; in Austria he personally shot a hundred partridges on each of three days: he shot four stags in one day in Scotland. It was of these feats that he wrote to Ettie when he was away; he did not ask her what she was doing or what she was feeling. He never told her what he was feeling. Perhaps he did not know this himself. In all his letters to her at this time there is only one reference to John Baring: this was when Willy was shooting in Austria and Ettie was in the Isle of Wight with the children. Willy wrote – 'My dearest, I have got two letters from you today, the last saying that John Baring had been down. I got a stag this morning, hit him four times, at what was said to be over 300 yards. The first shot would have settled him but we didn't know he was hit, in fact he was so far off it was difficult to see him'.

The pattern for men was not to ask questions, not to think, but to make jokes and to do one's duty: if this was not too difficult, it was perhaps because it was part of men's duty to fight and kill. It was like this in law, in politics, in business; with thought disencouraged, furious instincts were satisfied by ritual. And the pattern for women was to dissimulate, to come and go, to be worshipped by seeming to be first one thing and then another. And this was held to be the real world, the world of gods and goddesses; while those who cooked, sewed, dug the garden, cleaned stables, were smiled on but were thought to be insubstantial. This was the world of Henry James's *What Maisie Knew* and *The Awkward Age*: when children were bemused not so much by grown-ups' lack of morals as by their inability to think of anything being real except their fantasies about keeping one another in thrall.

Ettie continued to be known as a model wife and mother: Lord Pembroke wrote after she had been married five years – 'I congratulate you heartily on your marriage and hope to see you when the honeymoon's over'. Willy was known as a model Englishman: 'You ought to have heard what the Duke said about you at dinner last night, he suddenly said quite simply you were the finest man he knew'. Willy and Ettie played these roles convincingly to each other: 'Shall you be pleased to get home Friday week? Catts will, and then we will have a nice quiet month at home with Maxie and do our things'. 'There is no woman who can hold a candle to Catts in any way whatsoever, and it is no use their trying.' Sometimes when Ettie was away Willy stayed at Taplow and kept an eye on the children: 'I have been to tea with them and they were very well and messy, quite happy smearing buttery crusts over each other and sweeping everything in reach to the floor'. And he would tell Ettie not to hurry back – 'If you do it will worry me, and the doctors tell me I am not to be worried'. But he was quite often ill at this time, with sciatica and headaches.

Of Ettie's friends and admirers the one most likely to call a spade a spade was George Curzon: 'Blessed Ett, just as I go off I must send you a line to say how beyond measure sweet was the last night of you, the little, clinging hand under the table'. And from his tent in Kabul, in Afghanistan, where he was one of the first Englishmen to travel – 'I remember kissing you in the library on a blood-red sofa in front of the fire; oh would god there were a fire now and a sofa for you and me!' This was when he himself was engaged to be married. But more than most people in this world he lacerated and justified himself by throwing himself into his work.

Ettie's friends often dreamed of her, and they told her of their dreams, as if the information was important even if they did not know why. George Curzon wrote from Rawalpindi –

My dearest Ett,

. . . I dreamed we were all (i.e. our friends) staying with you and Willy as your guests at some fascinating country place – it was not Taplow – we used to sit out on the lawn and play some new and delightful semi-literary game in which we all wrote things on paper (I have since forgotten the game which is a pity) and I remember you walking about in a white frock urging us to compete and coming and concocting some Rabelaisian jest with me. Then it was the evening and I was sitting in my room. I heard a knock and you came in. I said 'Oh you darling do come in' but was somewhat dismayed to find you accompanied by Arthur B and Willy, both of whom had overheard my ejaculation but who expressed no surprise. However Willy retired and Arthur and you remained. Arthur said – 'We have been talking it over and have decided that you (i.e. I, G.N.C.) must propose Willy's health tonight and thank him for all the week' – for we had stayed with you for a whole week – 'and above all,' said Arthur, 'you must put in a few sympathetic words about his extraordinary bad luck throughout the week in losing as many as thirty-nine goals.' This seemed to me quite natural and I undertook the task. I can remember you and Arthur leaving the room and his saying as you did so – 'Don't forget the thirty-nine goals!' – nor have I – but what they are, I have not yet ascertained.

Whether or not George Curzon ever cottoned on about the thirty-nine goals – this was before Freud was famous – it was evident that her friends were often confused about Ettie: she was so dutiful and yet so divine; so loyal and yet so ruthless; but it was this that her friends found so bewitching in her – the power of ambiguity and of transformation. Children of all ages are obsessed by witches: they embody the sort of loves that are frightening to oneself. Ettie continued from time to time to have remorse. At the end of her 1893 diary – after she had listed, as usual, the Class I of her lovers – she resolved –

> To give up, surely but gradually, for his sake, to
> whom so much owes –
> To prey against remorse, because of nerves –
> Never to re-begin with others –
> To do very best otherwise –

– but then, characteristically, she somewhat complicated the effect; adding –

> Life is subtle and not simple; to be lived, not thought.

❧ EIGHT ❧

The third lover whom Ettie took on in 1892 was Evan Charteris, the brother of Hugo Elcho and brother-in-law of George Wyndham's sister Mary and a founder member of the Souls; a barrister by profession, a wit, an expert shot; a renowned raconteur and player-of-games after dinner. Evan Charteris combined something of the characteristics of both George Wyndham and John Baring: he was literary (in later life he wrote a biography of Edmund Gosse); he loved Ettie from the time he met her till he died (he married in old age but his wife loved Ettie too); above all, he was inexhaustibly attentive. If John Baring was Ettie's champion and protector, Evan Charteris was her familiar and scribe. He wrote her thousands of letters, sometimes more than one a day; he sent them by special messenger; he sent her telegrams. It was as if his voice, or his neat controlled handwriting, had to go on and on for ever as if to cover up – what? – silences in which ghosts might appear. Sometimes his sound was uncannily like John Baring's –

. . . I feel that my relations with her are of a nature that forbid real darkness and distress and that our love has such native grace and strength and carries with it such a hope of an ideal that in itself is powerless except for good – and I expect that the values and fullness of a life are measured more by the character of its purpose and the greatness of its courage than by either its achievements or its finished perfections . . .

– but with something almost maniac about it, as if the code in which they all felt themselves constrained to talk – for Evan Charteris too referred to a third person when he spoke of love – had taken over, and they were indeed talking to abstractions or just to themselves –

. . . Do you think I can really have hurt her? For the answer to be yes it argues such blindness to facts on her part that I can scarcely believe it – and yet if it is true could anything be more sad – such an ending to such a summer! dear! surely she knows that never for a minute when I am away from her am I really happy – that at any moment could she divine into my mind she would find under depression or seeming high spirits or passive content as when one wakes in the still country after the turmoil of London the same insatiable prayer – *always* to be with her, never never parted through day or night through all the years of life and beyond – how then could she think that there came a day quite suddenly when I might have been with her and did not want to be? . . . I may blunder and irritate and drive her to despair with my despair, but no love that has ever been given her or ever will be given her can claim even kinship with mine – others have loved her I know – but whose life has been love for her and nothing beside? who can tell her that no thought has ever flitted through their mind without it was filled with her presence – who can say that they live solely and only to see her and to love her . . .

The pattern was as usual – ecstasy, some unknown sin, repentance, gratitude for forgiveness. John Baring and Evan Charteris often found themselves with Ettie in the same country house; they would visit her on the same day in London; they would stay at the same time at Taplow. This did not seem to cause confusion, either to them or to her. Ettie would record in her diary – 'Talked with Evan in the morning: walked with John in the afternoon: Evan read to me in the evening.' There was no place for jealousy if love was to do with an ideal. Even when there were laments and recriminations it was as if these too were abstract exercises, the purpose of which was to help in the fight against deprivation and fear.

Dear Mrs Willy – I *implore* you to ask her to forgive me – tell her I was wrong and I know it – and to have hurt her and brought misery on both of us, above all through failure in our perfect truth, makes me utterly miserable. For I have no way, and no will, no desire in the world save towards her – and she must draw the clouds away from across the star of peace and make me feel it is shining again into the depths – because I love her *so*. Oh! will you plead with her for me and tell her that nothing is lost but that I feel only strengthened and vivified by learning again the ruin that lies in the loss of her love . . .

These protestations seemed to have no content – in none of the dozens and dozens of such letters were there any details of what the misunderstandings or quarrels were *about* – it was as if the letters were prepared forms ready to be posted when there was any need for reassurance. The general type of such a relationship was admitted –

. . . we are all of us trees or creepers: if creepers, then some substance to clamber on is necessary; if trees, then neighbourhood is necessary to share the burden of the storms. So dependence is a law of growth; and the greater one's dependence in love the greater one's happiness – on which principle I cast my faith in you . . .

– as was its evanescent nature –

. . . my meetings with her are like shooting stars – I look up and she is gone! – before even I have time to tell her that with my whole soul I love her . . .

– but this was the point. To be both a tree and a shooting star was indeed magical; and it was magic that a man who felt himself insubstantial required from his goddess in order to give him hope. The pattern of dependence, loss, anguish, reassurance, ecstasy, was that of a child with its mother; but then, since each was to some extent acting out the pattern within himself, the goddess-woman and child-man could exchange roles: she would become the child who laid her head on his shoulder, and he would be the parent who regaled her with his comfort and wit. One of the bonds between Ettie and Evan Charteris was the way in which they made each other laugh. In a world of hunger, palatable morsels could be made out of the vagaries of others.

I have nothing more of any light to tell you of Margot – she thinks she has made up her mind and is proportionately miserable – but she does not say anything about it to Asquith till the New Year. Really, to lose your wife, be made Home Secretary, and marry the woman you love in three years is too much luck for one man . . .

We duly went to Hamlet . . . Forbes Robertson is the best any of us has seen . . . he makes him refined and distinguished, an everyday mortal of exceptional cleverness, a man one might ask to a waterparty or select for a bicycling tour . . . Mrs P.C. makes nothing of Ophelia, and looks like one of the 'old family' selling flowers, and no one would judge her insane or incapable of pleading. Hamlet's irresolution was unhesitating compared to Mary's doubts about going round to see Mrs Pat: we discussed it all dinner, we debated it in between every act, and finally were left arguing in the gangway when every other onlooker had left the theatre . . .

The making of a funny story, the timing and turning of a phrase, offered delight like food. But still, all this wit and world-weariness seemed antidotes to some apprehension. Evan Charteris once wrote 'God what children of despair we are!' He analysed this to Ettie:

I believe low spirits as we have them are modern, a thing of the day, due to the intense consciousness and sensibility which prevail and which record every little outward and inward change. In robuster days with less analysis in the air people were probably less easily influenced; they took life more as it came, and paused very much less to consider the in-and-out and to-and-fro and pro-and-con of every fact: not that it matters much what they did, for the question is what we do, and how what we do affects us. But I'm sure it must come from that – from the vitality of one's nerves which lays one open to the minutest innovations about one. How otherwise could one be in good spirits today and bad tomorrow, full of hope in the evening and half way through the next day torn with despair? The main facts of life don't alter, nor its structure nor its general composition. It must be due to little modifications within oneself . . .

Of all Ettie's admirers Evan Charteris was the one most capable in their quarrels of answering back. He wrote to her: 'How you do bully and how unreasonable you are! You really introduce and maintain an element of *fear* in friendship . . .' But there was little venom in his stings: for it remained unthinkable that the relationship should ever be broken. In fact adoration seemed to be stimulated by periodic stings; this could call forth further reassurance. Letters from Ettie to Evan Charteris have not come to light, but there is one rough draft of a letter in Ettie's hand-writing which seems as if it might have been intended for Evan. This shows Ettie's way of using spells and conundrums to keep a lover in a state of dependence.

Your attitude is very incomprehensible. In one letter (I send it) you talk of 'the future' as if it were synonymous with the dividing of you and me. If that is so in your mind, what sanction or meaning can 'the present' have held? I thought that, as concerning our friendship, it had been a stable attitude in both our minds – subject only to the chances and changes without and within that we could not control. And if it was not to be that, how could it bring strength or peace to either of us, or be anything but a burden? As a leaping off-place to separate futures it could never have been anything but most unhappy . . . That is where you have brought about irretrievable disillusionment . . .

The threat of ending the relationship was used but was never carried out– it was the ultimate weapon designed to bring the other person to heel. Evan Charteris once or twice used it himself – 'I want you to realize that the perfect past has created no obligation; that you are free and un-fettered in your friendship for me' – but this was again always the prelude to reconciliation. Such a relationship could not finally be broken because then the whole framework of life would collapse. But it was the man, as the child, who nearly always had to say that he was wrong. A quarrel which had begun with – 'I thought I oughtn't to take *all* the blame' went through the stage of 'You have been more unkind than any woman ever was to a man she hated' and finished with 'Your letter has made me feel to the full depths of my being all the blame that belongs to me and all the havoc I have wrought'. And then there was just the voice of reassurance going on and on again –

You have *never* failed – if you look back you will see that the provocation has always come from me, in the shape of some impossible claim or wild mis-understanding or ill-controlled aspiration . . . the loveliness of your being, your courage and your power towards the highest, your truth and the immeasurable tenderness of your ways – these are part of you and one has devoutly known it – and to have loved these as I have loved them in you cannot have been waste . . .

Ettie went to France in 1897 with Evan Charteris: they travelled with Hugo and Mary Elcho and visited the chateaux of the Loire. This was the first of several trips abroad she made with him. Willy once wrote 'I have not the smallest idea who the party is or whether you have a motor or where – I gather Evan is with you as you say he has seen a doctor'. Evan was Ettie's guide through architecture and painting: she wrote – 'He is the most expert liaison officer between the laity and the arts'. It became a custom, after a time, to invite Evan and Ettie together to country houses; but it was still presumed that their relationship was one of mutual amusement and security.

There were one or two men during these early years whom Ettie was interested in but who did not play or dance to her accustomed tune: these were men who had siren-like qualities themselves, and so were in competition with her. One such man was Harry Cust. (Once when Evan Charteris was a struggling young barrister and was trying to impress an eminent solicitor he invited Harry Cust together with the solicitor to dinner; Harry Cust got uproariously drunk, and Evan Charteris sent him a telegram the next day saying 'You have ruined my life but it was worth it' to which Harry Cust replied 'That is a sentiment I am more used to hearing from women'.) Ettie wrote a short story called 'Proteus' which was said by her friends to be about Harry Cust: it was set in Venice, and the hero was a romantically demonic seducer. Ettie had been in Venice in 1890 when Harry Cust had been there with his friend Violet Granby.

Ettie seemed to be somewhat obsessed by Harry Cust. In 1913 Julian was writing to her wondering whether he and she were still 'resisting each other's blandishments'.

The despair that Ettie's lovers said they felt was to some extent only in mind: it did not correspond with the activity of their lives. But there is one glimpse of Ettie and Evan Charteris from the outside which confirms the view that Evan said he sometimes had of her. This is in a letter to Ettie from her old friend Betty Ponsonby (now Montgomery). Betty had been a friend of Evan Charteris's from childhood; she was in London in 1901 and she saw a lot of both Ettie and Evan. Ettie's cousin Bron Herbert had just come back from the South African War: he had been wounded and was being looked after in London by Ettie and Willy before having to have his leg amputated. Ettie used to take him for drives in her carriage. Evan poured out his troubles to Betty, and showed her a copy of a letter he had written to Ettie. Betty herself wrote to Ettie:

> 3 Lyall Street S.W.
> April 10th 1901

My darling,

I *do* feel so sad and anxious about dear E. Of course one trusts and thinks nothing extremely terrible will happen outwardly, but it is none the less fearfully sad inside. I am looking at the picture of you with the little boys – and I am thinking of your tenderest kindness and faithfulness to me all these years – and *then* I come face to face with the vein of Mary Stuart *cruelty* which *does* make me so sad.

I can't bear you having the faintest smile at E's agony of mind. There was something rather terrible in your coming in from the Bron drive, lovely, calm, kind; and in the little Burghesh bag hanging on your wrist being this cry of agony from the wrecked life of a man . . .

You see it seems to me so ringingly true and genuine those words from him. It is not like the love-making of I.G. who though he threatened it will *not* just kill himself. I can afford to smile at him with you, and to be amused at your unerring use of the *casse-coeur* right and left.

But with a friend of ten years unswerving love who has given up his whole life and soul to you the use of power merges into cruelty. I can't forget the despairing look he threw at me yesterday – as between one human being in great great trouble and another – and it sickened me with pity.

Now, you may *well* say two things –

(1) What then do you suggest is the solution of this situation? And, as you know, at present I *cannot* think or understand what would be best.

(2) I shall probably hear from you that this acute crisis is over – that it has been tided over again – that you comforted him a little, or that he is weak and will go on much the same.

Still even then do, do, keep from some things darlingest – you who are the essence of tenderest kindness – do not be unkind! And do not have the faintest smile with Bron, or me, or yourself, at knowing what your power has done in the way of using, absorbing, twisting and throwing about a whole life and soul!

I so tremble that you shouldn't be a little *tired* of the rows. Honestly I did hope that it wasn't so tremendous on his side as it is – that it was a culte, and in-love, and love-making, and friendship – but not this fundamental human suffering.

Well, my sweetest, I must stop – do write to me about it – you, kindest to me, will understand that I wish you could be like that with him.

B.

Ettie did write, and explained herself: and Betty wrote again – 'I do indeed see that I was mistaken in thinking that you could be even a speck mocking . . . I think I a little exaggerated under the impression of that day'.

❧ NINE ❧

In the summer of 1898 Julian was sent to a boarding school. He was ten years old. Ettie had taken him with her to look at two or three schools; this showed a rare respect for a child at the time. They chose Summerfields, near Oxford. When Julian left home Ettie recorded 'His fighting spirit leapt to the adventure, and he did not shed one tear, but he was sick several times on the journey from Taplow to Oxford'.

Ettie wrote to him:

My very very dear, It makes me miserable to think that when you open this you may be feeling a little lonely and sad, and I want it just to remind you how very *close* to you my love and thoughts are my darling, so that you can't feel quite alone. You have been such a wonder of all that is dear and brave during this last time at home – but as you step over the threshold into the new life I know that it must seem strange and perplexing just at the very first: but I have all trust in you, I *know* you will be brave and patient and overcome the things that may seem difficult at first, and do your very best, and be kind and truthful always. You have been such a good boy all your life, it makes me so happy to remember that (except for thoughtless things!) you have never done a *wrong* thing or been mean or unkind or cowardly – and you and I know the dear *wonderful* son you have been to me your whole life long. I can hardly think of what it will be to be without you, but there is the dear love and trust between us *for ever*, growing every year. You know that my whole love is yours, that I would do anything in all the world for you, from now till the day I die. That is why mothers' and sons' love is different to most other kinds of love – it never *can* change or alter – the constant blessing and joy ever since the very day that your yellow head lay on my arm. You remember the Latin sentence in your Prayer Book, and that it means 'Winter and Summer, And near and far, All my life and beyond.'

You know how I shall think of you and pray for you my darling that God may keep you always beneath the covert of His patience and that He may grant to you all your life long the love of Himself, and of the great and bright things of life – the things that are worthy to be praised. And that you may fight under His banner, and show forth His praise not only with your lips but in your life – and always be truthful and joyous and courageous and kind.

And I pray that He who above all things loved Love may bless our love together – you will not forget me? And if you are worried or troubled *ever*, write to me to come, and I will come from wherever I am as quick as the train will fly. Anyhow I am coming next Tuesday, and what a lot of things I shall hear, and *all* the things you do! I will write before that. God keep you, *dear heart*.

Your own
Mother

This was a letter from the heart. But if love had to be perfectly pure and ideal, what in return could a son give? Julian's letters from Summerfields were consistent in their assurance of happiness – 'I am getting on so well here and I like it so much . . . the boys here are so nice and don't chaff me much . . . I expect I will like the games very much'. Summerfields seems to have been for the times quite a kindly school: the 'chaffing' of the boys was sophisticated – 'Stafford is getting on awfully well and Horner and I have got a lot of chaps to stick up for him if he gets ragged about being a Marquis' – and the headmaster did not seem to indulge in too many of the punishments that were then customary. It was a special occasion when he was 'in rather a wax' and 'five chaps got whacked'. There were one or two boys who behaved as was to be expected – 'Asquith flourishes tremendously but he is an awful little bully; I believe he has thrashed every chap in his room'. But Julian himself did not seem to suffer; he gained the reputation of being able to look after himself. But what the school inculcated above everything was a spirit of competitiveness; and into this Julian entered eagerly.

A large part of his letters to his mother was taken up with telling her how well he had done each week both in work and games: this was how a mother's love was expected to be repaid. He was nearly always near the top of his class, and when he wasn't, he became anxious. 'I was top in Latin, top in Greek, 2nd in French, 2nd in English; I have never been so high up any week before . . .' 'Dane has got five marks ahead of me in Latin, I *must* catch him up . . .' 'I have just managed to scrape ahead of

Dane on Saturday and got the paper by *3 marks*, only just . . .' 'If I work
very hard I may gain 2 or even more places before half term; I will try
awfully hard to.' He usually won end-of-term prizes for English, French
or Latin. Ettie made it plain how much his successes meant to her. She
wrote in her Children's Journal 'Julian won the Latin prize for his form
and was also first in Mathematics and was carried back in triumph to
Taplow by his mother and Billy'. About his performances in sport, he
wrote – 'On Saturday I bowled five wickets and made about 40 (my
highest score yet) and am not out yet, I had got my eye well in; my last
scores were 4–2–2–3–2, all in one over!' These tabulations seemed to be
offerings to his mother. There is little mention in his letters of his
friends at school, the boys he lived with and played with.

In 1899 he asked his mother if she would send him a daily paper so he
could follow the course of the South African War. 'I am delighted with
the war news: I really think they will get Cronje at last, though I think it
was rather brutal of Kitchener not to grant him an armistice to bury his
dead.' After the relief of Mafeking he described how 'the whole school
changed and went into a field and flags were given out and we all lined up
and trooped round the field in procession 4 deep singing "God save the
Queen", "Soldiers of the Queen" etc. It was awful fun'.

Julian had met Lord Kitchener and had made friends with him when
he had stayed at Taplow just before he had gone out to be Chief of Staff
to Lord Roberts in South Africa. Julian wrote an account of this meeting
somewhat later when he was fourteen:

The first time I saw Lord Kitchener was before the South African War. I had
come home for the holidays and the first morning I got up before breakfast and
on going downstairs found a gentleman whom I did not know at all. He asked
me to come for a walk, and we went for over an hour. He found out that I was to
be a soldier, and asked me what regiment I was going in for, and how I was
getting on at school, and a great many other questions. He told me a great many
things about the army, and yet he never mentioned himself, and I had not the
least idea who he was. I enjoyed the walk very much indeed, and when afterwards
I was told who he was I was not at all surprised. It was easy to see that he was no
civilian; he looked a soldier from head to foot, and there was something about his
manner that showed he was no ordinary man, and yet he said nothing about
himself or his own doings. He spoke in a way that showed he meant what he
said, and it was easy to see that he was used to being obeyed. I think that on
seeing him for the first time one would feel an impulse to say 'that is a man who

would never leave what he had once resolved upon till he finished it to his satisfaction'. I should think it would be impossible to find features on which self-restraint and tremendous will are more clearly marked . . .

In the holidays from Summerfields Julian came back to Taplow to his ponies, his dogs, his bird's-nests, his fishing. He was now more part of the world of the grown-ups who came and went, for whom the large house was both a home and like a hotel. Ettie and Willy played with the children, encouraged endeavour; but about life at Taplow there was nothing cosy. Monica remembered as a young girl seeing one of her friend's brothers putting his arm round his sister's shoulders when she was hurt, and being amazed – 'as in our family, although we adored one another, we would have been too shy to be demonstrative in this sort of way'.

The summer holidays were the times when Ettie gave all her attention to the children: they would go away for six or eight weeks; Willy was sometimes with them and sometimes not. In 1896 they had gone to Loch Assynt, in Sutherland, and had fished and had watched their father shooting stags; in 1897 they had gone to St Pierre-en-Port in Normandy, where they caught shrimps and bicycled and learned how to swim; in 1898 they went to Swanage, where their brother Ivo was born, as unexpectedly as Monica had been. Willy was shooting in Scotland and Ettie tried to discourage him from taking the trouble to come south. He did, but only for a few days, and then returned to his shooting. Ettie told Betty Montgomery that Julian had 'heard Ivo being born standing just outside the door'. In 1899 the family went to Swanage again and in 1900 to Sheringham in Norfolk.

Nanny Wake and Harriet, the nursemaid, usually went with them on these holidays. In Normandy Miss Poulson, the governess, came too to help with the children's French. When Willy was with them they usually had a manservant, and when there was no cook in their rented house they took Mrs Neave from Taplow. (Taplow itself was sometimes let during these weeks – in 1897 to the King of Siam, who had an enormous retinue of sailors.) But even with servants, Ettie tried to give the impression of leading a simple life on her own with her children. A stranger remembered in 1899 at Swanage –

I was coming in one evening and I could see through the open windows Mrs Grenfell having a meat-tea with her children: they were all round her and the light from the lamp shone on her and made her look very young: the baby was on her knee, Monica standing near her, and the two boys on either side of her. No one was waiting on them – just she and the children, all supremely happy.

After the holidays Ettie and Willy would go off on their round of visits again: the women to their friendships; the men to their slaughter of birds. At Summerfields, Julian and Billy received a letter from Lord Kitchener:

Kronstadt

May 13th 1900

My Dear Julian and Billy,

Many thanks for your letters which caught me up on the march here, and I read them while our guns were pounding away at the Boers who were sitting up on some hills trying to prevent our advance. However they soon cleared out and ran before we could get round them. I wish we could have caught some of their guns but they are remarkably quick at getting them away and we have only been able to take one maxim up to the present.

Sooner or later we are bound to catch them but they give a lot of trouble. The Boers are not like the Soudanese who stood up for a fair fight, they are always running away on their little ponies. We make the prisoners of war march on foot, which they do not like at all.

There are a good many foreigners among the Boers but they are easily shot as they do not slink about like the Boers themselves. We killed a German colonel yesterday, and a Russian ditto a few days ago.

Now I must go back to work so goodbye.

Mind you work hard

Your affectionate friend

Kitchener.

This was when Julian was tabulating his cricket scores; he was also taking up golf. 'We both did the 1st in 6, the 2nd in 6, he did the 3rd in 3 and I in 5'. Lord Kitchener wrote again –

... We are catching a good many Boers now, I got 80 today, rather a good bag, they are not well off for clothes and their bags are generally without a seat.

Goodbye awfully glad to have heard from you

Yours always

Kitchener.

Another friend who wrote to Julian from the War was Bron Herbert, Ettie's cousin who had gone to South Africa at the age of twenty-three as a correspondent for *The Times* and had been wounded in the leg. He wrote –

What the Boers like to do is to sit on top of a very high hill with a nice flat plain below it and on top of the hill they have a cannon which goes 'pom-pom-pom-pom-pom-pom-pom' as quick as ever you say it; and every time it goes pom it fires a shell. All these shells burst when they hit the ground . . . They don't often hurt anybody, but they frighten everybody awfully, except General Buller, who is very brave and doesn't mind them a bit, and sits on his horse in the middle of them . . .

Then all our great big guns come up; some of them are long ones that are fired by sailors in straw hats, and some are little fat ones that shoot big shells straight up into the air that fall on the heads of Boers who are hiding behind houses and walls and who think themselves quite safe. And then when all these guns are firing away and giving the old Boers on the hill a jolly hot time out come all the soldiers and begin to march across the plain in great long lines wide apart so that they are much more difficult for the Boers to hit . . . And when they get close to the hill they fix their bayonets into their rifles and give a great cheer and rush up as hard as they can go. The Boers are more afraid of bayonets than anything else, and when they see them coming they run for their lives . . . So when our poor soldiers get to the top of the hill instead of finding a lot of Boers to kill as they had hoped all they see is the Boers galloping miles away over the hills and beyond. And that's the end of the battle.

I hope you've had a jolly good term and made lots of runs and got into the Eleven . . .

Julian did get into the Eleven and made a lot of runs, and continued to write home about his exploits. His letters are curiously impersonal: he had been taught by the men he admired that one did not talk about feelings. Men chalked up scores, and took wickets, and liked people who stood up for a fair fight – just as the Soudanese at the battle of Omdurman, where Kitchener's army had killed 10,000 with casualties to itself of 500.

Julian nearly always began his letters to his mother by thanking her for hers – 'Thank you so very much indeed for your awfully nice long letter, I did love it so very much'. Occasionally he was critical – 'I am so sorry but I think that paper simply piggish, do you really like it yourself?' He asked his father *Please ask* mother not to scent her letter paper'.

In 1899 Willy and Ettie went on a fishing trip to Florida and there chalked up their own scores – 'There is a new moon and blinding stars and the Tarpon are rising like minnows . . . Dad got two today and I got a 28 lb (!) Kingfish and nearly died of joy!' Willy caught a hundred Tarpon in three weeks, which was some sort of record. Ettie hated New York where 'they all scream and shriek and rush up and down in lifts and yell down telephones'. She admonished the children 'Be dear and good, I know you will, and do not quarrel, and wash your hands'.

In the autumn of 1900 Billy arrived at Summerfields. He was the same height and weight as Julian, and for his age he was cleverer; he was a more natural scholar and with the same eagerness to come out on top. Sometimes he seemed about to catch Julian up; but then Julian would move out of reach with some authority of his own. Julian and Billy seemed fond and proud of one another at Summerfields and they did not quarrel much now; though Ettie sometimes must have made their friendship difficult –

My darling Bill-boy,
    Your reports have come! . . . I must tell you a little about them. Yours is *excellent* – couldn't be better! You are *Second* in Latin Translation, *First* in Latin Composition, *Third* in French, *First* in Mathematics, *Fourth* in English. All the 'remarks' are very good indeed, and Conduct 'very good'. We are *so* pleased darling.
    Julian is *Third* in Latin Translation, *Second* in Composition, *Third* in Greek, *First* in French, *Seventh* in Mathematics, *Seventh* in English. His 'remarks' are good too, except in *Greek, Euclid*, and *Geography and maps*. They say he ought to have a good chance of his Form prize, with *more resolution and pains*. Conduct 'Good – but a little too joyous!' Of course this letter is for *you both*. Tell Julian *how* we both hope he'll 'buck up' and get the prize.

Julian began to love drawing at Summerfields: he wrote home asking for crayons and paints. This was one of the few requests that Ettie seemed slow in responding to. At twelve, Julian had very beautiful copper-plate handwriting. This was in contrast to his mother's, which was shaky and backward-slanting, and his father's, which was rounded but curiously fragile.

Julian was due to go on from Summerfields to Eton and it had been hoped that he might get a scholarship; but when the time came his headmaster did not think it was worth entering him, so he went to Eton to take the ordinary entrance exam. He did so well in this however that he was in fact put straight into the form which was usually reserved for scholars. From Eton, when taking the exam, he wrote –

There are lots of funny customs here – you ought to keep your hands in your pockets, you *must* not stop in the street and talk, you *must* always walk on one side of the road, you *must* not walk about arm in arm, you *must* not cross the street straight but have to go slanting . . .

During his last term at Summerfields he had, he told his mother, some sort of religious experience: there was a thunderstorm and – 'I suddenly seemed to realize God'. He did not talk of this much, but people at this time did feel a detachment about him unusual for a boy of his age; he seemed to be in relationship with a world inside himself. People used to say of Ettie that she seemed to come from 'a more rarefied world than ours': but Ettie's world was transcendent; Julian's was immanent. He was a very beautiful boy: in photographs of him at this time there is a sort of knowledgeableness about his beauty, as there is sometimes in paintings of animals in the company of humans. When he went to Eton the wife of a master wrote 'he was of the rather rare class of boys who are always men from the first'. A master wrote that the very sight of him in the street 'made his eyes fill with tears'. A friend wrote to Ettie – 'I used to think of that Greek epigram of the boy who was so beautiful he died'.

❧ TEN ❧

Of all Ettie's men friends during the years of Julian's childhood the most revered and authoritative was A. J. Balfour. Ettie had known him herself as a child: she remembered –

. . . a long afternoon under the trees and the charm and brilliance of the lazy talk, the excitement of rowing Arthur Balfour and John Morley on the river in my boat after tea, watching them all go down to dinner from the arch near the schoolroom, the breakfast next morning (already my favourite meal of the day) the despair at seeing them all go and – almost best of all – talking over and over every iota with Uncle Henry afterwards . . .

It was accepted that Arthur Balfour was the leading member of the Souls. He was slightly older than most – born in 1848 – and he seemed in an unusually practical way to be detached from, and thus able to be admired by, both the men and the women in the society around him. Somewhat androgynous, he could be seen as an idol. In Ettie's childhood he had been a clever but slightly ineffectual Member of Parliament; he was known for his habit of seldom getting out of bed before lunch, for his collection of blue china, and for his nickname 'Pretty Fanny'. Then in 1887 he had been appointed Chief Secretary for Ireland by his uncle Lord Salisbury the Conservative Prime Minister and almost at once his reputation changed. The Irish Secretaryship had been known as a graveyard for politicians; of Balfour's immediate predecessors Lord Frederick Cavendish had been murdered, Sir George Trevelyan had broken down, and Sir Michael Hicks-Beach had gone temporarily blind: but Balfour became the most successful Irish Secretary of his generation. The Irish troubles of the time were to do with flagrantly unjust laws by which tenants had to pay exorbitant rents to absentee landlords who had the power to evict them. There had been demonstrations; Balfour backed the police in keeping law and order, but set about pushing through Parliament measures which would enable tenants to become owners of their land. His nickname changed from 'Pretty Fanny' to 'Bloody Balfour'.

His style of achieving this was the style of the Souls: he was flippant, but he used flippancy seriously. When Irish Nationalists yelled at him in Parliament he pretended to be asleep; when he did deign to reply, instead of being argumentative, he was witty. He made charm effective. Perhaps this was only possible when in politics there did not seem much to be done.

As a member of the Souls he flirted with Ettie; but he was the one who remained god-like and almost out of reach, and it was sometimes Ettie's voice that seemed to go on and on –

4 St. James's Square S.W

My dear Mr Arthur,

How can I thank you enough. I have never in my life been one half so pleased with *any* present. You really do not know what delight you have given me by that darling little red heart and the lovely dainty chain – thank you over and over again, a thousand times over. It is *quite* lovely and I am overjoyed whenever I open its little case and look at it. You do not know what real pleasure you have given me. It will be such a happy remembrance to me always of a very great and dear friend, and I love to have had a present of any kind from you and *most* especially this beautiful one. You could not possibly have found anything I should like nearly as much. Thank you dear Mr Arthur from the bottom of my heart for it – and for seven years of kindness and friendship. You must forgive this hurried line before dinner, but I *must* thank you directly.

Yours
Ettie Grenfell

In the world into which Julian and Billy grew up and in which it was the pattern for men to make themselves infantile in front of women, they could have learned something of masculine dignity from Arthur Balfour. Ettie wrote to him in later years – 'You do not know what a great Idea you were in the boys' lives, as well as a most beloved presence: they most truly adored you, and in the strangest way you guided them – all unknown to yourself – as you do all of us who love you . . .'

Ettie's letters to Arthur Balfour are among the few of hers of this time that have survived: they are in the style that she probably sometimes used to her other admirers. But because Arthur Balfour remained somewhat disembodied, they contain none of the ruthlessness that she sometimes seemed to use to those who were more pressing. In Ettie's letters are the sense of wonder, the funniness – as well as the gushingness – that others found so attractive:

> Government House Madras
> January 10th 1892

My dear Mr Arthur,

   ... One feels to have woken up in quite a new world and I long for a new language to talk about it in ... the wonderful moonlight, dawn, *visible* vibrating heat, and those marvellous skies every evening: doesn't one feel always to have been colour blind and suddenly to have had one's eyes opened to see what orange and blue and scarlet really mean! I long to spread out my mat on the roadside like the Hindoos and just watch the strange rainbow life passing and passing; don't you wish we were all gleaming copper-coloured instead of mealy-white? ... We were at Bombay for a few days on the way here; oh! such a poisonous railway journey, exactly like being put in a baking oven and tied behind a London dustcart for two days in a strong wind. They had their 'Dignity Ball' at Madras on Monday night, it was such a very curious sight, the extraordinary English crowd and the grave sad Rajahs in the background with such sad patient faces. I think R. Kipling is horribly misleading about Indian Society, the women seem *so* washed out, flabby and dowdy: the men a little better, especially Generals over 82 who are quite spirited ...

One of Arthur Balfour's masculine accomplishments was to have written, in 1879, a serious philosophic work – *A Defence of Philosophic Doubt*. This pointed out confusions in some of the currently fashionable ideas about science: scientists claimed in the first place that only what could be sensed was 'real' but then demonstrated that in fact what was sensed was 'unreal': in his work, Balfour raised questions which modern philosophers of science are still answering. But Balfour made claims for religion: since science could not establish 'truth' but could only put up hypotheses to be knocked down, what gave validity to this process was still faith – something held by custom and tradition rather than achieved by reason. Balfour was unique amongst the Souls in that he took science seriously: but his attitude towards religion was representative of the Souls who, for all their sophistication, liked to appeal to mystery. Life on earth was a game, usually a sad one, and energy could be maintained only by reference to a life beyond. In 1893, when the Conservatives

were for a while out of office, Arthur Balfour went away to write his
second book of philosophy –

Hotel Gassin
Pau.
22.1.93

Dear Mrs Etty,

I always say you are the most amusing letter writer in the world: guess
therefore what my delight was at receiving a masterpiece like the one you
wrote me from your bed of sickness. It warmed me through and through as I sat
shivering in my fur coat over a smoky wood fire struggling ineffectually
against the rigours of a southern winter! I hope that on your side you have now
finally thrown off all remains of your feverish chill; though I do *not* hope that
you have found a doctor venal enough to allow you to go to Eaton – partly
because I think it would have been very bad for you; partly, perhaps chiefly,
because as I cannot be there myself I do not see why anyone else should have
the chance.

I have enjoyed my stay here very much, though my life has been of a
monotony of which you stay-at-home people can form no adequate conception.
As soon as the weakness of the flesh allows me to get out of bed and dress I fly
on one of the wings of the abominable little coupés which are here the
recognized means of transport either to the golf ground or to the tennis court.
With a due interval for déjeuner I cultivate one or other of the noble pastimes
till it is dark: then I come in, pile up the logs on the fire, put on my furs, and
sit down to write my Immortal Work till dinner. After dinner Alice [she was
his sister] and I play Bezique – two games and no more. I have taught her the
art since we came here: and I think I must have taught her well, for she
usually rubicons me and inevitably beats me. Fortunately we do not play for
money, and I hope that through this inexpensive channel to get rid of my bad
luck for the year. Bezique over, we read till bed time: sleep nine hours and
then recommence – an excellent way of getting through life, which only
requires an occasional very nice letter from a very dear friend to make it
perfect. Alas! that it will be over by next Wed, when we go to Paris, staying
there for a night, and crossing on Friday. Yours, A.J.B.

The book that he was writing was *Foundations of Belief*, which was published
two years later, and which gained a certain amount of attention; for the
Conservatives were again in power and Arthur Balfour was Leader of the
House of Commons. *Foundations of Belief* carried on the argument from
A Defence of Philosophic Doubt. It ridiculed the pretensions of rationalism or

'naturalism': naturalism could give no reason for anyone to trust in reason; for this there had to be a metaphysical framework. This was what faith built up. But still, such a framework contained little hope for this life; earth was a spark within a universe of ice, and heaven was won by an individual's wit and wonder. It was such qualities that he continued to appreciate in Ettie.

> Stack.
> Reay Forest. Lairg.
> September 2nd 1894

My dear Mr Arthur,
... This house is quite tiny, but the outlook quite beautiful, down the river Laxford one way and up the lochs the other and Stack hill hanging right over us at the back – my huge family wild with delight at anything and everything. It's a great thing to be at the stage when getting worms for the bait is quite an equal excitement to catching the fish! ... I walked 19 miles yesterday to the top of Arkle, so beautiful it was, the sea on three sides and miles and miles of hill and loch in the gleams of sunshine then the white mist rolling in all around and under one. It is such curious country all that side – *utterly* bare black scald-grey rock, it looks as if it had been *scraped* by the wind ... We had great fun our week at Bolton, what a *marvel* the Duchess is of spirits and energy; but I came to the conclusion after a week that no one *ever* has looked such a great age, she *must* be a hundred – those orange eyes and accordion-pleated cheeks and adamant figure – however she walked simply for ever on those clockwork legs ... I am reading Drummond's *Ascent of Man* with the greatest interest, I long to know that it's 'passed sound' by all you who know, I mean the scientific part. I think as a hypothesis it is much more *attractive* than Kidd's? I have been reading an old novel, *Wuthering Heights*, don't you think it is *quite* wonderful? It holds one like a spell I think, every page charged like the hour before a thunderstorm ... We are off to kirk at Lochmore where the Duke does a weekly 'record' through the prayers. Goodbye, my dear Mr Arthur. Yrs. E.G.

Arthur Balfour's closest friend was Mary Elcho – the wife of Hugo, Ettie's old admirer, and the sister of George Wyndham and the sister-in-law of Evan Charteris: there was something incestuous about the congregation of the Souls. Mary Elcho and Ettie were also great friends; one of the bonds between them being their grave attention to Arthur Balfour. Sometimes, however, they went in for amusements more extrovert, which cast an unusual light on the activities of the Souls.

Ascott, Wing,
Leighton Buzzard
April 29th 1895

My darling Mary,

I am writing to tell you of a glorious project we have formed, and am quite shaking as I write with eagerness that it should smile upon you – do *try* to think well of it as you read? It is to go over to *Normandy* at Whitsuntide for 4 days or if possible 5 taking over our bicycles, and go from one of those beautiful old towns to another, taking it *quite* easy, Alfred Milner knows the country well and undertakes to do 'Cook' . . . We ride slowly along the Seine on perfect and absolutely level roads and through lovely pasture lands and orchards just coming in for the end of the blossom and keeping always in touch with the *Railway* (on account of luggage) so that anyone who was the least tired would just nip in with their bicycle to one of those dear French trains that apparently always stop if one holds up one's hand! . . . and just go quietly on to the night's resting place. Or, still nicer, go by *boat* on the Seine river. There are *beautiful* old towns, churches, buildings of all sorts to see, he says, and little comfy *very clean* country inns. The projected party is –

1. Alfred Milner
2. 3. Margaret Spencer and John Baring
4. 5. Ettie and Willy
6. Mr Norton (a very nice boy)
These are *pretty* certain. Then –
7. Mr A.J.B. who I *really* do think would come with pressure?
8. Evan
9. Mary Elcho . . .
. . . if you could come you need not bicycle *at all* if it would be tiring . . . we propose taking *one courier* for the whole party, just to convey luggage (say we take just one bag each) and I think *one maid* between the four women just to do the dreary drag of packing and unpacking bags every day? My Martins speaks every language and says she'd *love* to come and do for us all? or we could take yours or *anything* you liked? You see the one point is to get *you*. . . .

Ettie's powers of persuasion in this instance failed (Mary Elcho was known as 'Napoleon' amongst the Souls and was a match for Ettie); neither she nor Arthur Balfour came. But a party consisting of Ettie, Willy, Evan, Alfred Milner, Mr Norton and May Balfour did go to Dieppe with their bicycles and then to Rouen and Le Havre and Honfleur and it rained and thundered and dogs barked all night and some of the party packed up and went with the lady's maid in the train (this is the one reference in Ettie's letters to Martins her maid). Willy had to leave them to go to Paris on business (he was attending a conference on Bimetallism) but Ettie and Evan and Alfred Milner stuck it out and bicycled thirty miles a day, and Ettie and Evan managed to have some romantic tryst at Pont de l'Arche (Evan reminded her on the anniversary – 'A year ago – Pont de l'Arche!'). This was the side of the Souls not much dwelt on – the walking or bicycling for miles over moors or rough roads, while maids and couriers went by train.

Arthur Balfour was important in the world in which Julian and Billy grew up not only because he was respected but because he would have taught them the value of observation and thought. But for all his serenity, Balfour's attitudes to life were still pessimistic; they were based on hope in another life, and a surrender of worry about this. For fifty years he was at the very centre of the social and political worlds; he brought the two together in that he influenced society to be intellectual and politics to be witty; he remained an individualist, hardly representative even of the party that he led. Julian would have loved the individualism and the irony: he hated the idealism and the world-weariness. Balfour foresaw the descent of Europe towards war: he was one of the few politicians who prepared for war, quietly and efficiently encouraging the building of new battleships and the production of new weapons; he also foresaw something of the social forces which would be at work after a war. But his appreciation of all this was in the light of his belief in another world; and this belief, Julian came to think, was what encouraged futility in this world. Arthur Balfour became President of the Society of Psychical Research; many of his friends, including Ettie, became interested in things like séances and ouija boards; they were searching for explanations, but not for change. Nothing, finally, seemed more absolute or interesting than death. Ettie wrote to Mary Elcho at this time about the death of a mutual friend – 'I have never so much felt the unintelligibility, the irreconcilableness: yet through the very extremity of suffering one feels, almost against one's will, the *proof* of Intention. Chance could never be so wildly, blindly, cruel? And in Intention, however inscrutable, one can rest'.

❦ ELEVEN ❦

The Souls did not meet so often after 1895. Arthur Balfour became increasingly involved in government – Lord Salisbury was frequently ill or away on foreign affairs and Balfour deputized for him as Prime Minister. George Wyndham went to South Africa – there had recently occurred the Jameson Raid and romantic Tories were getting ready for more serious exercises in imperialism. George Curzon, after years of one journey after another, married in 1895 and in 1898 went to India as Viceroy – though he still dreamed of Ettie, as had been his custom.

Viceregal Lodge Simla
Sept 11 1901:

For a whole night I have dreamed of you – no hope of reciprocity – they were wonderful dreams, lovers' dreams, in which things uncontemplated in life were realized in that glowing fancy haze. Now that I am awake again and am respectable it is a heavy shock to find that there is no love, no triumph, no embrace; not even the fugutive consolation of a kiss. Ah me!

Lord Pembroke died. Margot Tennant married Herbert Asquith. (Ettie wrote – 'Poor darling little Margot, I think she felt very sad and strained and "reactionary" rather as it all came quite near – she is not the very least in love with him and faces it, but I do thoroughly believe it will all go well ... Poor Asquith as white as a sheet too and has grown quite thin with emotions!') There were new luminaries from a younger generation appearing on the scene. Ettie wrote to Arthur Balfour about a weekend at Panshanger – 'Winston leads general conversation on the hearthrug solely addressing himself in the looking glass – a sympathetic and admiring audience'. The new generation were aggressive; they were in reaction against the self-deprecating irony of the Souls.

In 1892 Lord Pembroke had been able to write to Ettie about the election in which Willy had stood as Liberal candidate for Hereford –

Truly the detachment of we English in the matter of politics is sublime, almost ridiculous. There you are doing your best to frustrate and procure the condemnation of the six years work of your greatest friend A. J. Balfour; and here am I who am convinced that a Gladstonian victory is a very grave national disaster in itself and probably symptomatic of worse things to come writing to congratulate you on Willy's success.

But at the end of the century sides began to crystallize like those in war: men who met in country houses now were apt to find themselves in agreement. By the time Willy stood again for Parliament, in 1900, for South Bucks, he was a Conservative.

The violence that lurks within most societies had for some time in British politics been concentrated upon Ireland: in 1893, over the Home Rule Bill, members of the House of Commons had come to blows. Then with the rejection of the Home Rule Bill by the Lords, and after Gladstone's retirement, passions had suddenly cooled and the struggle was shelved. It was then that Liberals and Conservatives looked around for re-alignments. Some turned aggression as it were against themselves (the 'decadence' of the 1890s was that of elegant people with no one to spite except themselves) and some wandered in the corridors of power like ghosts as if searching for new fires in which to poke their irons.

For years the pattern of war had been that of small posses of British soldiers in distant lands fighting hordes of natives and winning with superior weapons. The exception to this had been the killing of Gordon at Khartoum; but this had been avenged by Kitchener at Omdurman. But shortly after this Kitchener hoisted the Anglo–Egyptian flag at Fashoda on the Upper Nile and Colonel Marchand hoisted the French flag at the same place and at the same time and there had almost been war in the Tom-Tiddler's-Ground of Europe: then Germany took over the port of Kiao-Chau in Shantung, and Britain took over Wei-hai-wei on the Gulf of Pechili, and again there seemed to be congestion on political musical chairs. There were even prospects of war, for a time, between Britain and the United States on the grounds of a boundary dispute between British Guiana and Venezuela. It was as if people were looking round for justifications for war; and politicians were having to scrape the diplomatic barrel.

The life of the Grenfell family had settled into its patterns – the winter

at Taplow, the spring when the parents went to London, the holidays
when children and parents were together. There were new crazes – you
could take your bicycles by train and explore the countryside; you could
skate, both on roller skates and on ice. The hunting, shooting and fishing
went on the same; as did, for Ettie, the reassurances and adoration.
There were times when Ettie's motives for soliciting these were questioned
– 'Of course you are a very attractive woman, and I think you well
measure your power, but I wonder why you trouble to pour into my ears
and eyes the double distilled honey of flattery?' – but this was written in
1897 by the 'I.G.' (Ivor Guest) of Betty Montgomery's letter to Ettie of
1901, by which time he was apparently threatening suicide. Ettie
herself sometimes wondered why she took such trouble with these
routines when she was most happy with Willy and the children: but she
had become accustomed to them, and needed them.

Willy occupied himself in his usual ways during the years 1893–1900
when he was out of Parliament: he climbed in the Alps, he took up fencing
again, he became President of the Four-in-Hand Driving Club, he
travelled as British delegate to international conferences on Bimetallism.
He continued to write to Ettie his careful, tender letters, in which he
told her not of himself, but of his movements.

Beyond the circles of their friends, their families, their Parliamentary
politics, their sports, Willy and Ettie did not seem to look much at what
was going on around them. They did not talk of social conditions. No. 4
St James's Square, which was where they stayed when they were in London,
was only a hundred yards or so from the Haymarket, which for years had
been one of the most flamboyant centres of prostitution in Europe. Its
speciality had been child prostitution. Moves had been made to clear up
the area: but the trade just moved to north of Piccadilly. Respectable
people who lived so close did not seem to notice any of this: at least they
did not talk of it. They had been trained that what was not ideal, in
some way did not exist.

Of the poor as a whole respectable people did not think too much:
there were certain areas of poverty allocated to them, which they called
their 'districts', and these served as justification perhaps not to notice
the rest. Ettie had a 'district' in Maidenhead where she visited the poor
in their homes and in the workhouse: she took them food and clothes,
sometimes accompanied by her children. The poor were grateful – 'Dear
Madam, May we ask you to accept the enclosed small present with every
good wish for the coming season from The Women of Your District'. One

day a year Ettie had them all up to Taplow; she described the scene to Arthur Balfour –

You cannot imagine what a day we spent after you left, the rain and the 'District' arrived together and very soon the latter were reduced merely to –
    wet black bundles = old women
    wet white bundles = babies
– and there we were, helpless, from 2.30 to 8. The boys and W played up nobly and had races and games for the children in the *downpour* while I herded with the very old and the very young in the tennis court where we had feeble games and feebler conversation and were miserable – and to so many of them it is just the *one* small 'out' of the year. Wasn't it cruel?

– but this was probably more than many such families did. And in the 1890s a 'district' must have seemed as foreign and strange as an under-developed country does today.

Ettie and Willy were not extremely rich according to the standards of the day: their total expenditure on housekeeping at Taplow in the year 1899 was £2,118. 6. 10½d. (this was Ettie's figure: she kept precise records). By far the most expensive months were June, when there were '3 Sunday Parties' and Ascot; and December, when there was Christmas. Even with the purchasing power of the pound being then about ten times what it is now (1975) this was not a huge expenditure for an aristocratic family in a large house requiring a dozen or so servants. Willy's income consisted mainly in rentals from the 3,000 acres of the Taplow estate: he also experimented with mining shares and with shares in Canada. But until 1913, when Ettie inherited her own fortune, the family had to take care about money. Willy and Ettie sometimes had the reputation of being rather mean (Ettie did not have good taste) but they lived up to the limit of their income. Each month Ettie filled in the columns of her Household Accounts in her careful, childish handwriting – 'Butler's book – £68. 5. 3½, Housekeeper's book – £28. 11. 1½, Cook's book – £71. 3. 9½' and then further details on the page opposite – 'Butcher – £43. 1. 1½, Fish-monger – £19. 14. 0½, Oilman and Lamps – £23. 15. 6'. She did this every month of every year: the process seemed to be some offering to those who really had to care about money.

There are no details of servants' wages at Taplow: these seem to have been included in 'Butler's' and 'Housekeeper's' books. But normally before 1900 housemaids would have been paid only a few shillings a week; butlers, housekeepers and cooks quite a bit more – and earnings by them would have been supplemented by tips from guests. Evan Charteris said he always tipped Mr Barrett Good the butler at Taplow half a sovereign and a whole one if he had no change; and there were often up to twenty weekend guests. But the matter of wages seemed to be of secondary importance even to lower-paid servants: the main question was whether or not they would be well looked after. A woman applying to Ettie for the job of housekeeper in 1900 wrote 'wages are a secondary consideration to me . . . I prefer a smaller Establishment to very large ones' (she had been a still-room maid with the Earl of Crewe). And Ettie did look after her servants even after they had become too old to work: 'I can assure you my dear Lady what I should have done if it had not been for you I don't know, you have been my Dearest Friend on earth and I can assure you I have always felt there was no one I could trust like you'. And when they were with her servants at Taplow took on a certain prestige: ladies' maids, valets and coachmen in the fashionable world all knew each other and formed their own society somewhat according to the status of their employers. When Mr Barrett Good, the butler, went to church at Taplow, he went in just behind Willy and they both wore top hats. A gardener wrote to Ettie – 'As I grow older I see more and more how much we are dependant on one another, and how the different classes fit into the framework of society, and then notice that honesty of purpose comes in everywhere . . .'

The rumours of war that had been gathering found substance in 1899. The Boers in South Africa had established a racialist state in the Transvaal; then when gold had been discovered there in the 1880s there had been an influx of English, French, Germans and Jews. These outnumbered the Boers; but the Boers allowed them no vote and few civil rights. The British High Commissioner in Cape Town was Alfred Milner – he who had acted as 'Cook' (of 'Cook's Tours') to Ettie and her bicycle tour in Normandy in 1895. Milner protested about the treatment of the British in the Transvaal: the Boers rejected the protest, and invaded Cape Colony. Thus a war began in which, at first, small posses of natives, as it were, seemed to be overrunning the hordes of a British army. For once the British could feel patriotic and romantic without guilt.

The South African War changed very little in Britain except perhaps that after victory it loosed new diamond-and-gold-millionaires upon the social scene in London. What it might have changed, but did not, was the image of the British Army as a body officered by professional soldiers trained to win, instead of a body officered by (which was nearer the case) an escort agency for young ladies and horses both at home and in the East. British officers in the Boer War were for the most part incompetent. Quick victory had so long been taken for granted, that people were surprised when battle was found not to be exciting.

Douglas Compton, Ettie's old confidant, wrote from the war –

We go on marching about week after week aimlessly and uselessly . . . we have come back here very slowly clearing the country thoroughly, taking away every living thing, and destroying all food. As I said before, it is a method that does not commend itself much to me.

Willy joined the Bucks Volunteers and went to a camp in Kent. He wrote how sorry he was that he would miss the summer with the family; also he was sorry he was too old to be in the war. Ettie wrote to a friend – 'These are anxious days, but what courage and faith one has about it all . . . My boys are aching to plunge in, and long for the day when we touch our reserves of 11 and 9!'

Ettie told one of her funny stories to Arthur Balfour. There had been a big shoot at a country house where Ettie had been staying, and her host had shouted at one of the beaters – 'Get back into the wood or I'll shoot you!' Then he had turned to Ettie and explained – 'This beat is particularly well wooded'.

In January 1901 Queen Victoria died. Ettie wrote to Mary Elcho –

Wasn't it beautiful and wonderful, so the *Truth of Death*, that triumphal procession, and the note of Victory, and the blaze and colour as she passed; and the quite *silent* crowds, more thrilling than any storm of Jubilee cheers; wasn't it exactly 'the beauty and the joy of living, the beauty and blessedness of death!'

❦ PART II ❦

Boyhood
1901—1910

A book about the past depends on what information is available: the Grenfell family were not at the front of public life and there is little in print about them; information for this book comes mainly from letters and documents left by Ettie Desborough after her death in 1952. There were thousands of these letters, in neat bundles, dated, so that there was the impression that what had survived had been passed for survival.

Ettie described her attitude to keeping letters when writing to Mary Wemyss (Elcho) in the 1920s. 'I came across a big box of letters and tore them up in the train . . . scattering a funny paper chase of scraps of paper so living 20 years ago. It is terribly like tearing up life – perhaps one ought never to keep letters – but among them were such wonderful ones from George, and I couldn't help saving a few from the rushing wind behind the train'. Ettie kept more letters from George Wyndham than she seems to have suggested to Mary Wemyss – all those, it appears that were of interest in themselves.

Letters cannot be too much trusted as purveyors of information; they are often written to impress, to justify, to amuse, to plead. A reader outside the context can misunderstand a situation. But letters which are passed for survival by the sender or the recipient have their own validity: the interest they have held in themselves is a mark of authenticity.

In dealing with these letters there is a feeling that a reader or a writer is being led on some paper chase like that in which Ettie scattered her trail out of the train; participation is being offered in some game like those which she and her contemporaries so elaborately enjoyed. There are clues, hints, false trails, sudden prizes. There are the codes that players in the 1890s used among themselves – John Baring's letters to Ettie, for instance, with their references to 'E' and 'C'. These references, at a superficial reading, could be taken as real: it is only if a reader or writer cares enough about the participants that he comes to realize they are not. Many of the dates have been torn from the tops of John Baring's letters which makes fitting them into the puzzle difficult: but the letters have not been destroyed, so that sense can still be *found with effort. Some affecting but perhaps potentially dangerous letters had been hidden in packets of quite different dates – Betty Montgomery's letter of 1901 about Evan Charteris for instance was in a bundle of family letters of the 1940s. There was one envelope of particularly passionate letters from Evan Charteris which had on the outside, in the shaky handwriting of Ettie's extreme old age, the word 'Alice' and 'Letters from E to A' – Alice being Ettie's old and great friend Alice Salisbury (Gore). But it is quite clear, to an enquirer who takes enough trouble, that the letters are to Ettie and not to Alice Salisbury; their contents can be checked against engagement books, telegrams, other letters. Ettie herself would have known that this might become clear: it was as if, by her false trails, she was just making sure that she would deceive only those who did not have enough care to solve her riddles: for those who had she had seen there were provisions – like the Sphinx.*

This is encouraging for a writer who might otherwise feel awkward about prying into other people's affairs; but not if these affairs have been laid out like a maze. After Ettie's death her papers went to her daughter Monica: Monica too went through them, sifting; she picked out bits for private circulation – always those that were cheerful, for she was censorious of the dark. But she, too, does not seem to have destroyed much of which she did not approve. Like Ettie, perhaps she had the confidence to believe that others would see things like herself.

After Monica's death in 1973 the papers were lent to the present author. Nearly all the quotations in this book are from these papers; when they are not, the source is noted in the text. (The chief exceptions to this are the letters that Julian wrote to Marjorie Manners: these letters are in the possession of her son, the Marquess of Anglesey.) Julian died when he was twenty-seven and was known as a solitary man; it is unlikely that he wrote many letters to people outside his family. And of these, none seem to have been destroyed. In any case, with the story being kept mainly to the trails and guidelines left in the Grenfell papers there is the impression of some of the participants having a hand in the unravelling themselves; which is an encouragement, when the story is critical.

There remains the question of what Julian would have made of a book about himself; for he did not live to leave his own clues and trails, and his mother wrote his memorial. But Julian, more than nearly all of his contemporaries, felt that he had something of his own to say; and during his lifetime he was mocked when he tried to say it. The collection of essays that he wrote and tried to get published when he was twenty-one was ignored: it was his critique of the society around him. This book has sympathy with Julian's critique: and any author likes to hope that his work may one day be recognized.

PREVIOUS PAGE Ettie
Grenfell.

TOP LEFT Katie Cowper and
Ettie in the eighties.
TOP RIGHT Willy Grenfell in
the eighties.
BOTTOM Mother and son in
1888.

Father and son in 1890: a page from Ettie's Children's Journal.

1890.

to forgive him, so he said "Forgive me. Millie. Amen!"

August 21. Max said today " Do you like Dada? I

think Dada's such a nice woman " He is so fond of little

Billy now, & said

one day " I

'alighted with

Billy — I like

'joy him "

Dada. Max. August, 1890.

TOP The Grenfell family, 1900:
Willy, Ivo, Billy, Julian, Ettie,
Nanny Wake and Monica.
BOTTOM LEFT Julian and Billy as
pages, 1897.
RIGHT Ettie, Julian and Billy,
1900.

House party in the 1890s: Henry Chaplin (host) centre, with monocle; the Prince of Wales to his left; Ettie Grenfell behind the Prince; Arthur Balfour behind Henry Chaplin; George Curzon fourth from left (standing); Willy Grenfell third from right (standing).

TOP John Baring with Monica.
BOTTOM Maurice Baring, Ettie, Evan
Charteris and Julian.

TOP Henry Wilson, Bron
Herbert (in chair) and Winston
Churchill, Taplow, 1901.
BOTTOM Monica and Archie
Gordon (with Elsie Graham).

TOP The Grenfell family on horseback,
1904.
BOTTOM LEFT Julian and Ivo, 1901.
RIGHT Julian and Lord Kitchener,
1902.

❧ TWELVE ❧

Julian went to Eton in 1901. Eton is unlike other English public schools in that it inculcates the patterns of a ruling class not only by making boys undergo the mixture of brutality and reassurance by which tribal loyalties are fashioned, but it provides a level of confidence and sophistication from which some boys can look down on these loyalties with charm.

When Julian had gone to Eton to take his entrance exam he had noticed the customs by which boys were taught to respect arbitrary conventions – hands had to be held in pockets, streets had to be walked in only on one side, crossings had to be made not straight but at an angle. When he settled in in the autumn term (or Michaelmas Half, as was the jargon) the brutality was there – 'There are a good many *brutes* here but I don't yet know of any in the house, and I think it's really quite easy to keep out of their way if you try'. But brutality was as usual not much talked about: it was accepted as training for the world outside. Julian wrote consistently to his mother that he was happy as he had done from Summerfields: 'I am very well'; 'I like it here awfully'. It would have been difficult to write anything different, and to be approved.

The thousand or so boys at Eton live in houses, forty or fifty to a house, with a housemaster in charge of each. Julian was in A.A. Somerville's house, which seemed kinder than most. 'Poor Horner is at a most terrible house and I am sure he is not having a very good time'. In domestic affairs the older boys at Eton have almost despotic power over the younger: this is epitomized in fagging – the system by which big boys can summon little boys and treat them like servants. 'The big chaps here are awfully lazy, one called me just then to fetch a book he had left at a chap's room at the other end of the passage.' It is unlikely that Julian in fact suffered very much from older boys; his alertness and good looks would have protected him. But at the end of his first term he was writing – 'The chaps who are brutes are beginning to leave me alone now and I am getting to know some of the others' – and this illustrates another pattern that was to become pronounced as he grew older, his way of never complaining about anything until the circumstances which gave rise to complaint were past.

The pressures from the family were more than ever that he should succeed. When Ettie visited him just after the start of his first term she discovered that he had been put in the form usually reserved for scholars though he had not taken a scholarship; she wrote to Willy –

I felt literally physically *sick* with happiness – isn't it *wonderful?* he is *above* Horner and the other scholarship boys! . . . Matron told us that only *one* other boy had done it ever since she has been at Eton!! He was so happy, and so darling and modest, saying he'd just 'happened' to get the questions he knew.

Julian did himself now seem to care less about success: his letters home still reported cricket scores and form placings, but without much interest. His style becomes even more formal, as if drained of forbidden feeling.

Ettie wrote in her Family Journal that Julian himself used to say that he passed through 'a very priggish inward state' during his early years at Eton. He was prepared for Confirmation, and set great store by the talks he had with his religious instructor Mr Bowlby. Mr Bowlby wrote to Ettie –

Talk after talk we seemed to get closer; and his quick intelligence, his fearless honesty, his love of all things noble, his loathing of all things base, called up the very best in one's own nature and longings. If you say I have helped him, it is equally true that he has helped me. It is wonderful – will you let me say it? – to have given birth to and trained such a boy.

A boy has some chance to live his own life at Eton; he has his own room, and he can to some extent work, walk, dream in his own time. This is the best of Eton. But he still has to become emotionally impervious: the conventional world, brutal and charming, is strong around him. To be an individual he has to build up a shell; and the danger of a shell is that after a time it can stifle the growth of the substance inside it.

There is a letter from Julian to John Revelstoke of this time which gives more of a glimpse of his life at Eton than most of his letters to his mother. John Revelstoke (his mother's lover) had given Julian the present of a horse.

                                                                          Eton. Windsor
Dear John,
     Thank you awfully for your glorious present, it is too tremendously kind of you; when I got your letter this morning I was so bumptious that the fellows

had to suppress me forcibly; it is really too ripping to be true – and *Robin* too!
I quite despise the 'Old Berkeley' now when I have got a Leicestershire hunter.
I am simply longing to see him. I hear he is going to arrive on Thursday.

Tomorrow I am going over to Taplow for Short Leave; the hounds meet at
Woodburn Green, 3 miles from us, so I shall get a ripping day's hunting,
Hurrah. I am going to ride Goliath, Dad's 17.2 hunter, whom I adore, but am
sure I shall never look at him again after seeing Robin. I have had five days up
to now this year, one an excellent day with the Bucks and Berks stag.

My stupid finger will bleed all over the paper.

I wonder if you have had any very good sport in Leicestershire this year:
there has been practically no frost, anyhow. The country would be very
frightening after this, where you never get more than one jump an hour.

I am simply enjoying my head off here, was there ever such a place? I have
got a ripping lot of friends, and that makes the whole difference.

I run 3 days a week with the Eton beagles, who are really a first class 15 inch
pack. We had killed 108 hares this half, 9 last – we had one fearful mishap,
3 hounds run over and killed by a G.W.R. express.

I am up to Macnaughton this half, for the 3rd time; he is fearfully keen, and
the division are a very hot lot, mostly tugs.[1] You must come down to Taplow
some time next holidays if you ever have time, and I will try not to be late (?)
this time.

I am being confirmed this half: Bowlby prepares me, he is a first class man,
I simply love him.

Do you think you could send me a photograph of you, if you have got one
anywhere at hand; it would be splendid for my room here.

It was too awfully kind of you to give me such a topping present, and I can't
thank you enough.

Yours very aff:

Julian

In 1903 there was a fire at night in one of the houses, and two of the
boys were killed. There were bars across the windows on the lower floors
of the house so that it was difficult for boys to get out or for rescuers to
get in. Julian described the scene to his mother – 'One great fellow is
supposed to have gone off his head . . . Kindersley is absolutely dazed, and
Caledon's hand is dreadfully burned'. He explained how it was thought
that the fire had started from a fuse. One of the chaplains had talked to
the boys; he had told them 'he was sure God would not allow a thing like

---

[1] Scholars.

this to happen unless it was for the good of the sufferers in the end. Then he absolutely broke down and sobbed, it really was terribly pathetic'.

The resulting attitudes of the authorities were typical of Eton. There was a sermon preached in the College Chapel which Julian thought 'far the best sermon I have ever heard'. The preacher suggested (Julian sent a copy of the text to his mother) that –

the call of God which summoned two of your number away was not meant for them alone but for us all . . . Are we not meant to go into his presence too – to see at least the train of his Majesty filling our temple now – the Lord sitting on his throne – so loving yet so stern – so unapproachable in his infinite holiness – in order that we, so hardly escaped from peril, may know our own sinfulness and feel ourselves unclean, unclean?

A few days later again, Julian described to his mother how it seemed probable now that the fire had been started not by a defective fuse nor even by a God who wanted the boys to feel unclean but by an arsonist:

It is quite true about the fellow who tried to set Rawlins' on fire ['Rawlins'' was the name of one of the houses to which the burned-out boys had been transferred; 'Kindersley's' was the house of the original fire] his name is Moore. A fellow found him on the passage watching a fire he had just lighted with the things in his grate; he asked him to put it out but Moore said 'No, don't, doesn't it burn rippingly!' The fellow then put it out, and Rawlins got some doctors down to look at Moore. I believe, but no one seems to know, that they said he was mad, and anyway he has gone away . . . Moore was the first fellow to get out of Kindersley's on the morning of the fire and the only fellow who had got his clothes on . . . All this seems to show that it was him who set Kindersley's on fire, but of course no one can prove it, and it may have been the fire at Kindersley's that gave him a sort of fire-madness . . .

It was this that was typical – the pattern of disaster, heroism, the claim that God was teaching one a lesson; and the whole thing packaged in purple preacher's prose. And after the discovery of human agency and madness still – this could not be talked about – there remained the need for preaching and justification. The bars on the windows of houses were removed; but God could find other ways to remind boys of their un-worthiness. Disaster was the proof of a loving God; how else could life be bearable? Guilt, with a kind and punishing God, was not man's respon-sibility. Such were conventional confusions.

Julian wrote to his mother every week and she replied and also visited him four or five times a term. His letters continued bright, but the emptiness at the centre remained. Taplow was only five miles away and he could run there and back during a half-holiday afternoon; he sometimes did this – and then could let his mother know what a good time they had had. 'I don't think anyone could have done more or had more fun in one day.' But still, he did not tell her about what was going on – apart from fun. He played the usual football and cricket and racquets and fives but he did not excel at these; what he did love were things he could do on his own, such as beagling. For this, he would even put off a chance of getting to Taplow. In work he was usually near the top of his classes though he now did not set so much store by these achievements. The one subject in which he was outstanding was the composition of Latin verses.

In 1903 Billy won the second top scholarship to Eton: Julian sent the news to his family by telegram. Ettie wrote – 'We were wild with joy and so many telegrams of congratulations came; Willy and I had a wonderful Marlborough House Ball that night – everybody's kindness and rejoicing about Bill!' (Arthur Balfour, who was Prime Minister, wrote to Ettie 'How proud I am to be Godfather to his sister!') Julian did not on the surface seem to be jealous of Billy; he would joke about Billy's superior scholastic achievements – 'I got First Class in trials and he got Distinction, the brute!' – though he once cried out about some achievement of his own 'that he will never do!' (Billy did.) But he would at this time (in Ettie's words) 'go and see Billy every Sunday afternoon and lecture him severely "for his own good": the interview invariably ended in a terrific fight – nothing made the boys laugh more in after years! . . .' This was when Julian was still suffering from what Ettie called his 'inward priggishness'; which was, perhaps, the beginning of his struggle to break free from his past. He did in letters sometimes complain about Billy's vagueness – and about his failure to show him letters from their mother meant for both. And Billy did, from time to time, have fits of aggression and depression at Eton. But what was noticeable was that when Billy was getting bad reports Julian usually did well – he won the school prize for Latin Verse – and when Billy was working hard again, Julian became ill. He got mumps in 1905 just before an important exam: and in 1906 before the same exam again he was seriously ill for twenty-four hours with sudden and inexplicable blood-poisoning and had to be taken home to Taplow. He did not in fact win any of the major school prizes which Billy won later, nor did he succeed when he tried for a scholarship to Balliol.

Julian's heart seems to have been most involved during his time at Eton –

together with running with the beagles and an obsession about keeping himself fit – in the editing of the school magazine, the *Eton College Chronicle*. He was one of two editors – the other was Ronald Knox – and he wrote leading articles, reports of school events, and poems. These achievements did not seem to call forth the same rapture from home as would have done successes in exams or cricket. Julian also took an increasing interest in the house and school debating societies. The proposals he spoke in favour of were – 'That Englishmen spend too much time playing football' (for which he was booed); 'That it was wrong for a country to expel Jews' (which motion was lost by three votes to four); 'That fagging should be abolished' (though he confessed that privately he favoured it); and 'That England is not degenerate' – for which proposal he was having difficulty, he wrote home, in finding any statistics.

He became the head of his house and a member of Pop – the self-electing oligarchy through which Eton boys contribute to the running of the school; which sets the conventions about who shall cross the road slanting and who shall go straight; who shall wear fancy waistcoats and who shall put sealing wax in their top-hats. In some ways Julian became a traditional member of Pop: he wrote – 'The Lower Boys are all *terrified* of me, they bring me my tea, get my bath, empty it, and clean up my room every day'; but in some ways he was different. A Captain of a house can, if he likes, keep an eye on new boys. Julian wrote – 'Poor Larry Melgund is fearfully backward; he is too delicate to play games and his eyes are too bad to read. Poor little fellow! What can he do? I go and see him whenever I have time'.

Together with Julian in Pop were the friends who were to go with him on to Balliol and later to the war – Charles Lister, Patrick Shaw Stewart, Edward Horner, Denys Finch-Hatton – and they and others formed a group which, after they were dead, was taken as almost mythical in that it seemed a brilliant culmination of an Eton tradition. Julian, while he was editor of the official *Eton College Chronicle*, started with his friends a rival paper called *The Outsider* – the aim of which was to mock the attitudes expressed in the *Chronicle*. This again was typical of the best of Eton – both to uphold tradition and to laugh at it; to have the confidence to stand back from, while feeling part of, the society in which one found oneself. This was an achievement, probably, of no other public school. *The Outsider* was –

a tearing success; the first edition of 300 copies was sold out in three hours and 130 of the second edition have gone already . . . but of course the great pity is that all the jokes, and the whole point of the paper, are purely Etonian . . . to anyone else most of it must seem perfect gibberish.

Some masters were offended at the jokes at their expense and Julian had to apologize. At the same time he was writing a farewell leading article for the *Chronicle* which was 'sentimental, more or less, but I think much the best I've ever done'.

The worst of Eton is that it is its very sophistication that makes growing away from it difficult. What has been inculcated is charm; and charm is a way of manipulating society. But charm lacks substance; so it is to society that a charming person is tethered, however much he dislikes society. He is beholden to others, because there is not much inside himself.

Julian told a story to his mother of how he was staying at the home of his friend Charles Lister when bound copies of *The Outsider* arrived. Charles Lister's parents were Tommy and Charty Ribblesdale who had once been bright and dashing members of the Souls. Now –

Ribblesdale sits in a corner glaring at Charles and snubbing him as often as he can; poor Charles seems to be having rather a down, but that has no effect at all on his spirits. Charty too gives him tremendous lectures now and then during which he always winks at me and Ronald Knox. Charles' bound *Outsiders* turned up the other day, and were very grimly received. Charty read out selections last night with a set face of boredom; at last Ribblesdale could bear it no longer and fell fast asleep.

It was towards the end of his time at Eton that Julian began to have the battles with his mother that he was to have on and off for the rest of his life. These, he said, were matters of life and death to him. Julian liked being on his own or with one or two friends; Ettie tried to involve him in her social life. Julian liked beagling, riding, fishing – he got permission to fish for perch in the lake of a nearby estate; to sit by the river in one of the master's private gardens – Ettie tried to get him to go to parties. In 1905 he wrote –

> Sound, sound the clarion, fill the fife!
> To all the social world say 'Hang it –
> I, who for seventeen years of life
> Have trod this happy, hustling planet

       I won't go woman-hunting yet,
       I won't be made a social pet!'

He went to some of her parties at Christmas, but not all. Still, he felt guilt about displeasing her. He wrote – 'I am awfully glad you told me about the Sinful Iniquities; and only wish you would more, and always. They are really so important, don't you think?'

Years later, a friend remembered a vision of Ettie and her two sons at Eton at the end of Julian's time there.

It was at some summer festivity, probably the 4th of June 1906; I was coming out from school yard when I saw the Grenfell party – the mother with her two sons and a small daughter. They were walking slowly along in the space between the school buildings and the long low wall on which only Pops were allowed to sit. The mother wore, I think, a green dress. She was slight in build, medium height, not so tall as her sons, holding herself straight, very straight, with an evident air of authority, almost of divinity.

On 4 June each year – a sort of Parents' Day – it is the custom for sixth-form boys to make orations to the assembled company. These orations are chosen by the boys and are usually taken from the classics – those skeletons of Western education for three thousand years. On 4 June 1906 Julian (it was his last term) chose the passage in the *Iliad* where Hector has run away from Achilles because he, Hector, knows he will be killed; and then is persuaded to stand and fight by Athena, the goddess of war. She has disguised herself as one of Hector's friends so that Hector trusts her; but in fact she is on the side of Achilles. Athena gives Achilles back his spear when Hector has got it from him, so it is Hector who is killed. The *Iliad* was considered edifying for boys and parents – a hymn to slaughter and betrayal.

One of the last letters Julian wrote to Ettie from Eton concerned the death of his old nanny, Nanny Wake.

Surely the great maxim is to take everything, and especially death, in the most natural and cheerful way that we possibly can, without letting ourselves be absorbed for one instant in the little petty things or forgetting the great mysterious background that there is to everything. The only way must be what the Greeks insisted upon, and called 'the mean', '*to metrion*' . . .

❦ THIRTEEN ❦

Ettie's way of casting her spell over people was by means of what came to be known as her 'stubborn gospel of joy': this was the name that one of Julian's contemporaries gave to it, referring to Ettie's way of insisting that everything must, regardless of appearances, be all for the best, because to suppose otherwise would be unbearable. And to many of her own generation Ettie was in fact simply a bringer of joy: the number of letters she continued to receive year after year from people telling her she was the one person who brought light into their lives, on whose power they depended for sustenance, is amazing. Her children's generation were initially often more suspicious: it was Cynthia Charteris – the daughter of Mary and Hugo Elcho and niece of Evan Charteris – who coined the phrase 'stubborn gospel of joy'. In later years, when discussing Ettie with a mutual friend, Cynthia Asquith (she had in 1910 married a son of the Prime Minister Herbert Asquith) tried to analyse this. The friend said that his 'quarrel' with Ettie was about her 'constant battling against life'; about the fact that 'her deliberate activity made her mechanical and prohibited any real friendship or the finest companionship . . . she never "blossomed" . . . was never "a rest".'[1] Cynthia Asquith agreed that Ettie's presence was like 'an electric light'; one that 'made one blink' and of which a man at least 'had not got control of the switches in his own hands'. About Ettie's power with women Cynthia Asquith told a story of how once she and Ettie and a group of friends had been discussing a woman's looks in a desultory way when the woman herself came into the room and Ettie exclaimed 'We have all been saying how we would rather look like you than any other woman!' Ettie's white lies had become proverbial (Margot Asquith once said 'Ettie has told enough white lies to ice a cake'); but they still seemed to work. People were 'unveiled like an

[1] Lady Cynthia Asquith, *Diaries 1915–1918* (London, 1968), p. 396.

Egyptian mummy' by Ettie; or 'carried off bound to her chariot-wheels'.[1]
The children of the Souls objected to what they called 'Ettyism', but
they did not have much to put in its place: and in the end they were
mostly charmed by it. Cynthia Asquith wrote that she herself found the
'anti-cant' of the 'Coterie' (as the children of the Souls came to be called)
'suicidal to happiness'; and that she herself had more sympathy with
Ettyism. The cynicism of the Coterie was personified by Cynthia's
brother-in-law Raymond Asquith: 'there is an insidiously corruptive
poison in their midst, brilliantly distilled by their inspiration, Raymond'.[2]

Julian was not deeply involved with the Coterie because at Oxford he
was too much of an individualist and after that he went abroad; so that in
his battles with his mother he was never opposing her 'stubborn gospel of
joy' with an equally conventional cynicism; he had his own gospel, even
his recommendations for joy. What he found false and objected to in
Ettie's gospel was both its naïveté and her promulgation of it in the
fashionable world. It was in this respect, he felt, that she was the same as
the cynics: they played the same strict game on different sides. The real
battle was between those who depended for the ground of their gospels on
the social world, and those who felt seeds of joy could only grow within.

To understand Ettie's dependence on people round her – and, as a
revolt against this, Julian's passion for independence – it is necessary to
remember something of Ettie's own infancy and childhood. Ettie's mother
had died when she was a year old; her father had died when she was two;
her adored brother had died when she was eight and the grandmother on
whom she depended when she was thirteen. Sickness and death were not
hidden nor drugged in the 1870s; pain went on in the home, and children
were within the perimeter of things now seen usually only by hospital
nurses. When Ettie's brother Johnnie was dying his illness lasted a whole
winter; the doctors from the first had little hope though they did not know
what his illness was. This was another characteristic of the age, that
suffering was inexplicable. Ettie was sometimes with Johnnie – an aunt
wrote 'I took poor little Ettie in to him as he lay asleep' – and was
sometimes taken away. Then she herself felt 'desperately forlorn without
Nanny and Johnnie, from whom I had never before been separated'. This
account was written by Ettie over seventy years later. When her grandmother died who had been 'my refuge and strength ever since I could
remember' there was 'added to the sorrow all the wretched embarrassment

[1] op. cit., pp. 394, 396.

[2] op. cit., p. 79.

of a child in grief; the shame of tears, the utter impossibility of expression'. Such calamities to a child have no counter-weight in experience: the loss of someone on whom one is dependent seems total; it is as if life's structure has been taken away. If such losses are repeated, there is induced a terror which perhaps can be warded off only by a determination that things shall not be so. This is possible; but at the price of fantasy. This was Ettie's predicament.

There had been a tradition of melancholy in Ettie's family: her father, Julian Fane, had reputedly died of a broken heart after the loss of his wife: her favourite uncle, Henry Cowper, had seemed to be overwhelmed and to waste away after the death of his favourite sister. There was also this tradition of incestuous feelings: both her father and her Uncle Henry had carried on adoring correspondences with their mothers. Julian Fane had written a poem every year to his mother on her birthday: 'If the sonnets I have written reflect something of a sick man's doom they do but bear like everything else I write to you the impress of reality'. His last, written a month before he died, ended – 'O Mother, I clasped Death, but seeing thy face, Leapt from his dark arms to thy dear Embrace'. He was forty-two. Incestuous feelings can be the result of terror about potential loss: the result of such feelings is usually depression or fantasy. What else can happen to a man about such terror – or his mother?

The sister whom Ettie's Uncle Henry had loved was her Aunt Dolly, the mother of Bron Herbert – he who had been staying with Ettie after his return from the Boer War and who, according to Betty Montgomery, had caused such distress to Evan Charteris when in her carriage. Bron's childhood had been as full of catastrophe as Ettie's and in some ways even odder: his father was Auberon Herbert, whom Dolly had married when still emotionally attached to her brother Henry ('You don't know how it preys on me sometimes having left you . . . much as I love A, I don't think anything can be the "all over" thing you are to me'). She and Auberon Herbert had four children: the eldest, Rolfe, died when he was ten after a drawn-out illness like that of his cousin Johnnie; Dolly herself died four years later; the remaining children – Clair, Bron and Nan – were brought up by their father Auberon who was what Wilfrid Blunt called 'the last of the uncompromising individualists of the Victorian age, the most consistent and ablest' though he was 'slightly touched in his later years with eccentricity'.[1] Auberon Herbert had briefly been an MP: he was a passionate advocate of the rights of minorities and of people in primitive

[1] Wilfrid Blunt, *My Diaries 1888–1914* (London, 1932), p. 570.

countries; of individuals in any fight against state compulsion and control. He did not believe in sending his children to school, and in the 1890s, when they were in their teens, he was living with them at Portofino, in Italy. He had been quarrelling with his son, Bron; and his eldest daughter, Clair, shot herself. Clair left a note saying –

I shoot myself feeling that I had better not continue to live – that I have only made myself and other people unhappy by living – and I hope that by my death I may perhaps undo some of the mischief I have done and help to bring the family together again. I used to think that I might be of use to Bron. I now feel that I shall only do him harm and add to his difficulties and therefore it is best to shoot myself.

Bron Herbert played an important part in both Ettie's and Julian's lives: he was in age and in character somewhere halfway between the two. To Ettie he was the member of the family who had been through some of the same experiences in childhood as she had: he also loved her, and perhaps thus satisfied some incestuous fantasies in herself. (It had been to her aunt's brother, Alwyne Compton, that Ettie had nearly become engaged when she was seventeen; to his brother Douglas Compton that she had also been devoted during childhood.) To Julian, Bron was a man from his mother's world but who by upbringing and by habit was close to his own ideal. In the mid-1890s Auberon Herbert had taken his two remaining children to live in some huts built by themselves in the New Forest. There, Wilfrid Blunt reported,

their way of life is the most uncomfortable imaginable. They have no fixed hours for meals, or for getting up in the morning or for going to bed. The first regular meal is said to be at half past two in the afternoon, and there is another at twilight in the evening, but they do not seem to sit down to either meal. Auberon sits in a summer house during part of the meal while the children run in and out, and he has constantly to get up to rearrange his clothing which is of shetland wool shawls and jerseys, and the children are called to put up and take down wooden screens on this side and that as the wind may seem to blow and not to blow . . . Nan, with inexhaustible patience, humours and serves her father; and Bron is almost equally good to him. This is the best tribute that can be paid to Auberon's system of education, but it is clear that there must be a breaking point somewhere. I don't know which child to admire most, the boy or the girl.[1]

[1] op. cit., pp. 235, 236.

This was a life that Julian loved; the way that he found it easiest to be with people. It was even the kind of life that he said he loved in war.

Auberon Herbert had seemed something of an enemy to the Cowper family: he was an enemy, certainly, to Ettie's precise routines. When Bron came back wounded from the South African War Ettie rescued him from the unsuitable huts in the New Forest and took him to Taplow to prepare for the amputation of his leg. Here Julian learned to love and admire him. But Bron soon came under the spell of Ettie's more personal routines –

Dearest Ettie,

Your letter made me very happy and yet a little sorry too – sorry that you should have ever imagined a cloud on the blue sky of our happiness. I have the profoundest conviction that it is to be one of the most permanent things of my life. Do you know that you have filled a place that has been vacant ever since Clair's death . . . You and she are the only two women I have ever looked up to for the sympathy and help and encouragement that a woman can give to a man . . . You are so to speak in the world, but not of it . . .

Julian came to see Bron as the figure in his youth most like himself. (He does not seem to have seen much of Bron's father Auberon, although he sometimes teased Ettie about his liking for 'Uncle Auberon clothes'.) When he left Eton Julian used to go and stay with Bron in Yorkshire:

I've had the time of my life here; I had no idea it was possible to like anything half so much; real sport, such a relief after the ant-fed partridges in wire remises; walking hard all day and killing a few *wild* birds. Bron has been in gorgeous form, I do love him, we've walked 11 hours each day in torrential rain and at the end his leg got bad and I think it hurt him a lot but he was golden about it.

Bron was twelve years older than Julian; he was something of an older brother, a father, and a demonstrator of what life could be. Julian wrote 'What an angel he is . . . a really *great* man'.

Sometimes Bron made a stand against Ettie: and in this too he was like Julian –

Dearest Ettie,

You have most unluckily forestalled me as I was, when your letter came, on the point of writing to you on the subject of parties. The fact is that I intended – so far as I am able – to stop going to them. This, though you may not think it, is quite serious, and the result of much thought. They are not the places where one sees one's friends, at any rate in a satisfactory manner, and as I do not intend coming to London this summer more than I can possibly help I should be more like a fish out of water than usual . . .

If ever you are at Taplow without a party – which is, I fear, impossible – I would love to come; supposing, that is, that you would let me. But as you know I see nothing of you except sometimes at the other end of your great lawn at your parties; and as I suppose you know too, you are the person I far prefer talking to . . .

But then, when he separated himself from Ettie, he, like her other lovers, seems never quite to have got over his resulting sense of loss; and in this, again, he was like Julian.

Bron inherited the title of Lord Lucas on the death of his uncle Francis Cowper in 1905; he became an energetic member of the House of Lords. Under the Liberal Government he was made successively Under Secretary of State for War, Under Secretary for the Colonies, and President of the Board of Agriculture. He continued to enjoy his wild life and his horses. Then in 1915 – in spite of his wooden leg, the fact that he was thirty-nine, and had been a cabinet minister – he left politics and joined the Royal Flying Corps and became a pilot. A colleague wrote 'There was a touch of other-worldliness about him even before he became an airman'. Still, after his first flight – 'he came down a different man from the one who had gone up and was different ever afterwards as if he had made a journey into the springtime of the world and brought back a breath of it'. He was shot down and killed in November 1916.

There is a look of Ettie in the photographs of Bron: the hooded eyes; the control; the vulnerability and arrogance. There is also something of Julian – the knowingness, such as there is in paintings of animals. Julian hoped to go into politics just before the beginning of the war: it was just after Julian's death that Bron decided to join the Flying Corps. Julian, Bron and Ettie all seem to have been representatives on some battleground over which issues of pain and reparation were contested. Julian, even more than Bron, was a champion in the battle against the emptiness of the society around him. When Julian was killed in 1915 Bron wrote to Ettie –

Wrest Hospital   Ampthill
29.5.15

My dear Ettie,

Nothing I can ever write or say will either convey to you what I feel or help you. You know I was fonder of him than of any other living man and never can anyone else be the same to me that he was. It was not merely that we had so many things in common, and that I was never so happy as when I was riding or shooting or fishing with him; I think he personally counted for more.

When he came back, as he used to do after years abroad, he brought into one's life, stale and stuffy with all the things that seem so small just now, great gusts of fresh air. His standpoint was always so honest and open and brave it made the conventional point of view seem such a travesty.

You remember how in his early boxing matches he used to get knocked out so often, and how later on he got just the necessary amount of balance which made him so fine a fighter. It seemed to me that process was steadily permeating everything he did. He no longer overrode his hobbies like he used to when he wrote his attack on the smart set any more than he did his racehorses; and the result was he used to win. We used to write to each other very little, and so when he was away I didn't follow all this; but each time I saw him he used to make me feel at once the great expansion that was going on in him. And now when the fulness of the powers that were in him seemed in sight though he had not reached them, he is gone. In these short months he made himself a name as a soldier only to be killed.

I cannot tell you the aching gap it has made. I think of all the happy times we had, his spirits, his keenness, his skill, his intense enjoyment of everything that boy or man, sportsman or poet, loves: of the way he made everyone adore him: of the way he was centre of all he did: and it seems that a great part of my life is torn from me.

                                                                                Bron

❧ FOURTEEN ❧

The hollow that there had seemed to be at the centre of Julian's feelings at Eton was a reflection of an emptiness felt in the political world outside: this was the time when there were passions but not much for there to be passions about: when politicians moved like ghosts in corridors. Eton was part of an educational system whose strength had become fossilized; its languages were elegant but dead. In politics the belligerence which had once seemed necessary for survival – chaos had often had to be fought like sickness and death – now seemed trivial; but at the centre, there was no other force to take its place.

In 1902 Arthur Balfour became Prime Minister. Willy Grenfell was now a Conservative MP. Neither seemed to have much enthusiasm for his job. Of Willy Grenfell in the House of Commons Bron Herbert wrote that he 'hated it with all his heart'. And soon Arthur Balfour was writing

Ten years of leading the House of Commons has given me an unutterable desire for change, and I never go upstairs to bed without thanking heaven that, in a very brief period, I shall have left my official residence and gone back to the comfort and repose of my own home.[1]

Arthur Balfour was a politician suited to this age; not passionate himself, and prophetic of what was happening. During the three years that he was Prime Minister the issue into which politicians did manage to channel their passions was that of Protectionism versus Free Trade: a subject about which, Balfour said, he himself had no convictions because it was one properly only able to be dealt with piecemeal and not by blanketing slogans. Under his leadership politicians let off steam while he got on with measures of practical importance – the implementation of his Education

[1] Letter to Joseph Chamberlain 2 Nov 1905; quoted in Kenneth Young, *Arthur James Balfour* (London, 1963), p. 250.

Bill arranging state aid for schools; the re-organization of the country's defences. Balfour pursued the latter aim largely outside the area of party politics. The emptiness at the centre of political life, he had foreseen, was one which men with arms would finally rush in to fill. He said that one reason he stayed in office so long while his colleagues wearied him with their trivial abuse was to make sure that his measures about defence would have reached a stage at which the Liberal Government that would follow him could not undo them.

At first it was thought that France would be the enemy; after the Entente Cordiale of 1904, Germany. Balfour did not seem to think it important to worry too much about what particular instance might start a war: with war in the air, some cause could be found for it. Balfour's politics were close to his philosophy: men were driven not by reason but by need; reason was largely used to justify need, and the best an individual could do in such circumstances was to keep his head – and his faith in another world in which reason might be operative.

In this world, man was 'a mere cork dancing on a torrent which he cannot control'. And the torrent moved from one ice age to another. What might be of interest in this world was the force and direction of the movement: 'What is going on here is a faint echo of the same movement that has produced massacres in St. Petersburg, riots in Vienna, Socialist processions in Berlin'.[1]

Of Balfour's colleagues many had this feeling but few his composure. George Wyndham had been made Irish Secretary in 1900, and in 1903 he saw through Parliament his Irish Land Bill by which Irish tenants were given aid to buy their land. Then MPs managed to find some irregularities in the behaviour of his Under Secretary, Sir Arthur MacDonnel, and they hounded George Wyndham till he became ill and resigned from office. Another victim of the time was George Curzon: he, too, as Viceroy of India, had tried to help the people he governed to become responsible for their own affairs; but in so doing he came into conflict with the army and was worsted in a struggle for power by the Commander in Chief in India, Lord Kitchener. It was as if the benevolent and amused paternalism of the Souls was cracking – George Curzon too became ill – and a tougher world was taking over. Ettie's and Julian's new friend, Lord Kitchener, was a representative of this world. Ettie once told Arthur Balfour one of her funny stories about Kitchener. She wrote –

[1] Kenneth Young, op. cit., p. 255.

The question of enemies came up; somebody said to K, 'How do you treat yours?': he said quite simply 'Oh, I have *no* difficulty; you see, such awful things happen to them quite independent of me.' So we said, 'How do you mean?' and he said, 'Well, George Curzon lost his wife; Sir Edmund Ellis lost his and his son was eaten by a crocodile; and Sir Denzil Ibbetson died of cancer.'

Then when George Curzon was returning from India disappointed and in pain (he suffered from some spinal dislocation) there were none of his political friends to greet him at the station – which would have been customary for a returning Viceroy. Many of his friends were in fact staying with Mary and Hugo Elcho in Gloucestershire, and Ettie described the scene in another of her funny stories –

We were all at the Elchos the day they arrived and were trying all Sunday to concoct a telegram of greeting which all, including A.J.B., could sign. Nothing less jejune seemed to evolve itself than 'Glad you're back'. Hugo Elcho said, 'If we don't look out, it'll turn into "Glad your back's worse".'

Bitchiness was seeping into the eternal springtime of the Souls.

Arthur Balfour and George Curzon were like Wagnerian gods – aware that their style of paternalism was doomed, but still with enough care to want to see what they had worked for carried on. Balfour was the only one able to be amused by this. He resigned from being Prime Minister in 1905, and watched from the sidelines the outcome of the 1906 election in which the Liberals were returned to power with a huge majority and the Labour Party for the first time won more than fifty seats. He wrote – 'I am profoundly interested in what is *now* going on'.

Ettie had lamented – 'Has our poor kingdom ever been in so many political pieces . . . I wonder if it has ever happened before for both parties to split simultaneously?' This was in 1905, when the Liberals too were scattered over Free Trade. But she had her own reassurances. 'The only anchorage seems to lie near those buoys who still float serenely, tranquilly, accepting only responsibility for the *possible*, and with a sort of unity within them quite detached from the hurricane.' One such buoy was Arthur Balfour; another was Kitchener.

Julian had written of his second meeting with Kitchener after the Boer War –

. . . he looked just the same, except that he was a little more sunburnt. He said that he wondered what the Boers would think of our life over here in the summer, going lazily on the river on boats and lounging about all day, and he said that they 'did not look at life that way'. Whatever was going on he seemed to pay the greatest attention to it, even if it was not of the slightest importance. He saw me catch a pike once, which got into a deep bed of weeds and took a very long time to land, and he proposed that we should get up early next morning and see if we could have any luck. The next morning there was a high wind and frequent showers of rain, an ideal day for fishing, but one when most people would prefer to be in bed. He was dressed before the time and came to my room when I was still in bed. We managed to land two nice fish that morning, and Lord Kitchener seemed very pleased, while he could not help laughing as he just slipped the landing net under the biggest we had yet seen and it gave a sharp turn, made a frantic rush, and broke the line. Lord Kitchener cannot stand two things – state dinners and being photographed.

Willy at first did not seem to be affected by the personal venom that was creeping in upon the Souls ('It is a great pity that George C has had to resign') but he as much as anyone wanted to get away from the public vapourings. He described meetings at which he 'struggled in vain against an overwhelming sea of ceaseless platitude'; politicians who uttered 'indiscriminate, nauseating and stentorian encomiums'. He had hoped at one time that he would be made a junior minister: then it became too obvious that he was out of place. A gossip-columnist wrote –

Standing well over six feet in height, with the frame of a Hercules and with health and strength written in every line of his manly face, one wonders what can induce him to desert the country and outdoor exercise to spend hours every day in the House of Commons and in the even duller committee rooms attached thereto. One unconsciously returns to one's childhood dreams and feels that such a man should for ever be performing heroic deeds such as slaying dragons or killing giants . . .

There were rumours that he was going to be offered the Governor Generalship of Canada: he wrote to Ettie – 'I believe the Canadians judging by the papers would have liked us to go'; but the offer was not made officially; and when it was, years later, it was Ettie, apparently self-effacingly but effectively, who did not want to go. In 1905 she had just given birth to her fifth and last child – her daughter Imogen. Julian wrote 'What fun it will be when we all get down to Taplow again with the baby.' Billy wrote 'How too splendid about little Oxygen'.

The honour that Arthur Balfour did provide for Willy on his resignation in 1905 was to make him a peer. Ettie wrote to Balfour to thank him:

'It never seemed possible to believe it really could happen, partly because one wished it for him so very much'. So Willy moved out of the House of Commons and into the House of Lords. He had difficulty in choosing a title. He toyed with the names of various neighbouring localities: Julian wrote from Eton –

> Hail Grenfell, from the House for ever free!
> Hail Grenfell, Grenfell never more to be!
> Hail! Thou hast reached the mountain peak of fame;
> Thou hast a peerage; hadst thou but a name!
>   O Marazion's the Jew
>   And Butler's too prosaical
>   Taplow's not good enough for you
>   And Beauvale's lackadaisical;
>   Marlowe recalls vulgarity –
>   The river-tripping cockney;
>   And Bray suggests hilarity –
>   The laughter of a dokney.
>   'Lord Maidenhead'! – Oh how disgust-
>   ing! 'Fordwick' – Oh what foppery!
>   Be fair, be just, and be St Just;
>   To me that's just tip-toppery!

Willy chose to be called Lord Desborough (the title of St Just was chosen by another member of the Grenfell family some years later). Willy had been made a peer for his involvement in local rather than national politics; also for sport. In 1903, at the age of forty-eight, he had taken up fencing seriously again and had become a member of the English Epée team; he fought in international competitions in Paris and Brussels. A year later he was captain of the team when the English beat the Belgians and only narrowly lost to the French. He wrote – 'We have done much better than I expected and better than the score makes out, as we suffered in the judging which is more important than the fighting'. He became Chairman of the British Committee for the Olympic Games which were to be held in London in 1908.

People in Ettie's world had become increasingly obsessed by games. Arthur Balfour kept the month of August or September free every year for golf. He wrote to Ettie –

I have done nothing important or distinguished since we met except to win the handicap prize, value £4.50., at N. Berwick on Friday. This has caused far more emotion and surprise in my family than did my becoming Prime Minister. Doubtless also it is more important.

Herbert Asquith, who became Prime Minister two years after Balfour, also spent a month in Scotland every year at golf: he sometimes played with Balfour, even when they were enemies at the height of political passions. Balfour also had a passion for tennis. Mary Elcho told a story about how he had once hit her in the eye with a ball and she had not thought it proper to tell him, although for a time she was almost blind.

The addiction of the older generation to golf and tennis while Armageddon or whatever it was loomed closer across the Channel was countered in the younger generation by a growing contempt for games with balls; but Julian at least had a growing love for other kinds of sport. After he left Eton he involved himself more and more hectically with hunting and shooting: he kept a game book in which he recorded every fox chased and every bird or animal killed. But he still preferred to be on his own. He came to dislike the mass partridge- and pheasant-shoots at which his father excelled; at which scores were kept as if birds were breaks in billiards. The point of sport, Julian wrote, was to 'take us back to the land, back to real things, bringing the elemental barbaric forces in ourselves into touch with the elemental barbaric forces of nature'. This was fundamental to his protest against the society around him. By these means he thought the power of Armageddon might be propitiated: it was only being tickled by competitive games.

A friend of Ettie's wrote to her in later years describing another memory of Julian at this time.

Julian stayed out in the woods quite late, not coming home for dinner, a moonlit night. He came in suddenly through the window after dinner among us all in our stupid evening gowns, and looked round at us like a man in a dream, and only said 'Where's Mother?' He passed through, and found you, and came back arm-in-arm with you, telling you how wonderful it was outside in the woods, and how you must come out and feel and see it.

Julian's love of sport was to do with killing; but killing of this kind was to do with the earth, and was understood by poets. Julian wrote –

The love of sport is the love of primitive things, strength and speed, dash and courage, stealth and cunning; and these are seen more often in pursued than in pursuer. The man who is fondest of sport is the man who is the most interested in animal things and in the animal. He is the man who finds an almost sensual pleasure in the speed of the greyhound with its spring, swing and stretch, so true that it hardly seems the truth; in the glorious first burst from cover of a pack of foxhounds on a good scenting day with blood in their cry; in the almost terrifying tension of the pointer working up to a good running covey. He is the man who loves best the whistling wing-beat of the flighting duck, wildest of birds; the flash of the leaping salmon; the jerk of the stag's head when he first 'get's the wind' and you must shoot quickly or not at all; the long slinking stride of the fox and his ultra-feminine cunning; and the speed of the hare when she first finds out it is business this time and lays back her ears.

This was written by Julian when at Oxford. The poetic impulse was traditional – the connection between love and death. Julian went hunting and shooting with Bron Herbert: Bron Herbert had written of his life in the wilds – 'I reign supreme: I am an autocrat on an island and everybody has to bow to me: we live the lives of gods and dogs in one'. It was this, for Julian, that was a contrast to the life at Taplow – with its exact plans and routines, its ball-games and its paper games, its charades and acting. (A guest wrote to Ettie – 'I shall remember *always* with almost more pleasure than anything else you writhing and twisting on the parquet floor in red velvet . . . your conception of the part of a serpent's tail being one of the greatest triumphs of modern Art!') But Julian's revolt against games by turning to primitive life was also a turning away, for the moment, from what he knew was serious. For men are in fact not gods nor dogs; and battles, not only for poets, have to be fought in the mind. And there is one question that he seems never quite to have asked – if a man has to hunt in order to keep in touch with reality – to kill in order to love – then what are the origins of these experiences that a man has to destroy love to show his regard for it?

❧ FIFTEEN ❧

One of Ettie's more recent exemplars and confidants – who seemed to demonstrate in the literary world as Arthur Balfour did in the political both the emptiness at the heart of society and the probable futility of one man's nevertheless worthwhile efforts within it – was Maurice Baring.

Maurice Baring was the younger brother of John Revelstoke; he had been at Oxford with Bron Herbert just before the Boer War, and Ettie used to see him when she visited Julian and Billy at Summerfields. He became a diplomat and then a writer; he had a genius for languages, being fluent in French, German, Italian, Spanish, Danish and Russian. His success during his early years as a writer was as a parodist: he wrote a number of books – *Diminutive Dramas, Dead Letters, Lost Diaries* – in which by putting himself into other and mostly fictional personalities he played games with his own and with readers' erudition. The skill was in the form: nothing of substance was being stated.

Ettie's upbringing had been literary: she had discussed Provençal songs with George Wyndham and quoted Swinburne with Douglas Compton; the games that the Souls played in the evenings had often been to do with parodying or copying writers. These games Ettie had continued with her children. In 1901, for instance, in a tea-time competition about who could write the best 'Epitaph to a Fisherman', Ettie had made references to *The Compleat Angler*, Willy had turned out an eighteenth-century couplet, and Julian had written –

> He who caught gudgeon
> The length of a yard
> Now lies in a dudgeon
> In Taplow Church Yard.

Maurice Baring's letters to Ettie are full of private references and puns;

he seemed to be luring her, by making her guess his allusions. Sometimes his language becomes almost private – as if by this too he were drawing a magic circle round the two of them. He used and expanded a language that had been started in the Baring and Ponsonby families of his parents' generation (his aunt was Lady Ponsonby, the mother of Ettie's old friend Betty); this had been the language of Ettie's childhood. 'Spangle' was to flirt, 'relever' to gossip, 'dewdrop' a compliment, 'heygate' conventional, 'brahms' condescending, 'bird' happy, 'ridge' a depression, 'dentist' a heart-to-heart talk. Sometimes Maurice Baring had to explain a word to Ettie –

Poopsy means poopsy-brained when one is quite wanting: it comes from G. Liddle's fatherine who always thought he was staying at an hotel when he was at home . . .

Ibsen doesn't mean Ibsenish or Ibsenite but means sometimes obvious, sometimes 'cru' outside – what everybody has always said or thought: an Ibsen pen is an ordinary pen not a stylo . . .

– and sometimes he would send to Ettie two or three letters in the same envelope, each one being a parody of the sort of letter that might have been sent –

Dear Mrs Grenfell,
    It must be very wonderful to have a mind like yours. I have never read a word of Balzac but shall do so at once . . . Yes, how wonderful Le Pere Goriot is! The black sordid Misery of the table-cloth – and the glaring satin gowns and the plush carpets of Anastasie – it is as you say almost *too* horrible. I liked what you said about its being 'a shock to one's system like having typhoid' and one's finishing it 'trembling with pitiless cruelty and horror'. . . .

Dear Mrs Grenfell,
    Your letter about Balzac was exceedingly suggestive. I do not think however that Balzac supplies man with a philosophy universal as that of Shakespeare or of Goethe. He can scarcely be said to see life steadily and see it whole. I trace the Germanic element in Balzac's character – the Germanic element which blending with the Celtic racial instinct produces such a curious complex result causing him to appear so little French while in reality he has so little of the German – I trace this blend to the migration and immigration of an Indo-European Persian stock from Marseilles to Touraine in the first century

BC caused by the decay in the carpet-making trade in that town in which these Graeco-Persians so eminently excelled. Balzac was of this stock . . .

– and only after all this, the god of frivolity having been propitiated, saying something of what he himself felt about Balzac; though even here the statement was dressed up –

Dear Madame Sottise,

Yes I've read Pere Goriot. I think it is wonderful; but I haven't got a tremendous culte for Balzac – I think it's fatiguing reading – not the least Borax – but fatiguing like a strong cigar or black coffee. He sees all the world through a huge glass that distorts everything and fills all the milk-kans with steaming tea. I think he's one of the writers who create a see into another planet where the people are quite different – George Meredith is another. Miss Austen and Tourgenieff are in this particular planet . . .

– Madame Sottise, the name by which he often called Ettie, being itself a joke originating from Renan's 'O Madame Sottine que vous êtes belle!' which had once been misread by Ettie, so that she had become Sottise – silliness.

Maurice Baring wrote dozens of letters to Ettie playing such games, making her guess, teasing her; forgetting sometimes the answers to his own riddles ('"wis whom" gives me brain stoppage: I don't know what I said'). The wit, the erudition, seemed to be used as a charm, a defence; but against what? When he had first met her he had told her that he loved her, amongst others –

. . . I've got a skillion things to tell you about Bron. He is so golden that I didn't know he'd got such a tremendous adoration culte for you – the other night I had a little dinner and Bron came – after din when we were punching type healths it was Bretted to drink the health of the most adorable woman you knew and to say the Xtian name. Bron said 'Ethel' and I said 'Priscilla' – then Bron asked me privately afterwards like Nicodemus in a black corner of Balliol Court whether I had meant the same person as he had and I said yes. Then I think I went up 60 in his estimation and he said '*But she is far the most charming person in the world.*' Then he said 'She doesn't like me a bit' – I washed this – and he said 'No, I know I haven't got the way of it with women somehow.' Then he told me how you used to birdsnest together a long time ago and we blocked you for about an hour. And when I washed you off the block and blocked something else Bron said 'Do let's go on talking about what we were talking about just now . . .

Maurice Baring and Bron Herbert were of a younger generation of Ettie's adorers; Maurice Baring prostrated himself in something of the old style, but being a writer, he was able to stand back and also play games with himself for so doing; though the feeling was the same –

Oh Mme Sottise, Mme Machiavelli, Mme Fargueil, Mrs Willy, Mrs Etty, Mrs Grenfell! If you only knew the cloud of CARPET that arises between one and *anybody* however nice after one has been with you! one ought to go through a sort of quarantine of milk before one is fit to go into society . . .

I simply can't do without it, your letts are like stars or like arsenic or strychnine or anything you like but I *must* have them (spelicans again I suppose) (or glib) (or Mrs Hunter) . . .

Chère . . . Renan would describe you as going to heaven like this – 'Madame Sottine monta au ciel et fut presenté au Seigneur. Le Seigneur remarqua à part au Saint Esprit que Marie Madeleine n'était après tout qu'une femme assez fade – "Voila une femme" dit-il "qui m'aurait compris." "Sans doute," répondit le Saint Esprit séduisant, et il pensa avec pitié que son illustre collège aurait été une facile proie à cette femme subtile. "Quel dommage que ma petite affaire ne s'est passé au XIXieme siècle!" pensa-t-il.' – I think this is enough blasphemy for one evening but Allah is very broadminded . . .

The image of divinity was the same: it was against the power of this, perhaps, that all the jokes were summoned. But in Maurice Baring's poetry there were no jokes. This was a time when romanticism in poetry went easily into decadence; when feelings of humility towards a loved one became ways of lamenting the emptiness of a mirror:

I have got several poems in my mind; I don't know whether I shall ever write them. One is to be called 'The Modern Circe' – a ghostly creature on a phantom Isle so far from turning men into pigs gives them five minutes block then sends them away and they think they have had a molaire and go away consoled; but something remains and they never get rid of the sight of her Fargueil eyes and the sound of her silver relevage and all the horizon round her island is studded with white sails and all the air melancholy with sighs; and seek as they may they never find her island again. Is that no-block? or is it worth punching?

Maurice Baring did in fact write a poem called 'Circe', which was published in a volume called *The Black Prince* which he dedicated to Ettie. The sixth stanza of 'Circe' is –

There in the emerald evening she bestows
A silent pitying audience on her slaves;
And thence they sail into a long despair;
Around her isle dark vapours seem to close.
Before them lie unending wastes of waves,
And dazed they think the vision blest and fair
Was but a mirage of the mocking air.

The image that a poet is in thrall to – in defence against which he cracks his jokes and writes his poems – is inside himself. A poet knows this; but still – how can he defend himself?

Maurice Baring dedicated another early poem to Ettie, 'Sigurd', in which an angel comes down to Siegfried when he is dying and offers him anything he might want in another world: Siegfried chooses oblivion, because to live in any world, with or without his love Brunhilde, would be too painful. Maurice Baring wrote another poem about Sigurd later and dedicated it to Archie Gordon – a young man who loved Ettie and whom Ettie loved and who was killed in a motor accident in 1909.

Ettie was an inspiration for some of Maurice Baring's satirical sketches (as well as possibly for his novel *C*, mentioned earlier). One of his *Diminutive Dramas, Ariadne in Naxos*, presents a scene which might have been enacted by Ettie, Evan Charteris and John Baring – or indeed by Maurice himself. Ariadne is in her London drawing room and she is expecting one lover Theseus and, in half an hour, another lover Dionysus. She tells her maid to show Dionysus into the dining room if he arrives early. Theseus comes in an agony of remorse for some fault he can't quite remember; he begs Ariadne to forgive him, which she does not quite do; but she uses his self-humiliation to make sure that she gets rid of him on time. Then Dionysus comes in, and he and Ariadne settle down in front of the fire. This sketch, cut out from the *Morning Post*, was amongst Ettie's papers some fifty years later.

To write of Ettie as an angel of death and deception as well as the source of all goodness and light was not odd at this time when those who welcomed her 'gospel of joy' believed at the same time that there was not much worth-while in this world but only in eternity or oblivion. This was a characteristic of the age – an optimism allied insanely with an expectation of Armageddon. This was a style in politics, literature, teaching: the optimism was perhaps a defence; the doom even its justification. People are often cheered at the prospect of battle. But both the energy and the apprehension were to do with games; there was still not much observance of reality. A clever young man who moved in Ettie's and Maurice Baring's world at this time was Constantine Benckendorff, the son of the Russian Ambassador in London. He described the atmosphere from an outsider's point of view. He went to stay at Bron Herbert's house Picket Post in the New Forest. During the day there was strenuous exercise, riding or swimming 'in all weathers in the newly established swimming pool at the bottom of a steep ravine'. Then after dark Bron Herbert would assemble his guests and –

a sort of intellectual carouse would begin, consisting of a series of sharp skirmishes where no subject, even the most outrageous, was barred, so long as it led to an argument. Those arguments would sometimes go on deep into the night when sometimes the rising tempers would be cooled by a moonlit ride through the Forest. It must be admitted that the more an opinion or a theory flew in the face of all existing evidence the more welcome it would be as a subject at Picket Post. The contention, for instance, that the earth was flat, and that the contrary was impossible to prove, was at one time a favourite one of Maurice Baring's; with, I think, Hilaire Belloc amongst others in strong support; while I, the professional navigator, led the opposition. The strange thing was that the ring of bystanders, which for once included Bron, seemed to have no strong conviction one way or the other, and were more impressed by the ingenuity of an argument than by its factual merit.

This brings me to an observation on the education of nearly all the public school and university men with whom I came in contact in those days. Superbly trained to use their brains deductively, they appeared to me to give a minor place indeed to any factual scientific knowledge of the kind that would be at the disposal of every secondary schoolboy on the continent . . . Nature was observed only for its picturesque qualities – 'bird bores' and fly fishermen, with their limited range, perhaps excepted. . . . The same sort of blank wall of indifference and relative ignorance was met when I occasionally tried to get some idea about the activities of local government in England . . .[1]

This was the pattern – that in a world increasingly dependent on the achievements of science those responsible for the overseeing of these achievements had little interest in science and none for scientific method. The attitude of mind which tries to refute an hypothesis by experiment rather than to enthrone it by argument was taboo. When Julian went to Oxford he found that to talk about personal observation was slightly

[1] Constantine Benckendorff, *Half a Life* (London, 1954), pp. 95, 96.

indecent: the convention was, that elegant fancies were required to get through this vale of tears. For at the end, death was real anyway.

As a journalist Maurice Baring was present at scenes of historical importance. He was in St Petersburg just after the abortive revolution of 1905; he does describe this scene, but he makes no mention of the forces behind it – of Marx, Trotsky or Lenin. He called his autobiographical book *The Puppet Show of Memory*. He seems often, in his attitudes and his philosophizing about life, to be representative of Ettie. During the 1914–18 war, after Julian and Billy had been killed, he wrote –

If there is any meaning in life at all – if life isn't the practical joke of a spiteful imp or the blunder of a blind and fumbling fool – then there must be something beyond this life . . . and if one is inclined to think that life after all may be a bad joke or a stupid blunder then one is faced with the difficulty of accounting for the blossom, the fields, the honeysuckle, the sunsets, the dawn, the nights, the Parthenon, Shakespeare, St Francis, Beethoven, Velasquez, Shelley – the very existence of such radiant creatures as Julian and Billy . . .

This was Ettie's faith: it was the same argument for faith as that of Arthur Balfour. It was the fashionable argument for God – that there had to be a God just because this world was so horrible. The assumption was, always, that man could not be responsible for horror (nor for beauty); there had to be a God because otherwise responsibility was unbearable. To believe in a force 'beyond' which could turn terror into sunlight was a necessity. It was the sort of faith that Maurice Baring had in Ettie.

Do you know what washed away my ridge? It was I thought I was having a 'manque de foi' towards you, and that even if it was true I had no business to think it. I had no business to reason about my faith in you no more than a Catholic has any business to reason about his faith in the dogmas of his creed. I thought this, and all ridge was lifted, leaving only my old unalterable trust in you which would surmount and survive anything in the world; which nothing could affect, nor alter; which was, is, and will be for ever as long as I live . . .

This was the sort of statement of faith that women had been taught to call forth – by which men had been taught to live – a means of sustenance like a breast. Maurice Baring in fact became a Roman Catholic in 1909: he wrote to Ettie –

I knew not only that you would understand but you did understand . . . I believe anyone 'saves his soul' in his own way . . . and whereas some people I

know get on without a church others can't . . . The paradoxical root ideas of
Xtianity are not to me preposterous because human life and all religion seem to
me a gigantic paradox . . . I must have all or nothing and with nothing I cannot
exist; I should have blown out my brains.

Most of Ettie's adorers of her own generation in fact lived till an old
age – Evan Charteris, John Revelstoke, Maurice Baring – though all
these died childless. It was her admirers of her children's generation who
died young. But then – were they not lucky? This was what the older
generation asked – what they said they would themselves have wanted – if
there had not been the younger generation to be so lucky. This was how
the older generation comforted itself. In 1916, after the death of two of
Ettie's sons and of the sons of many of their friends, Maurice Baring
wrote to Ettie on the death of the latest –

> I am sorry for us, but not for him.
>
> For him it is a privilege and a prize beyond anything
> he can have dreamed before the war.
>
> To say it is a waste is to me like saying the frankincense,
> gold and myrrh of the Three Kings was a waste –
>
> – or a waste to give an engagement ring to someone you are
> going to marry whom you love . . .
>
> But Oh! we shall miss him –
>
> Shan't we miss all the others more for missing him –
> But then what do *we* matter?

❧ SIXTEEN ❧

Ettie wrote in her Family Journal of the time just before Julian went to Oxford –

It must have been about this time that very vehement discussions started between Julian and his mother, generally on quite impersonal subjects, but not infrequently ending with both disputants in tears. They each held very strong opinions, and could not bear the other not to agree absolutely. This went on from time to time for three or four years. Julian's mother sometimes felt mildly depressed about these arguments, and used to think how dreadful it would be if anyone ever overheard them and the very plain speaking on both sides; but Julian wholly approved of them, and used to call them his 'fight for life' . . .

Julian went up to Oxford in the autumn of 1906. His fight for life was both with his mother and with the rest of the conventional world that seemed to have staked its faith on insubstantiality and death.

Julian at Oxford read for Greats – the examination for a BA degree which was based on a study of classical and modern philosophy. The corner-stones of this study were Plato – who held that logically there was an eternal world of ideal forms of which the sensible, everyday world was a shadow; and Aristotle – who held that, granted this ideal world, a man should strive to conform to it ethically by the training of his will. For both these philosophers reality was to do with processes of mind; and actual experience was subservient.

At Oxford at the end of the nineteenth century the leading contemporary philosophers had been T. H. Green and F. H. Bradley. Both were 'idealists'; they had led a reaction against the 'empiricism' current earlier in the century. Empiricists held that actual experience was primary; but admitted from this it followed logically that a man was no more than a bundle of unconnected sensations. This encouraged the idealists.

Fashions in philosophy alternated between idealism and empiricism, like the hem of a skirt going up and down.

There could be no outcome to this dispute because no criteria were accepted to which to refer it; and argument was a game that required two sides anyway. There was little desire to find a form of study which would relate what went on in the mind to what was observed in experience – a form of language which might embrace the two.

When Julian arrived at Oxford he at first felt rather lost. He wrote to Ettie –

> Balliol College
> Oxford
> Sunday 21 Oct.

Dear Mother,

. . . I am liking this place ever so much more now. I was really *bored* the first week although I didn't want to say so: of course it was the last thing I expected to be, or thought I would be in any way possible. I know exactly why it was – no exercise. There were the people I simply love, and everything new, but just *nothing* to do, work or play, and you know what that means to me. It seemed to take such an age to get started, and to be just the same with everyone else, and in such a short time getting such a slow start was so rotten. I hated it because I was very ill (from mere inertia) and very impatient at the same time, which was fatal! Also I was naturally longing all the time to be at Eton again, which never happened when I was doing things hard in the holidays. But now it is entirely different as everything has started. I row hard every day . . . I box too in the mornings sometimes . . . so get quite enough exercise!

I go to Greats lectures and do Greats work already, which is a new sort of plan here, and I love it, as it is mostly ethics and philosophy which simply thrill me. I am going to ask if I can do more lectures . . .

Julian often felt ill: this was a continual undercurrent to his otherwise abundant energy. He had had blood-poisoning when working for scholarships during his last year at Eton, and again when he had been due to go away for a week in the summer to play cricket. In January 1907 he 'grazed his arm' while out hunting and had to put off going back to Oxford for a week. In the summer of 1907 while staying with friends in Scotland he got a temperature of 105° which the local doctor called 'very inexplicable' and his mother made an all-night dash by 'motor, ferry, train, dog-cart, ferry, motor' (Family Journal) to be with him. The same summer when he was in camp doing preliminary training for the army he cut his hand in the propeller of a boat and his mother had rushed to be with him again.

Julian tried to fend off these feelings of sickness and of being out of place by violent physical exercise. He also worked hard academically. In 1907 he wrote to his father – 'I eat very little and am quite emaciated: I'm working now with both hands, day and night.' He rowed for Balliol in the races at Oxford in February, and in the Ladies' Plate at Henley in July. He kept a horse at Oxford, and hunted and rode in college steeple-chases. And he boxed.

The Boxing Competition came off last night. I had trained down to a shade to get to the weight (11st 4lb) but I was very fit. I beat my first man to death in 1¾ rounds, and they had to stop the fight or I would have killed him outright. As it is he is pretty bad. In the final I fought Turner, neck and neck for three rounds, the best fight I have ever had. It was almost point for point, and we were both helpless at the end. I nearly knocked him out twice, and he all but got me out once. The referee, a swell London man, gave it to me; but the three judges, Oxford men, gave it a tie as to boxing but gave *him* as the winner on footwork! So he won! But I don't care a bit, as it was a draw really, and a fight worth living for. I *did* love it, although quite terrified. I am working. Love to Dad.

This was to his mother. This was what his mother liked; this was what mothers and sons had been brought up to like; Julian's descriptions of boxing are like Homer's. Violence had been for thousands of years what gentlemen did. Julian tried to understand this.

A contemporary, Ronald Knox, wrote of Julian at Oxford –

He had this Greek love of form, but not for its own sake . . . Strength, speed and skill were to him the assertion of the dignity of man . . . I can fancy that even rowing would appeal to him primarily as an instance of a man's 'scoring off' the conditions of nature. (This is an exposition of his philosophy of the time, not of his feelings: this is how he liked to be thought of.) He did not exalt muscle over brain: he knew that cunning is, at least as much as strength, the weapon of the noble savage; and, as his tutors knew, he had an unusually good brain. But I think he would have always preferred to assert it by superiority over wild nature. Making entries in his game book was, in that first year at any rate, a solemn ceremony; though we laughed at him and he laughed at himself even as he did it . . .

This was his philosophy and not his feelings: but then, what were his feelings? He filled in time with violence in order to stop feeling ill; he

asserted his superiority over nature – why? What was it he wanted to kill?
He went through other traditional motions of Oxford arrogance –

. . . The Master sent for me and said . . . that if I view-halloed in the quad and
brought in pigs and poultry and ragged the dons and threw rolls of paper up into
the trees and the roller down the cellar steps and tried to undress the Marquis of
Tavistock in the street on cold nights – and *much* more – he was afraid the college
would have to lose a prominent member for a number of days . . .

– but he did not go in much for this sort of thing. Billy did more of it
three or four years later. Julian had the reputation at Balliol, in the words
of another contemporary, Tommy Lascelles, of –

an almost monastic asceticism. Except for occasional binges, he never had a drop
more drink than was good for him . . . He was essentially an un-clubbable man
. . . the only genuine egoist alive, I should think, who would have been
genuinely happy as Robin Crusoe.

He did not talk much about his work in philosophy: it is probable that
he came to agree with Billy who wrote from Balliol four years later –
'Philosophy is the greatest nonsense, as all sensible people must know by
now; but it makes the brain revolve'. But the almost total separation of
philosophy from an interest in what life was actually like meant that those
who looked for models to which they could refer feelings and conduct
turned to literature. Classical literature was on the curriculum for Greats.
In the battles that Julian had with his mother they talked about literature.
Euripides was being translated at the time by Gilbert Murray, and these
translations were fashionable. They missed much of Euripides' irony –
Euripides' genius being not only to describe the primitive passions that
run the lives of men who are under the impression that they are free but
by pointing out this situation to encourage men to think – and turned
Euripides' subtlety into a tragic romanticism like that of Swinburne. It
was probably because of this that Gilbert Murray was so popular. In 1907
and 1908 Julian and Billy and their mother and their friends corresponded
about these translations: they used them as models by which they could
talk about life. Like this, Ettie could keep up with her sons; and they
could all try to express, in a world otherwise dominated by form, something of their feelings.

In 1908 Billy wrote from Eton –

My Dearest Mother,
    I am so very glad you love the Gilbert Murray. I think Pater's explanation

of the almost inhuman cruelty and beauty of the Bacchae is by far the best;
Agave and the sisters are punished for having denied the Divinity of Dionysus
. . . Agave's worship of him is only a form of madness sent on her by the god,
a manifestation of his power and godhead and the means of her punishment . . .
I should love to talk to you about it. Could you come and see me here Monday
afternoon, before you go to Scotland? . . .

The Bacchae is the play of Euripides which deals with the questions that
obsessed him above all others – what happens to the dark forces which
exist in everyone when they are denied? And what, apart from denial, can
be done about them? Pentheus, the King of Thebes, and Agave, his
mother, have denied the divinity of Dionysus the god of passion; they
have insisted on the rule of order and light. As a result Agave becomes an
unconscious and wild devotee of the dark god, instead of paying him
respect in the gentle way which, it is suggested, is possible. The god then
secretly enters into Pentheus, who chooses to watch his mother's savage
rites: his mother and her followers tear him limb from limb. *The Bacchae*
was performed at the Court Theatre in London in 1908: Ettie and Billy
went to it. Ettie wrote – 'Nothing could persuade me against the beauty
of these plays: I haven't had such a fulfilling experience for years'.

The play of Euripides that Julian and his mother loved most was
Hippolytus. Ettie called it 'almost the most beautiful bit of print my eyes
ever fell upon'; Julian learned much of it by heart, and quoted from it on
his deathbed. The particular dark force in *Hippolytus* is the lust which a
stepmother feels for her stepson. Phaedra, wife of Theseus, falls in love
with his son Hippolytus and keeps this secret and becomes ill. When it is
found out, and Hippolytus has rejected her, Phaedra kills herself. But
Hippolytus is killed too, for Phaedra has left word that Hippolytus tried
to seduce her. In fact, Hippolytus loved only birds and animals. The song
that Julian quoted on his deathbed and which Ettie said he loved better
than anything else in the world was sung by Phaedra when she was longing
for herself to be like Hippolytus; to be able to assuage her passion in
the woods –

> O, take me to the Mountain. O,
> Past the great pines and through the wood,
> Up where the lean hounds softly go
> A-whine for wild things' blood,
> And madly flies the dappled roe.

> O God, to shout and speed them there,
> An arrow by my chestnut hair
> Drawn tight, and one keen glimmering spear –
> Ah, if I could!

This song seemed to be a bond between Julian and Ettie; as if through it, if in no other words, they found echoes of their predicament.

The third play of Euripides that was much discussed by Ettie and the circle around her sons was *The Trojan Women*. Ettie wrote to Patrick Shaw Stewart – who in some ways took the place of Julian in her affections while she and Julian were having their battles –

> How more beautiful than anything The Trojan Women is! Hecuba! – and that marvellous scene between Menelaus and Helen and her! – and how beautiful the things she says are! 'I that bare Hector' – and – 'Even as the sound of a song' (on p 41) and – 'Thou deep base of the World' (on p 54) and – 'Ah what a death hath found thee, little one' (p 68) that loveliest speech . . .

The Trojan Women takes place after the sack of Troy when the Greeks are handing round as slaves the wives of the dead Trojan heroes. Hecuba, wife of the Trojan King Priam, is the central victim: with her are two of her daughters-in-law. To one, Andromache, Hecuba is pitiless when Andromache weeps for her murdered child. About this scene Ettie wrote – 'Andromache is the only one I don't much like: she has a rather carpet-atmosphere?' And towards the other daughter-in-law, Helen, Hecuba is even more savage; mocking her when she tries to explain that the Trojan war was not her fault – she could not have helped eloping to Troy with Paris since she had been under the spell of the dark god of love. Hecuba, in a jealous rage, demands that Helen shall be killed in the name of order and retribution. Ettie wrote – 'Do you think in the controversy between Hecuba and Helen Euripides is really on the Hecuba side – I do – and that Helen's speeches are special pleading, marvellously "clever" and cunning – but G.M. doesn't take that view?'

Ettie identified herself with Hecuba: what she liked most ('that loveliest speech') was the scene where Hecuba mourns her murdered grandchild in a hymn of self-lacerating ecstasy, her chief regret seeming to be that the child had not died in battle –

> Ah, what a death that found thee, little one!
> Hadst thou but fallen fighting, hadst thou known

> Strong youth and love and all the majesty
> Of godlike kings, then had we spoken of thee
> As of one blessed . . .

This was the 'side' which Ettie felt herself, and Euripides, to be on.

Greek tragedy portrays, and by this perhaps hopes to propitiate, the primitive passions in men which are largely unconscious; these can be glimpsed by an audience even if only dimly by the characters themselves. Ettie was a woman of primitive passions: she had from her childhood a great need for love and reassurance. An audience is not freed from destructive passions by observing them: Euripides wrote at the time of the Peloponnesian War when Greek civilization was almost destroyed by self-laceration. But in tragedy, complexities can at least be recognized. Julian in his love of primitive life did seem to be trying to propitiate dark forces in some way like that of Hippolytus; but Hippolytus was destroyed by Phaedra's love for him; this was a force he could not propitiate by transpositions of destructive feelings. Julian also tried to fight destructiveness with knowledge: but he did not have time. What Ettie (and most of her world) said they liked, were stories of a wife's rending lust for her step-son; of a mother's wild jealousy of her daughters-in-law; of an old woman's threnody over the dead body of a child. When Julian told Ettie he was fighting for his life, his claim seems to have had substance.

❦ SEVENTEEN ❦

When Julian was at Oxford he was seen himself as somewhat godlike. Contemporaries wrote –

He just took the whole of life in both hands, enjoyed everything in it good and enjoyable, pursued fiercely all that was false or hollow or humbugging, feared nothing in it, loved much, and yet with all his clean-cut directness there was no subtlety, no humour, no fancy or whimsicality which did not appeal to him strongly. There are simple people and there are subtle people, but Julian was both. . . . I shall never forget how impressed I was when Julian first came up to Oxford – there, as you know, men fall into sets; there is the riding, horsey, Bullingdon set; the rowing men; the 'saps'. Julian knew nothing of sets, but just did everything and shone in them all. He rowed, and he hunted; and he read, and he roared with laughter, and he cracked his whip in the quad all night; he bought greyhounds from the miller of Hambledon, boxed all the local champions; capped poetry with the most precious of the dons, and charmed everybody from the Master of Balliol to the ostlers at the Randolph. And he was the best of friends and the dearest of men. The only things he couldn't stand were pose or affectation, and he could be a terror to the occasional Maudle still to be met with at Oxford . . .

(Lawrence Jones)

His thoughts seemed always to be a genuine part of himself, because they were his and not another's. His notions of how life should be lived were widely different from those which are generally received; but his practice showed a much closer agreement with his theory than commonly obtains between the creed and the conduct of more conventional persons. He was impatient of all restrictions and artifice, and consequently of most of the forms and standards of what is called civilised life . . . There was something primitive in Julian, a simplicity, force and directness which were almost savage, but tempered with a natural courtesy and grace which gave him the finest manners and a smile which was indescribably charming and intimate. Intimate, according to the somewhat exacting standards of the day, I should doubt if he ever was, even with those who knew him best. To me at any rate he seemed to have a spirit essentially solitary and self-contained, opening more freely to nature's solicitations than to man's . . .

(Raymond Asquith)

There is a story in one of Miss Kingsley's books of a West African medicine man who found himself at death's door. He applied all his herbs and spells, and conducted all his well-worn rites before his idols and with his friends' intercessions – without any effect. At last he wearied of his hocus-pocus, and took his idols and charms down to the sea shore and flung them into the surf and he said 'Now I will be a man and meet my God alone'. Julian, from the time I knew him, had flung away his idols and had met God. His intense moral courage distinguished him even more than his physical bravery from the run of common men, and his physical bravery was remarkable enough . . .

(Charles Lister)

Julian fought, and protected himself; it was in solitude that he won his battles. His friends warned him that his self-containment might not always be sufficient –

In the days when he was the most vigorous man alive he always used to boast that he could feel absolutely no interest nor take any pleasure in the society of any living soul but himself . . . I used to tell him that if you build everything on one single key-stone, and if anything goes wrong with that keystone, the bottom is apt to drop out of your universe . . .

(Tommy Lascelles)

– but the question was still unasked – what was it he was fighting? The battles he was having with his mother were on the surface at least a continuation of her trying to make him more sociable and what she called 'affectionate', and of his refusing her blandishments. He still would not go to many of her parties, and he kept himself to himself at Oxford. But this was scarcely a matter of life and death. It was true he sometimes poked fun at Ettie's friends and lovers – 'Poor John was rather in the dumps, had you been giving it to him?'; but these were mainly jokes. Then around 1908 Ettie became involved with a new lover, a young man eighteen years younger than herself and only three years older than Julian,

and it was then that the passions that had been lurking beneath the surface
between Julian and Ettie seemed to emerge.

Archie Gordon was a son of the Earl of Aberdeen, the Lord Lieutenant
of Ireland; he had been at Oxford when Julian and Billy had been at Eton
and had often come over to Taplow. Here, in the absence of his parents,
he seems to have been received more and more as a member of the family.
He, like Julian, was bright and strong and curly haired: he had the same
reputation for sunniness and energy, but not for rebelliousness. Socially,
he was everything that Julian was not; and in her battles Ettie seemed to
take him as a substitute for Julian.

At first he had been ostensibly a friend of Monica's, though she was
eleven and he was twenty –

> Balliol College
> Oxford
> May 28th 1905

Dearest Monica,

I am afraid I have been a long time in thanking you for your photograph
(with which I am very pleased). As a matter of fact sending letters 'to be
forwarded' bores me, and I do not know your address. Last night, however, I
met your mother dining with the Asquiths in town, and she gave me the
information I wanted. She also had the kindness to sew on a button on my
coat that was coming off in the middle of the drawing room . . .

> Dec 8th 1905

Dearest Ca,

I was prevented from answering your letter yesterday because I went to
Hatfield. I had a splendid time there, though it was only for one night. I
dressed up as a lady in a dressing-gown of your Mother's, a beautiful pink
creation, with a lace mantilla and diamond brooches on my hair. Very
becoming, but very hot . . .

And Ettie wrote to Mary Elcho –

. . . Monica and I paid a three-day visit to the Asquiths and had the utmost fun –
the house teeming with Balliol boys including Monica's principal 'spangle' – and
she had a *glorious* time, and I exploited all the fragments cast to Mothers –
Raymond was quite delightful, and Archie Gordon . . .

Monica was still only twelve; Archie Gordon was twenty-one; Ettie was
thirty-eight. But all the participants seemed to know the rules of the

game. Mothers, not daughters, were allowed to pick up crumbs. Archie Gordon was before long writing to Ettie herself –

> 1 Beethoven St
> Berlin
> Nov 3rd 1907

My D,

Our first winter day here – a freezing east wind and a yellow evening exactly like Scotland – but you don't know Scotland in Winter! I have just finished a week of much dissipation and a good deal of silly depression but I feel as bird as anything this evening in a quiet way. At these moments I think I feel the desire for the far-away things strongest of all but not *sharpest* – the prevailing sensation is the wonderfulness and value of their existence. I got your Johnson and have just begun it, and am looking forward to it *immensely* – thank you so *very* much.

. . . I *do* want to be nearer you, E. dearest – I *ought* to be. I am not feeling as though I was *doing* much here. Much too distracted. Bless you. You are dear. Yrs A.

Archie Gordon was training to be a banker. He was affectionate, sociable, went to parties, played golf; he adored Ettie uncritically: he held the fashionable belief that life was rather depressing apart from ideals. To Ettie, he must have seemed what she was trying to make of Julian. Evan Charteris wrote of Archie Gordon – 'His youth had the peculiar gift of making others, divided from him by a generation of years, feel no barrier of age . . . In this way he enlarged the area of friendship, and was able to attach himself to anyone with whom he chose to make friends.' This was at the time when Julian, at Oxford, was establishing his reputation as someone who 'didn't make many friends because he didn't want many friends; he made hardly any at Oxford outside our small Balliol gang, and he didn't swallow every one of them either' (Tommy Lascelles). And when Ettie tried to make him 'affectionate' like Archie Gordon, Julian fought this –

Our controversy is quite impossible as a controversy because you start by denying the only point which makes it one – my having no faculty for 'affection-ateness' . . . It's no good trying to improve what you haven't got. I'm trying *awfully* hard to do that with my affectionateness; but either it's not there, or it's got into the hell of a dark corner . . .

This was at the time when Archie Gordon was writing to Ettie –

Hotel D'Italie
Brescia
April 12th 1908

My V.D,

... I wanted to write you such a real reflection of happiness and sun ...
Every day we have talked of you and thought of you, in all the lovely places.
But I am going to *tell* you all about the *things* very soon ...

My beloved E., I can't begin to speak of all the joy of seeing you *often* and
much, I trust, during the next weeks. I have the whole universe waiting to be
talked about, and all my life to be submitted to you. And my love precedes
me from here, warm from the sun and the joy that there is here.

Bless you and keep you. Yr A.

Ettie accepted this sort of affectionateness: she was not getting it from
Julian. For a while in her relationship with Archie Gordon she even
seemed to be the pursuer – a contemporary remembers Archie Gordon
leaving a dinner-party early one evening and running to meet Ettie who
was waiting for him under a lamp-post. But much of the passion seemed,
as usual, to be in the mind. Ettie did not object when Archie Gordon
travelled in Italy with another woman (he wrote to her 'V. has just made
a devilish effort to seize and read this letter: we have a little common
sitting room between our bedrooms, and I have granitely rejected her
blandishments'). And it was in the mind that there soon began to be
established the sort of ties by which her adorers were secured to Ettie.

Vice Regal Lodge
Dublin
May 8th 1908

I have just come off the rough sea, driven up in the rain and got your letter.
And now I am feeling the blank, dreary misery which once only before I had a
taste of. The very memory of that other taste is another blow at my heart, for
to whom but *you* should I turn when in trouble, *you* whom I have wounded and
wronged?

Why am I writing to you? All that you say is true – there is nothing for me
to say in excuse – if *excuse* were a word that were possible in such a connection.
And yet no human power could prevent me from saying what I have to say.
For the truth of my love and trust for you is the truest thing that I know, and
tho' I have by my amazing *irresponsibility* made it possible for you to have
doubts, I have to bear witness to the light that is in me. My darling, you who

know me will know the sadness that is in this letter, the bitter remorse, the aching to heal the wounds I have made myself. All the things striving for utterance – all the memories *choking* me with grief.

I know you will be all right whatever you do, and yet I *must* plead – I feel the other things being beaten down by my one great and simple faith. I *can't* lose you. I had better write nothing more. I am losing my thoughts.

My friend of friends you will always be, tho' I should never see you again. For the things that are in the past are holy.   Yr

A, who loves you and yet gave you pain.

PS   Will you send a telegram to say you have got this letter?

This letter might have been written by Evan Charteris, George Wyndham, John Baring: the letters of Ettie's lovers seem to follow some blueprint for joy, sin, guilt, repentance and forgiveness. The sin here as usual is not named – it might have been making physical advances to Ettie or not making physical advances to Ettie; it might have been making advances to someone else, though this is unlikely, for Ettie was on good terms with Archie's other women friends. But this did not matter; what mattered, even, was that the sin should not be named. For Ettie's power, and the responses of others to it, was in dreams; and what was of concern above everything was that a dream should not be broken. Archie Gordon wrote of –

an extra wave of *thinking* and *wanting* that happens to be on me this morning . . . perhaps it is a dream about you a few hours ago that brought it on . . . I *love* waves like that which suddenly slide up and tumble you over; and the temporary-loss part gets no vestige of a chance against the *volume* of everlasting-possession-happiness.

Sometimes it seemed that possibly he was waiting for his dreams to become real –

I have just come back from the Polignac ball where I spent half an hour wandering sadly among unknown crowds thinking how perfect it might have been. You don't know how perplexed and sad I am because I know something has happened and I have no vaguest notion what it is – and it makes me unhappy.

Never for one moment will I waver in trust, I am certain, but I can't avoid gnawing anxiety, and speculations will keep thrusting themselves on me which I have to fight to keep off.

I come back always to the thought that *nothing* could come between us and it does good and helps me to wait patiently. But may it be soon, E dearest?

I can't imagine that *none* of my letters and tellys have reached you. One last Friday, one at Wednesday AM, a telly the same night.

You know I would wait seven years and not weaken, don't you? but it wouldn't be without pain.

I shall be at the Hotel Foyot, Rue Tournai, from today.

I was beaten today by a put in the champs.

Your ever loving and wasting

A.

Ettie's family and friends knew of her involvement with Archie Gordon. It was customary for a fashionable lady to have a 'culte', even such a young one, if it could be thought of as a dream. Betty Montgomery wrote to Ettie later – 'What a strange thing it has been in your life, that bright star-like radiance sweeping through for three years!' Willy was away much of the time, either fencing (he wrote to Ettie 'I began with the Captain of the German team and pursued him to the ropes and got in a rib-roaster') or occupied with organizing the Olympic Games. Julian and Bron were the members of the family who objected to Ettie's dream: Julian wrote about a proposed summer holiday – 'Bron seemed to think Glen Goich splendid but too near the smart set; and he says you must promise not to have Archie Gordon in the house ever'. But in such a battle, with so many transpositions, what would it have been to win?

In 1909 Archie Gordon seems to have tried to become engaged to Violet Asquith – the 'V' with whom he had been in Italy and who was, and who remained, Ettie's adoring friend. In the autumn of 1908 he and Violet had been staying in a house party in Scotland and she had fallen over a cliff: she had been given up for lost, and then had suddenly been found. Archie Gordon had described the scene to Ettie – 'she had *no* concussion, which was surprising, as she had apparently *fallen* on the back of her head among the rocks'. After this, there are no more surviving letters from Archie Gordon to Ettie: there are indications that he, she and Violet Asquith all corresponded, and that their letters have been destroyed.

Then at the end of 1909 Archie Gordon was driving a car near Winchester when another car ran into him and he was thrown out. He was taken to Winchester hospital, and it seemed that he would die. At first only his mother was allowed to see him. Ettie began a vigil, at first away from his death bed, that she was to repeat later, and much more closely, with two of her sons. She sent bulletins to her daughter Monica –

. . . Archie goes on well but I fear there is still great pain. And another sad thing is that his mother says he longs all day long to see Violet and me but the doctors (so wisely and rightly) forbid his seeing *anyone* but his mother . . . Vivi has been wonderful – so strong and brave – I think they really will be married now if only he gets well – and then he'll feel it was worth it all!

Monica was a student learning German in Dresden. She had another letter from her mother in a fortnight's time telling her that Archie was worse; that Ettie and Violet Asquith had been summoned to his bedside –

Dec 15th

My own little Casie,

. . . My darling, I am writing to you because you are so absolutely here in my heart – your love and sorrow just as if you were sitting by me – at a time of shipwreck like this all the little things like time and space shrivel away and only the big ones like Love and its triumph and eternity seem to count. That is why we must not hold too clamorously to keeping Archie here – or feel with too much anguish that his bright spirit should leave us for a little while. His radiance is *ours*, and all his goodness and happiness and love cannot die to us. I do not want any of us who he loved ever to have a *dark* thought of sadness about him, it seems as if it might almost hurt and confuse *him*, in whatever land he be. I should like always to feel thanksgiving for him and praise and *joy* whenever we think of him, he could never have borne to cause us grief or that we should think of him in relation to dark and sombre sorrow. He himself was so utterly ready to go – when he was ill a week ago he said to his mother 'I have done so little with my life yet, do you think it is wrong to be so content to go?' The things that were eternal were always very near to him, the very pivot of his life and spring of all his sunshine – and his faith that all was ordered and ordained never left him. I like to think he hardly *knew* sorrow . . .

And Monica, aged fifteen, replied –

Darlingest,

Have just got your letter. Oh my poor poor darling Mummie, but *how* true everything you write is! Brave heart, 'Vous êtes si philosophe ma très chère'! – and we *won't* let sorrow creep into our lives, will we? They were indeed not given us to pass in mourning . . . *What* a thing true, staunch unfailing love is . . . Even when I'm in the blackest moods, when I think of you and our love it revives my energy and love of life . . .

The same day Ettie had written –

Royal Hotel
Winchester

My own little girl,

It has been very wonderful. I met Ld Aberdeen in London, and we travelled here together, arriving at 8 pm. He was alive, conscious, and *so* happy – he looked up with his *beaming* smile – and said rather weakly 'Darling'; then slowly 'I knew you'd come'. We had a long talk, only his voice weak – all the rest just Cha himself, and *so* happy. We stayed with him all the night, his father and mother, Violet and I – and others in and out. He was conscious till 3, and died at 7. Very very peacefully. Once he said 'Love to Bill and Ca'. Another time, very faintly 'Goodbye'. I kissed him, and he said very feebly 'It has been very wonderful, hasn't it?' I am writing down everything he said, and will show you. Violet was beyond *all telling* – her strength, control and unselfishness. And oh! those poor parents – they have been so marvellous and *so* heartbreaking – I have just been in to them. I am going home tonight.

He looks beautiful in a way I can hardly tell you – so thin, and the beautiful *lines* of his face showing clear – the nose very fine and thin – and the beautiful brow and the hair and setting of the eyes; and a look of *radiant* happiness – I know you will like the thought of that, and be able to *dwell* on it – my own dear.

Your Mummie

❧ EIGHTEEN ❧

The story of Archie Gordon is relevant to the story of Julian because it illustrates something of what Julian was fighting against and perhaps even foreshadows his defeat. Julian's battles with Ettie were contemporaneous with her and Archie Gordon's relationship during 1908 and 1909; this latter pattern was one from which Julian thought he could remain aloof, but part of it was inside him and he could not. It was a pattern that perhaps defeated many young men around 1915.

The pattern was to do with Ettie's insistence on order and light and her denial of darkness; her fantasies that there was no darkness even when there was; and the damage that can be caused by such illusions, because they can be reconciled with reality perhaps only in a circumstance of death. About life after death, that is, anything can be imagined as real: and so, when there are confusions, death can be seen as a blessing. In Ettie's and Julian's feelings for each other there were confusions, and dark ones: it was these that, by Ettie at least, were denied – or were transferred, in a dream, to Archie Gordon.

There seems to have been no taste, touch, smell, in the love between Ettie and Archie Gordon. In *The Bacchae*, when the wildness of the senses was denied ferocity went on in the heart. Julian, with his impatience of dreams, was a challenge to such ferocity. But for the same reasons, he was potentially its victim.

Death was welcomed in dreams because any shining light could be imagined about it: it was still hard to live with in reality. But it could be written about, and thus light be kept alive. 'I am writing down everything he said, and will show you.' And if what is wanted is a story that is orderly and bright, then what can be better than one about eternity? Like this, the loved one is simple and unchanging. The story has an end; but those left behind can continue with their threnodies.

After the death of Archie Gordon Ettie and those around her became like Hecuba and the Chorus at the end of *The Trojan Women*. They wrote to and fro –

> Dear Arthur,
>   . . . It is difficult to describe the beauty of his face after death. He had grown very thin, so that all the lines were quite fine and clear, and the beauty of the brow and eyes seemed instinct with happiness. It has been truly 'the beauty and the joy of living, the beauty and the blessedness of death' . . .

> My dear Ettie,
>   . . . This will be a sad Xmas for more than one; yet not after all for *him* . . .
>   (Arthur Balfour)

Maurice Baring wrote a poem –

> Gaily he rode into life's tournament,
> Gaily he ran at tilt to win the prize . . .

And Ettie wrote a poem –

JOINED

> By mute communions, by salt sad kisses;
> By passion's web, that with restless strands
> Wove us together; by the unplumbed abysses
> Where we have gazed, and never loosened hands . . .

And even Billy wrote –

I know how wonderful your love for him was, and God knows he loved you more than anything in life or beyond. It must be happy for you to think that you never failed or disappointed him once – as a sort of guardian angel in his life . . .

The dead were not to be pitied but those left behind: this was, as usual, the message. And even the living might be permitted to be happy because the dead would want them to be; now, they need not feel separated from the dead who were in glory. At the back of this insistence on the glory of death and the non-existence of sorrow was the terror that sorrow might be too difficult to handle: Ettie seems both to have had this terror and to have been a protection for others against it: from her resoluteness, they got support for their own defences. When Archie Gordon died

Ettie's correspondents were both commiserating with her and were saying – Thank God at least for you, because you make things all right for us. Monica wrote – 'Oh Mummie, don't be sad – do remember how we love you and what you mean to us all.'

And Billy wrote – 'God knows I could be miserable enough thinking how poor a friend I was to him . . . he always the giver and I the taker . . .'

This was perhaps the deepest fear – not so much that one might not be loved – this could be assuaged by passionate reassurances – but that one might not love – this was what assurances from others could not fill. A child, when a loved one is taken away, feels itself responsible – what else can a child feel, with no ability to distinguish between itself and others? A grown-up can distinguish; but not if fear of loss has become too set. Then, there is the experience of the unknown sin at the centre – the wrong for which one feels responsible but cannot remember why – the hollow which insatiably demands forgiveness. It is against this that a wall of fantasy is built up; but protection only perpetuates the emptiness. And there can be no real healing, because a real touch might revive the original love and pain.

It is striking how often Ettie's correspondents spoke of their melancholy – a melancholy which, when they were not talking about it, they said need not exist. Most of Ettie's lovers spoke of their melancholy; then denied it. Sometimes whole families seemed to become melancholy in turn; passing it round, as it were, as if in a game of hunt-the-slipper. Herbert Asquith wrote to Ettie of his wife Margot doing a cure – 'she stays in bed every day until about 2.30 or 3, then gets up and about 4 has a round of golf, then dinner and a little bridge, and she is generally in bed by 10.30 or 11'. Then he himself was 'for the time being a mere vegetable, lying late in bed and reading indifferent novels and playing still more indifferent golf and wondering in odd moments why and for what possible purpose I was created'. Then his daughter Violet, after the death of Archie Gordon, became ill and 'her strong will has been *set* on getting ill, which seems to me such a cruel selfish and shallow view of death'. This was the description by her stepmother Margot. Margot added, apparently inconsequently but aptly – 'I have such awful difficulty in understanding the value of appearances: they mean nothing to me you see'.

One of the oddest outcomes of Archie Gordon's death was that it brought Ettie and Violet Asquith even closer together: it was as if they were enabled to love each other – perhaps to love at all – through the love-and-death of Archie. Violet Asquith wrote –

Sometimes I feel it's almost a waste that we're always so happy together, because in these moments of sharpest anguish and lowest ebb I long for you so – and then when you come the need of help seems almost to have melted before the joy of seeing you: I *can't* be unhappy with you ever.

But what then was it that was longed for – joy or pain? In fantasy, these were joined; this was the protection. In anguish the loved one could be held, and so – where was pain? A fantasy of anguish was required – to be safe from a real one.

Sometimes sorrow did break through to Ettie. She wrote a poem inspired by a children's book she was reading to Imogen –

> O show me the road to laughter town
>   For I have lost the way.
> I wandered out of the path one day
> When my heart was broken, my hair turned grey;
> And I can't remember how to be gay
>   I've quite forgotten how to play;
> It's all from sighing and crying, they say.
>   Baby, take me to laughter town
>   For I have lost the way.
>
>   Feb 2 1910

But then, within a month or two, she was writing to a new young admirer – Patrick Shaw Stewart, who was in age even closer to Julian than Archie had been.

                                                              3 April 1910

D.P.

I think of you so often . . .

I have just got back my letters to Archie (I didn't know I'd written so many letters to *everybody* there is in the world!) – they don't tear and wrench like other people's letters to one, and remind of so many *little* things – of course all the big ones don't need remembering. It is all strange as it slips into perspective, isn't it, *worse* than one thought and yet better too. 'Reality lay behind the pain; and Reality – though seas of grief may first be plunged through to find it – is always joy . . .'

D.P., you'll come here, won't you, April 16th – and would it be quite imposs to join us at Panshanger a day or two before??

                                                              Love, E.

There is something awe-inspiring about Ettie's manipulation of joy-through-pain: her insistence that reality was what she said it was, and if it wasn't, it had better be. She succeeded with her gospel in converting most of those around her. And if she punished heretics – which she did – might this not too be a benefit – after they were dead?

This was a time of decadence in literature, when categories became confused – love and suffering, death and joy. Ornate young men subjected themselves to cruel women: cruel men decked out like women dominated girls like boys. Here too the confusion was the protection – with no distinctions, the mind was free to defend itself as it liked. The death of others could be a delight because it could be a victory for oneself; death of oneself could be a triumph because it could seem like a story. And what could be blamed was a wild and malignant God; but then, God must be a joy, or nothing else was bearable.

It was a time of decadence in politics. In 1908 Arthur Balfour gave a lecture at Cambridge entitled 'Decadence'. He said that there were times in the histories of societies like senility when 'there spreads a mood of deep discouragement, when the reaction to recurring ills grows feebler . . . when learning languishes, enterprise slackens, and vigour ebbs away'. It was possible that by the disciplines of science a society might revitalize itself without waiting to be swept away in the processes of evolution, for in science men had an instrument with which to stand back and observe both the world and themselves. Science was an 'instrument of social change all the greater because its object was not change but knowledge'. But still, it seemed unlikely that a society could revitalize itself without much of it being swept away.

It was a characteristic of Ettie's generation (and indeed of generations that followed) that in spite of lip-service to objectivity and knowledge passions remained primitive. People had been trained to possess and to kill; they justified this by talk of duty. Perhaps this had once been necessary: it was now dangerous, but they did not question duty. It was something that, like life after death, could be dreamed of as required.

People in Europe at this time were spoiling for a fight like drunks outside a pub on Saturday night. Willy sat next to the Crown Prince of Germany one night in 1909; he wrote to Ettie – 'I had an amusing dinner next to the Crown Prince and we discussed the relations between Germany and England; he would apparently like to fight someone more or less, but not England, because he says we are brothers.' (Arthur Balfour might have known that brothers are people who fight.) The particulars of a fight did not matter: one was just needed, by the heart.

It was against all this that Julian had his battles – and in parallel to

Ettie's and Archie Gordon's loving and dying. Julian protested against fantasy; he himself became ill; he looked for sense and discrimination to stay alive. He pursued health in the outside world but felt the sickness in himself. He had almost won his battle against this when, some time later, there was suddenly all the killing outside.

❦ NINETEEN ❦

Julian's letters to his mother during his first year at Oxford had been mainly to do with his work and sport and undergraduate affectations. This style continued through 1908 though more anarchically –

The great amusement this term is lying in the quad and singing from 8 to 1 every night. Charles has been away for a week canvassing for Russell at Wimbledon; he played cricket the other day in black trousers and brown boots. Bones has (literally) shaved his head with a razor because he says there is no one here he wants to please. Denys has taken a season ticket to London and spends all the time in the train. Everything is going splendidly, and I love this term, especially the rowing. I am getting on with my army work . . .

Charles Lister was Julian's closest friend at Balliol. Julian called him 'the best of all, a wild mind absolutely and wholly uninfluenced by contact with civilisation or people'. Charles Lister had become a socialist at Eton; he had collected £75 for the 'Russian People' after the abortive revolution of 1905; at Oxford he joined the Independent Labour Party and campaigned at Wimbledon with Bertrand Russell on the issue of Women's Suffrage. He would sometimes have what Julian called 'a large trades' union congress in his room', when 'crowds of the roughest men I have ever seen' would flock into Balliol and ask 'Where's the 'On C. Lister?'. In 1908 Charles Lister was sent down for a term for being inadvertently rude, when drunk, to the Dean of a neighbouring college. His friends put up a tombstone to him with the biblical inscription 'I wist not brethren that it was the High Priest'.

  Julian was not a socialist in politics because he had no interest in politics; but he had the emotions of a socialist, writing with contempt of –

those who value for its own sake the wealth, the magnificence and the display; those whom conventionality forces to keep servants and whom competition forces to keep an army of servants; those who rate the worth of themselves and others by the amount of these things that they possess and the show that they make of them.

He disliked politics perhaps because of the febrile atmosphere of the time; also, because he was going into the army.

Ettie wrote in her Family Journal 'It had been tacitly settled from their earliest years that Julian was to go into the army and Billy to the Bar. Except for a brief wish to be a scavenger Julian never wavered'. Julian did indeed waver: but what was 'tacitly settled' in the Grenfell family was powerful.

Julian had to do extra work above the work for Greats if he was to pass his army exam. He wrote in 1908 that he was 'living the quiet life and working all the week and dashing off in a buggy with a fast pony every Sunday to fish in odd corners of Oxfordshire with the greyhounds running behind'. It was at this time that he seemed always to have greyhounds with him – Hammer and Tongs, Dawn and Dusk, Melbourne – which he said he loved more than people. But he did begin to be interested in girls (he was twenty). Before, sexuality seems to have gone into work and play: there had been no trace of homosexuality at Eton.

He went to stay with the Lister family in Yorkshire and flirted with Charles's sisters Laura and Diana. 'Laura I think is wonderfully beautiful, but rather ridiculous, she languishes so openly, but I like her v. much: I'm not sure I don't like Diana better, she is exactly like Charles, with a little more dash, she rides like hell-flame.' He told Ettie – 'I'm really having quite a wickedly good time here': but added – 'I'm getting terrified of Nemesis . . . the Hippolytus spirit has had almost too crude a renaissance'.

His trouble seemed to be that he could not take the girls he flirted with lightly: he wanted – what? – to know them, to make love; but it was, of course, taboo for an unmarried young man to make love to an unmarried young girl. He could only do this with tarts, and respectable older women. Julian seemed to want to propose to the girls he flirted with. This became a family joke. When he had injured his hand while training in Norfolk he had sent a telegram to his mother telling her he had proposed to his nurse (this had resulted in his mother coming to him at once); when he wrote to her about Laura and Diana Lister he assured her 'It will quiet you to know that I have not proposed to *one soul* while I have been here'.

And then, back at Balliol –

... I'm rather *glad* to be back here; I had rather a surfeit of the fair sex at the end of the holidays and began to feel a crying need for Essex, roughness, and a 'world of men'. I like Laura very much 'as a friend'; she says I treat her like a 'good chap'. It was rather hopeless talking to her because we always both of us said exactly the same things and made exactly the same jokes at exactly the same time. It got quite oppressive ... Rough dinner tonight. Stag stunt. Hurray!

Young men were driven to rowdiness by the taboos: even permitted sexuality was a risk, either of scandal or disease. Consolation could be found in 'Essex' – the world of men. It is unlikely that Julian became sexually involved with anyone at Oxford. Flirtation, like longing, could be prolonged: but this made one ill.

I work very violently every day, and row, very ill; mental concentration only has the effect of making each stroke a sort of convulsion; and the more will-power there is on the one end of the oar the less water there is on the other ...

Julian's feelings of sickness came on him increasingly at Oxford. And he began to suffer from sudden and apparently inexplicable outbursts of temper –

I had a fearful row with a cabman last night; he demanded a preposterous fare and I suddenly lost all control, tore him down from his seat and shook him till bits began to drop off him. I never remember being so *passionately* angry in my life before, and why I can't imagine. It would be awful if murder always entered one's heart on being overcharged a shilling. Luckily I only shook him, and left him alive, gasping out wild threats of vengeance and the police courts.
    Archie has just walloped in from Stanway ...

Julian wrote about his rage; about Archie; he could not see, or admit, a connection. This was when Archie Gordon was writing to Ettie 'I come back always to the thought that *nothing* could come between us'; when Ettie was writing to Patrick Shaw Stewart praising the beauties of *Hippolytus*; when she was writing to Julian complaining of his lack of affectionateness, and Julian was writing to her – 'either it's not there, or it's got into the hell of a dark corner'.
Julian defended himself against her by mocking his mother's style –

I went and did a soshial last night to widen my circle of friends and my general horizon: the Bullingdon dinner – all the pin-heads there! They *are* such good fellows!! and now I know what a miserable fool I've been shutting myself away from my fellow men, but thank God it is not too late! and I believe that last night I laid the foundations for some golden friendships which will blossom out and change and colour the whole of my life. Do you know a man called Philip Sassoon?

It is so good of you, mother dear, to send me sermons: you *know* how I love reading anything of that sort; and if *ever* you have got any about, *do* send them on to me – tracts, or anything, you know! You are so thoughtful: and what a thing it is to have a good mother!

It was when he was being ironic to his mother that he perhaps managed best to handle his feelings: but it is difficult to be ironic about something that affects one closely. And it was Ettie's talent to appeal to seriousness. Soon, Julian was defending himself more carefully.

I did love your letter. I think it all most awfully good and true, and that I ought to agree with it even if I don't . . . I think 'schemes of life' are the only really interesting things: they are certainly the only things which really matter . . .

Character is *the* thing that you can mould and make for yourself; it is the result of continuous working upon the faculties which one starts with. The faculties are natural, born in one, mere chance. Character is the direct opposite of chance; every single thing you do influences it. It is the net result of what you have been doing by free choice since you were born. It only comes into contact with chance and predestination in the fact that it is founded and based on natural faculties. Of *course* there is 'superlative free will' in character.

But character *is* built on faculty to start with, and you must have the faculty as a basis. And my whole point is that this faculty of affectionateness has been left altogether out of my composition. I really believe this; things people say and do, and things in books, often seem absolutely incomprehensible to me; I've no standard in myself by which to know or judge them; they simply hit me and fall off again – solid crystal. Of course you will say that I had the faculty just as much as other people but that I've killed it; you said so the other day; but there I rather disagree – I don't believe I've set my face against things . . . I utterly agree that the building up of character is for its own sake a blank dead thing with no ultimate end . . . one must have some end, drifting is useless . . .

I am just beginning dimly to see *my* end I believe; very little and very dimly, but still a beginning . . . Honestly, I can't understand Love at present; I can't 'think it'. But once you get a big ideal, and the all-round expansion of a big ideal, I believe you begin to see and touch what you never did before and find a great deal more 'world'. I'm sure an ideal won't come to me through love; perhaps love will come to me through an ideal . . .

Julian's rejection of 'love' was a rejection of the form in which love had been presented to him – the cycle of adoration, guilt, humiliation, ecstasy. It was a rejection of his mother's so-called love of him – which too was an attempt to stop him living his own life and make him guilty. Then, the cycle of penance and forgiveness could get under way. It is cruel of a mother to tell her son that it is he who has killed his affectionateness: this is what he would fear anyway, with a child's vulnerability and lack of discrimination. If in fact a child's affectionateness is killed, this is usually the fault of a mother. One of the ways a mother kills it is by making him fear – by perpetuating dependence and pain.

Julian wrote –

Did you hurt my feelings? Not ½! Isn't it a pity I'm so *frightfully* sensitive; life becomes almost unbearable under the strain! However, I actually liked Sunday in spite of the anguish you caused me, and the utterly incoherent and inexpressible workings of my great brain. Are you well? And the catarrh? My down is gradually merging into a sort of semi-conscious state with total cessation of all feeling, which is rather blissful; I am now on a par with a living sponge, or a polypus, or the higher vegetable world. Work, riding and boxing all go on in a sort of dream . . .

Julian bashed himself about harder and harder. He had a new horse, Buccaneer, who 'jumps very big and quite clean . . . there were three gates in a line and he never touched one'. He won the Open Heavyweight Race at Oxford – 'having backed myself on Buccaneer at 4:1 and won much gold'. In a boxing match – 'I started *shockingly* badly; my tummy was all wrong, and my eye about a foot out. I felt awful. The man murdered me in the first round and all but had me knocked out; I knocked him out in the third, but it was a fearful narrow squeak!'

It was inside that he began to feel rotten: 'I feel such a rabbit, because there's nothing actually wrong with me, only I go on getting more and more dead and miserable and I can't work or do anything'. He did glimpse a connection between these feelings and the ways in which his mother was attacking him – 'Of course if I have got one (a faculty for affectionateness) all the time, then the things that you repeat are obviously and doubly true and I'm too bad to live!' But he could not believe that she meant this. He puzzled – 'I've got nothing at all *bad*, but I'm just stone dead in myself, there must be something wrong . . .' In the winter of 1908 he agreed to see a doctor: the doctor said he was 'overworked, over-trained and *starved*' (Family Journal). He had not been eating, ostensibly in order to get light for horse-racing. He went to Panshanger to stay with his aunt

Katie Cowper to recuperate. This was the time of his twenty-first birthday: the celebrations, both with the family and with the neighbours and the tenants, had to be postponed. He wrote from Panshanger to Ettie –

I slept $21\frac{1}{4}$ hours out of the last day, 11 hours in bed and $10\frac{1}{4}$ in an arm chair; and the remaining $3\frac{3}{4}$ (sic) I ate surprisingly. I do not leave this house, I talk a little sometimes in my sleep, and I sit facing books. I am well and happy. Do not think of putting yourself out to come down here.

What Ettie seemed to want was to keep him a little boy: like this, there was a proper way of loving him and being loved. This is the impression given by the insertions that she made into his letters when, later, she published them in the Family Journal – the impression of how much *he* had loved *her* as a little boy. Ettie's letters to Julian have not been preserved: their tone can often be imagined from his replies.

Julian was better in the spring, and went to stay with Bron Lucas and the Listers again in Yorkshire. He wrote home – 'I'm glad my family expresses itself glad with me at present: only sorry that it likes me better in depression than in elation'.

One of the ways in which his mother came particularly to fight him was over women: and this was one subject about which Julian and even other members of the family managed to see that Ettie was wrong, if not why. Ettie had not objected when Julian had been seeing a lot of Laura and Diana Lister: the Listers were old friends of the family (their parents had been Souls) and in any case Julian had made it clear his feelings were not serious – his masculine activities took precedence over Laura and Diana.

It is almost impossible to talk introspective shop about the intricacies of your companion's life and character when you have just stopped rowing and are just going to box with a hunger past all understanding and a perfect craving for milk out of a jug.

This was no challenge to Ettie's supremacy. But then Julian made new friends, who were rivals to Ettie's world: and Ettie did not like them.

These were Marjorie, Letty and Diana Manners, daughters of the Duchess of Rutland – who, as Violet Granby, had been with Ettie in Venice in 1890 and about whose lover, Harry Cust, Ettie had written her romantic story with its glamorous and seductive villain. The three sisters were known amongst their friends as the 'Hotbed', or 'Hothouse' – an allusion not to bed, but to a greenhouse – they being renowned for their exotic affectations. (However Julian wrote 'I am not sure that they are not a good deal more natural in their hot-house than most other people in the open air . . . They are born professionals – that is really the secret of their coldness and their enthusiasms – and perhaps their 2nd-ratedness.') Julian became a friend of all three, but especially of Marjorie, who was the first girl he loved.

He would write to her asking her to come down to Balliol –'O Marjorie this is too splendid, you really *will* come on Sunday? . . . remember to bring your racy knickerbocker suiting.' Marjorie wanted to be a singer or a painter: but, like Julian, she found herself in a world in which to be an artist was unthinkable. And she too was often thus made to feel worthless by a jealous mother. Marjorie was over four years older than Julian: it would thus not have been easy for them to talk of marriage. But then, in this orphaned world, what else was there for them to do?

I *do* want to see you again. I'm glad you thought I was 'good' at Wantage; I was indeed! All the 'self-sufficiency' we used to talk about disappears when I see you, and I have to fall back on the 'iron will'; which is really hardly equal to the strain! But I'll go on trying to be good, and as little of a bore to you as I can . . .

The taboo on sexuality for the young except in ways that were likely to be distraught was the means by which the old kept their power over the young; their own sexuality being such that they would be likely to feel envious. It was assumed that considerations of family were primary (Julian wrote to Marjorie about one Balliol weekend: 'For God's sake don't come then because I shall be booked for family duty'); and although he tried to encourage Marjorie to become a singer ('It would be too splendid if you made a "career"') he did not seem to see much hope of this. He could joke with Marjorie about the world around them –

There was a large social gathering at Taplow last Sunday; strange to say, it was rather jolly, as everyone forgot they belonged to the smart set and got extraordinarily intoxicated every night; never have I imagined such a scene in one of the homes of England; it was a great improvement.

But although he made it clear to Marjorie what he felt about her, he could not escape from the conventions that made love castrating. He wrote 'You are far too strong, and far too good at everything; it's quite disheartening'.

Ettie would not have Marjorie nor any of the Manners sisters in the house at Taplow – not, that is, until Julian was out of England. There was no sensible reason given for this. Julian wrote to Ettie 'You're a regular cold draught in the Hothouse'. Billy wrote from Oxford when Julian was becoming ill – 'Marjorie was here today and most delightful . . . She has the best *poss* effect on Juju's spirits, I can't imagine why you're so obtuse about her . . . For *Lord's sake* have her and Diana at Tap'. But he added – 'Nevertheless not my will but thine'.

In the spring of 1909 Julian was still arguing with his mother about unsociableness. He tried once more to deal with her animosity with reason. He had tried to stop her coming to Oxford where she pursued him with arguments, because he said he had to work. Then

Dear Mother,

I want to write an archbaker because our talk on Sat made me rather sad: and I'm going to be rather 'logical' because as you say it's the Only Way. I think you know that I'd do most things to make it easier between us: our 'getting-on' is the one thing I *really* care for. But I think the one heygately imperative duty is to be true to oneself and to one's own things; that's the one thing one must not tamper with. Our difficulty is that our 'things' are radically opposite – it's no good blinking it – it makes our friendship much more difficult but much more wonderful and worth having. And I *did* love the thing you said about nobody having the least jurisdiction over other people or the least right to judge their lives. You like the smart set: I like the solitary life – or few people at a time. That is God; and we had better leave him alone. The one set you hate is the Hotbed: *the one set I like is the Hotbed.* That is God: and I cannot see, and I'm sure you cannot either, that there is the least obligation on me to give them up for you. I like them – more than I told you the other day when I knew I was hurting you and wanted to throw a sop – and I should hate myself for meanness and disloyalty if I gave them up. I feel quite certain that you really agree with this position. That is the jolly part – I feel really so sure of your judgement.

But I think you have lapses and inconsistencies. You implore me to smoke less cigarettes, and the next day you give me a case. You implore me not to live the solitary life, and die of mortification directly I like anybody! You say 'Of course, it would have been quite different if you had gone to Panshanger; but going to Hartham!' It is really rather hard to see the ethical enormity of going to Hartham instead of to Pans, don't you think? As to the smart set – you implore me to work, and cry if I don't dance nightly. I've told you this is outside my life and that I feel no obligation to do it. But that is quite different from giving up friends, and I should simply love to come with you if you would like it; what I can't understand is your wanting me to . . .

Julian saw something of what his mother was doing – the 'having-it-both-ways' (or 'double-binds' as psychiatrists call them) by which people, but especially mothers, try to make themselves always seem right and others always seem wrong; and thus keep power. This was what Ettie did with most of those she wanted to love her. Julian saw this, but could not see why: and thus could not really believe it. He could not imagine that in this way his mother might simply be bad: if she was, things were not bearable. To maintain his vision of her he had to perform the volte-face which was the way of Ettie's lovers – to say that she must be right after all and he wrong. But Julian did not really believe this either.

But the real difference between us which hurts me is my callousness and your sensitiveness; that is what I sometimes feel will stop us going on. I *loathe* hurting you: I loathe not saying what I mean and what I think and what is in me. It is our old compact that I shall say what I think and not mind your feelings, which is so hard for me to keep. The alternative is putting on the stopper, and then goodbye to everything. And I really feel that after talks like Sat that it is no good. I would not have written if I did not care about it so immensely; I have been logical because it is my only way. I've got none of the higher or tender feelings, and a heart like a bad warty granite. It's my fault – but you must take me at that or not at all. And it's really just as much a duty for the most sensitive person in the world to be what he is and to say what he thinks as for a stone quarry; and just as deadly to friendship if he doesn't.

All love. J.

There was confusion here: Julian knew in his heart that he was the sensitive person and his mother the stone-quarry; that he was the loving one and she was not; that he was happy if she went her own way while she would hurt him if he went his. But he could not be explicit about this: if he truly hurt her by saying it, it might be he who would be destroyed. So he had to keep up the fiction of himself hurting her; which was what she wanted him to say. He could not even use the threat to get away from her: it was so obvious he had nowhere to go.

He did make a gesture of getting away. This was when Ettie was staying in a hotel in Newquay with Evan Charteris and Mary Wemyss and Arthur Balfour – and Archie Gordon came to visit them. Ettie had still been lecturing Julian about morals. Julian wrote –

Balliol College
Oxford
June 2nd 1909

Madam,

On mature consideration I have come to the conclusion that our differences
in view with regard to the moral sanction, Good and Evil, and the social
conventions, are so wide as to make further intercourse imposs between us: and
I thought that such a decision ought, in order to save confusion, to be made
public as soon as poss.

I went to Pans for a night yesterday: bloody weather, 8 good fish netted. The
Hotbed junior and Laura and Diana are at Pans . . .

This was a bit of a joke. What was far more serious was that Julian had
begun to write that spring the collection of essays that was to be his true
challenge to Ettie: his attempt to sort out for himself and for others what
he thought about his mother's social world of guilt and pretence and
imposition; and to suggest what individuals might do about it before it
carried a larger world towards perdition.

❦ TWENTY ❦

Julian's book consists of seven essays – 'On Conventionalism'; 'Sport'; 'On Individuality'; 'On Calling Names By Their Right Things'; 'Divided Ideals'; 'Selfishness, Service and the Single Aim'; 'Darwinism, Theism and Conventionalism'.

'Conventionalism' is an attack on 'the hall-mark of the English' – the belief that 'a thing may be immoral or inadvisable or unpleasant' but this does not matter so much as that a man 'should think and do as others do'. This belief is harmful because

a man's point of view and a man's method of life are his own and if he is made to conform to a fixed point of view and a fixed method of life it will kill his soul . . . A man can only see the facts of life as they appear to him in the light of his nature; if the attempt is made to compel him to look at them in the light of some other man's nature he will not see them at all.

The result of conventionalism is fantasy: it 'substitutes a stupid, formal makeshift world for the real world; it turns life into a game, and a bad game at that, say Halma'.

One of the forces which fosters conventionalism is competitiveness: it is by always having to keep an eye on others that a man in fact becomes tied to them. The world of competitiveness is the world of 'etiquette, of manners, of social advancement; its atmosphere is the pungent atmosphere of afternoon tea'. Opposed to this, a free society aims to produce 'the greatest number of individual men: society does not want a fairly good all round man, it wants a man who will do one job and do it well . . . A Society is just like a machine; every single piece of machinery must do its own work or the machine stops'.

Above all –

conventionality's terrible power consists perhaps chiefly in its grip on the cradles of our race. It's talons fasten relentlessly on the new-born infant; and just at the time when the future man is utterly at the mercy of any influence, when his own judgement is not yet formed, and his whole outlook and view of life depend upon what he picks up from others, then conventionality reaps its easy victory. Just at the time when impressions sink deepest, and anything believed sinks ineradicably into the soul, conventionality envelopes him like a pall, thrown over him by his parents and his relations. If they take the conventional view, what hope is there that he should avoid it? For the very essence of conventionality is to force itself upon others, and the child is in duty bound to take all that is told him as the literal truth. He cannot see for himself what is black or white, right or wrong; it is at once his necessity and his duty to believe others . . . None escape, except those hardy souls who refuse from the very first to believe that a gentleman is a man who wears a top hat. Helped by the spirit of contradiction, these people spend their lives in one long battle for their own independence, through misery often and through pain. Everybody else thinks that they are mad, and they are of course conscious of this, and it drives them to further extremes. If everybody thinks a man mad, the probability is that sooner or later he *will* become mad; through no fault of his own, but because self-consciousness is forced upon him . . . Thus not only does conventionality ruin its own slaves, but it irritates also the independent and drives them into revolt against the existing order of things.

'Sport', Julian's second essay, has been quoted from earlier. 'Sport' in the sense that Julian uses the word is the opposite of competitiveness; it is a means by which men come into harmony with nature and with themselves. Large pheasant-shoots and tennis for instance are the opposite of sport; they are games depending on formalities and the keeping and settling of scores. Sport is a means by which a man learns how to find something real – a connection between nature and himself. Sport is hunting, coursing, shooting for food, fishing: by these not only are the forces of Dionysus appeased, but a man has learned to make them almost gentle. Sport does involve killing: but all life involves death. And by honouring death, as it were, a man can come to terms with what is most difficult for him. But if he insists on competitiveness – on violence made artificial – then dark forces may overwhelm him.

'On Individuality' describes the enemy of the conventionalist. The individualist will take –

nothing on trust, nothing unless he can see a reason for it, and unless he can see *his* reason for it. He is unpopular with the moralists because he will not take ready-made morals, he is unpopular with the social stars because he will not twinkle to order, he is unpopular with his party because he will not bind himself to a set creed. But the real cause of his unpopularity is the determination to live his own life.

And so – 'the strong man has first to harden his soul . . . If he wants to be consistent he has to be defiant'. But his offensiveness is in fact only defensive: 'his attitude is "live and let live", and he is only aggressive to those who refuse to let him live'.

A force that conventionalists will use against him, in addition to the appeal to competitiveness, is the call to duty and self-sacrifice: like this, they can plead for their conventions against his reason. But 'if the choice lies between reason and virtue it would be well to prefer rational sin to irrational morality because there would be no bounds beyond which such morality would not go'. Virtue without reason, that is, is no virtue: and the appeal to 'virtue' is, most often, simply a means by which the conventional put pressure on individuals to conform. The fact that the appeal to self-sacrifice goes hand in hand with the exhortation to competitiveness is the proof of this: the two ideals are contradictory; they have no common substance except as weapons to make men conform. And yet it is by these fantasies that the conventional say that they live and die. This is one of the central insights of Julian's book – that the ideals of the society around him were wrong not just in the way of morals but in that they had no content: it was fantasy that was bringing society to despair.

Such had been the ideals of the Pharisees: they were the ideals of the smart set of 1909. They made a man 'care less for what he does than for the way in which he does it: care less for being the best than for making other people think that he is the best'. They are the ideals of a politics in which 'no call is made on a man for opinions of his own; his business is to take the opinions of others, to repeat them and to repeat them again'. The effect of all this is that a man loses the power of thought; he loses that which distinguishes him as a man.

True battles go on in the brain: this is where an individual can sift, compete, judge, sacrifice. 'The cerebrum is the battle ground of conventionality and individuality.' This battle is productive of life: conventional battles are productive of death. The mind, for comfort, may want to yield to conventionality; but –

vae victis if the invader carries the day! For the conventional habit of thought soon draws scales over the eyes of the soul. Thought, if it is to be truly thought, first comes out of the self and then becomes the self . . . The brain which receives the conventional and ready-made instead of grinding its own mill is a rubbish heap of dead matter.

In 'On Calling Names By Their Right Things' Julian applies these insights to Christianity. Each man accepts the god he wants: what conventional Christians have accepted is a god that demands self-denial while allowing those who say they believe in him to practise self-assertion. This split between what is professed and what is done – or perhaps the confusion of all categories because 'self-denial' can in fact be used for self-assertion – results in any conventionalist being able to do just what he likes; which is to do what is 'done' without thinking. In a world of no clear meanings there is no substance but only convention – the looking over one's shoulder to see what others are doing. It is only by standing back from the chaos of convention that things can be seen as they are; can be evaluated not by catchwords but according to merit. 'A virtue is a virtue so long as it actually does good. Self-sacrifice is a virtue so long as it leads to self-realisation.' A proper valuation is always practical: does such a course of action lead to happiness or does it not. Thus the world can be viewed, not dreamed of. And this is in fact what true Christianity taught.

When Christ condemned worldliness he condemned the conventional view that money, power, position, are the important things; he did not condemn the world as it was created, for that would have been a condemnation of God, but the world as we have transformed it . . . He condemned the view that life consists in competition about trivialities, and he damned those who try to force this view on other people. He condemned the 'worldly' man and the 'man of the world'; not the man who is in the world and who tries to make the best of it.

Ideas and ideals must be based on fact, not on fancy. Their origin is from fact, and their stability remains only so long as they remain true to their origin. Far from being degraded by any such connection they are lifeless and meaningless without it. Our idea of beauty is derived from all the beautiful things we have ever seen, it did not descend to us from the clouds . . . Once we say that true beauty is something of another calibre than the beauty we see in the tree, then we destroy the roots of beauty altogether; we root it in nothingness. Directly we say that virtue is something different from that which makes life worth living, we destroy the foundations of virtue. Instead of ennobling virtue we make it inane . . . Instead of being content with its foundation upon solid fact, we found it upon empty air . . . Religion is not a sense of the supernatural, but a super-sense of the natural.

'Divided Ideals' elaborates the idea that the driving forces behind conventionalism are envy and jealousy – 'the feeling that I have done something and I will gain the greater glory for it if you cannot, so I will make it my business to prevent you doing it even if it is my profession to teach you how to do it'. It is for this reason that so many of the instructions in education are absurd and contradictory – like this, teachers can remain feeling superior to their pupils and safe. As a nation we are jealous: 'we are afraid that we may discover our error and have to change or remodel our conventional opinions or some equally terrible thing'; but this fear of change is a fear of life; there is safety in stasis, in contradictions where anything can mean anything, and in death.

This is an age of Divided Ideals, and so of divided lives, for it is impossible to live a single life under many aims. Self-development and self-sacrifice, getting what you want or giving it up for other people, knocking other people's heads together or offering them a choice of cheeks on which to exercise their fists, these are but examples of the hopeless antagonisms between divided aims in which we have plunged ourselves and quite unnecessarily . . . life is impossible according to the present ideals.

If, however, a man could be brought to see that 'both of the two contradictions are good in their own way . . . that the contradiction is only an invention of our minds . . . that the ideal is composed both of self-development and of self-sacrifice but that it is one ideal, the promotion of the general happiness' – then, life would be possible. This is the point. Without the fantasy of ideals we could be like people trying to decide between the 'Great Northern and the Midland route to the same place: the G.N.R. would get you there quicker one day, the G.C.R. the next'. The means of choosing could be learned; they would be to do with what was practical. As it is we dither, imagining that different railway lines are absolutes. Or – 'It is as if we divided the white of egg of life from the yolk and then expressed surprise because it did not hatch out into a harmonious chicken.' But perhaps after all people did not want eggs to grow: divided ideals arose from a fear of life that was a fact. They were held by people who preferred to search for a heaven 'where the beauty of the idea atones for any result'.

'Selfishness, Service and the Single Aim' recapitulates –

In the last essay it was held that two things cannot be considered as contradictories if they are means to one and the same end; that service and self-development only contradict each other when each is supposed to represent the whole end of man instead of a means to that end

and adds – 'but it would have been nearer the truth to say that they are two interconnected routes, the two lines work together in combination, and the journey can best be accomplished by changing to and from one to the other'. For – 'service requires ability if it is to be useful'; and ability requires an aim if it is not to go round and round. Conventional people might in fact from time to time behave as if they recognized these truths, but they had to deny that they so behaved – this was what caused the confusion.

Also –

The philosophic objector may declare that matters become no better even if a connection can be established between self-development and unselfish aims, because at the bottom of everything lies the fundamental dualism between our own good and the good of other people. Your ideal of happiness, he will say, is no solution; it is your own happiness or the happiness of others, for they are vastly different things. Now all this attempt has been to show that they are *not* different things, but coincident in the long run, and that therefore the ideal of happiness is one and single. If a man breaks the laws of society he hurts not only society but himself.

This is true if the laws are good; and if they are not, he can help to make them good.

For what is good for all must necessarily be good for each; a man's happiness is necessary to the happiness of society and the happiness of a society is necessary to the happiness of the man. And the laws necessary for the society are laws which do not interfere in the least with his personal liberty; they enforce neither the top hat nor the conventional thought of which it is the symbol; the greatest enthusiast for freedom need not tilt against them. The ideal of happiness is one ideal after all, for the happiness of the many makes only the same demand on a man as his own happiness makes; and if he refuses to bend to these demands he will at one and the same time lose his own happiness and ruin that of others.

Society only works well, that is, if each man is performing his individual function; and he can only do this well if society is respecting him for being himself.

'Darwinism, Theism and Conventionalism' extends the argument into the context of evolution. 'If the fittest survive, it must be that those who wish to survive should fit themselves, as far as in them lies, to the world.' There need be no quarrel between Darwinism and Theism for the proper attitude of a man towards the world – that of learning from it and adapting himself to it by learning – should be the same whether or not the world has a creator or protector. In either case, that is, a man should be concerned with paying attention to available evidence. Nor should there be a conflict between evolutionists and those who believe in a future life; their behaviour should still be the same in this life – to learn from it. A creed for both evolutionists and theists 'enforces as a first duty the looking of facts in the face and the adapting of ourselves to them as best we may'. It is by this that there is a hope that the world 'can actually be made better through our agency'. For although evolution may depend on the agency of chance, yet men, by learning and adapting to facts, may yet make themselves ready for the operation of chance, and so by this even influence its effects. For what otherwise might die, might then live. Against this reasonable and active and hopeful gamble the conventionalists set up their defeatist creeds – the religions which tell men to look for nothing but another world ('an imaginary creation of that God whose creation they have just refused') and insist on 'virtues both unsuitable to life and destructive of life – contented humility, needless asceticism, wholesale mortification'. Equally defeatist is the creed of 'conventional' Darwinism, in which 'man is represented as a mere plaything of the elements, a helpless log on the ocean of circumstance . . . so much material in the hands of world-forces'. The drive at the back of both conventions is the same – a fear of thought, an anxiety about inquiry, an anger about change; a preference to say 'Lord I am a sinner' or 'I am helpless' because like this there is no responsibility and no demand; and a man can move, as is easy if this is what he wants, towards death. For such a person – 'any reference to facts is condemned as if one had talked of unnatural vice: any theory founded on experience is treated as if it were founded on a muckheap'. Such a creed is a reversal of all values: illusion is called reality, and life is called death. There is no hope for such a person 'except the hope of losing the present. The virtues after which he strives show neither rhyme nor reason in this life . . . they can point to no pleasant results for himself . . . he must continue to aim at the un-reasonable until his own reason dies from want of exercise'. And then – 'his reason, his purpose, his adaptability to the world lost, he must devolve into the barely animate growth from which he evolved, and thence again into nothing'.

At the back of Julian's short book was the conviction that the contradictory but professedly absolute ideals with which he had been brought up were leading to a communal state of mind which suffered from something like schizophrenia – the precedence of fantasy over facts – which in turn would lead to disaster. For how, he asked, can a man be both ideally competitive and ideally self-sacrificing at the same time except – Julian did not quite pin-point this but he implied it – in something like a major war? The society around him was beginning to search about, it seemed, for some such enormous competitive self-sacrifice just to prove itself not ludicrous. It was against these patterns that Julian fought – for complementarity rather than competitiveness, for learning and adaptation rather than sacrifice. He thought that a man could stand back and see something of himself – even of his own primitive passions – and by this, he could be less primitive. In fact, this was man's prerogative. For there were these abilities – and these connections.

The world is real . . . it is composed of a multitude of apparently disjunct purposes which are ultimately one because the great world purpose is ultimately one. And it continues only through the continuance and cooperation of these separate purposes of which mankind is one – and the next in reality because the next in individuality. So long as the purpose of men continues and evolves, so long and no longer does man continue and evolve. The moment that his purpose wanes, the moment that he becomes quiescent and loses touch with the world and with the world system – that moment is the beginning of his devolution, disintegration and death.

❦ TWENTY–ONE ❦

Julian wrote his book when he was twenty-one. It begged some questions and chased some contemporary hares: but it is an astonishing work for a boy to have written in 1909. It produced ideas that were only becoming accepted into jargon some fifty years later – those about the schizophrenic symptoms of a society programmed upon contradictory premises; scientific thinking depending on the elimination of error rather than the verification of truth; the possibility of standing back as it were from patterns of mind so that there can be some 'learning about learning'; the suggestion that by these means men might see themselves as agents in evolution rather than victims because they might adapt themselves to chance. These were ideas thrown out, to be discussed: they were taken up by no one.

It is not surprising that Ettie hated the book: she saw it only as an attack on her whole way of life, which it was, though Julian would have seen it as much more than this. It called Ettie and her friends not only conventional but – stupid! This – after all the originality and brilliance of the Souls! It even suggested that Ettie's methods of upbringing were wrong – when she was known as an ideal mother!

Willy does not seem to have recorded any reactions to the book at all. Perhaps he had so far removed himself from any form of intellectual effort that when he came across a book that said that the curse of Englishmen was to remove themselves from any form of intellectual effort, he did not understand it.

Fifty years later Monica wrote in memory of this time – 'Julian sat up all night for a spell writing a philosophical work . . . He showed it to us all as it progressed, and was chaffed a lot. I wonder if some of it was good?' This was probably representative of the family attitude at the time. A chap who wrote a philosophical work was naturally chaffed a lot. And

then when the whole thing was dead and buried, someone might wonder –
Was it any good?

Even Julian's contemporaries at Oxford did not like the book. In the
words of one – it was as if Julian had 'gone about with his intellectual
fly-buttons undone'. Undergraduates could, properly, talk of Plato versus
Aristotle, of determinism versus free will, of idealism versus materialism;
but an attempt to connect these abstractions to experience was treated like
sexual assault. Freud was writing around 1909 about the connections
between sexuality and thought – of the fears that the conventional had of
both.

One contemporary, Tommy Lascelles, had some admiration for the
book. He wrote in his diary about a visit to Taplow on 26 July 1909 –

J. was in the middle of a series of slashing essays on Today; airing rather
petulantly all his many grievances against the outward forms and manners of
modern society. Some of them were good, and they were all fresh from the cow
. . . but he aims at an impossibly crude kind of life; the pendulum has been
swung too far back by the atmospheric pressure of Taplow weekend parties.

Tommy Lascelles was right about the influence of the atmospheric
pressure of Taplow: what he did not see, as no one did, was that Julian's
suggestions were to do not with a pendulum, but with getting away
altogether from swings to-and-fro. His book was to do with the reaching
of an area of mind from which such processes could be viewed and
assessed. Tommy Lascelles's diary continued – 'Lady Desborough hated it,
they say; and Pat (Shaw Stewart) who has also read it, was quite flummoxed
by so profane an attack on that by which he lives and has his being'.

This was the point that people saw – the attack on that by which they
lived and had their being. Their counter-attack was, as Julian himself had
foreseen, to make out that he was mad – as indeed it could be supposed he
was, since in his loneliness he suffered his depressions. Monica, in her
account fifty years later, said that Julian wrote his book when he was
'suffering from melancholy' and that he 'got better the moment it was
finished'. From contemporary evidence this is the opposite of the facts:
Julian was in fine spirits when he was writing the book, and fell into his
deepest melancholy when it was ignored and rejected. But the myth of
madness was established. Billy wrote a few years later about a book of
Nietzsche's that he was reading that it was 'just a pirated reprint of
the book on Philosophy written by Juju when he was temporarily
deranged'. Julian's book does indeed have affinities with Nietzsche,

though not with the popular idea of Nietzsche – who, like Julian, was made out to be talking about politics when in fact he was talking about mind. This counter-attack succeeded: Julian tried to get at least some of the essays published; he took them to the editors of *The National Review* and of *Punch* but they 'of course' (Tommy Lascelles's words) refused them. Ettie was a friend of most of the leading lights in the literary establishment of the day. In any case, it is unlikely that they would have understood Julian.

The book was put away and was not mentioned again – except once by Billy, once by Monica, and once each by Bron Lucas and Patrick Shaw Stewart after Julian was dead. It was not even brought to light when people were making something of a cult of Julian as a dead hero: it would not have been helpful in the business of glorification. The book remained, in typescript, at the bottom of an old tin trunk, till it was dug out by the present writer sixty-five years later.

Monica wrote of the year and a half between January 1908 and the summer of 1909 as the happiest time in the life of the Grenfell family: 'all that year I used to walk, elatedly, just a little above the ground'. The climax to this time, Monica said, was the spring of 1909 when Billy won the Newcastle Scholarship at Eton – a classical scholarship open only to Eton boys but of almost supernatural importance to Ettie and her friends. Maurice Baring telegraphed – 'More delighted and happy than about anything that has ever happened.' Patrick Shaw Stewart (who had won the Scholarship himself) wrote – 'the most undeniable of all earthly triumphs; earthly but with that unique touch of the spiritual added by SS Mark and Luke'. This was the background against which Julian's book was ignored and mocked. His attack, however, must have left some traces. Monica recorded that after that summer the family never quite so easily walked on air again.

The book was also written and rejected against the background of Ettie's affair with Archie Gordon; the beginnings of her affair with Patrick Shaw Stewart; of her justifications concerning affectionateness and joy. Julian did not talk of this; but it is here that Ettie would have felt something of his anger. But Ettie could fight back. Archie Gordon and Patrick Shaw Stewart were ideals of what Julian might be: they were successful, romantic, sociable, brilliant. In attacking the standards of the conventional world, what was it he was attacking?

The friendship between Julian and Billy did not seem to suffer too much. Julian made one caustic remark about Billy's staying on at Eton a

year longer than necessary in order to win the Newcastle Scholarship –
'How is Billy? Surely not *still* at Eton' – a remark which was changed by
Ettie in her Family Journal to 'Has Billy written yet from Eton?' (Ettie
often quoted letters falsely in the Family Journal, to the effect of making
the family seem more adoring than they were, especially to herself: for
instance, to Julian's long and sad letter to her quoted on p. 142 she added
the sentence 'Anyhow I love *you* till all's blue' which is not in the original.)
But when Billy followed Julian to Oxford at the end of 1909 he seemed to
refuse, as Julian did, to let himself be set in competition. He won the
prizes for work and for games: Julian maintained his own authority. Billy
wrote of him at this time – 'He is a splendid creature, beautiful as a
panther, and no woman can resist him for ten seconds'. However he
added 'I wish I did not feel such a centipede beside the real *men* of the
world.'

Billy was known as a large, affectionate, gentle person; but one who for
short periods could be insufferable. Whatever violence was in him came
out in more conventional ways than it did with Julian. At both Eton and
Oxford there were times when he had the reputation of a bully. His
relationship with his mother was always more intimate and affectionate
than Julian's; he would write to her as 'My dearest one', or 'My darling';
while Julian wrote 'Dear Mother'. Billy seems to have moved easily
within and between both Julian and his mother's world; he was 'quaint',
quick-witted, a 'character'. He was the brother whom Monica loved best.
No one in the family seems to have been quite at ease with Julian.

In the summer of 1909 both Julian and Billy were staying with Bron
Lucas and the Listers in Yorkshire: they shot and rode; Julian was in
good spirits; he was with some friend who was an 'artist'. (Billy wrote to
Ettie 'Julian has been with his artist who has a cockney genius . . .': this
was changed by Ettie in the Family Journal into 'who has a cockney
accent . . .') Julian wrote 'This place is God's place: I feel a different man
after I have been here ten hrs – I *did* feel rotten all the time at Taplow –
it's a grand life; out by 7.30 till 7.30, 4 greyhounds, 40 couple staghounds,
14 horses . . . grouse, duck and hares; 2 ponds full of trout . . . no bloody
women.' But he did not really disdain women. Nemesis was lurking.

Julian was writing to Marjorie Manners more ardently in the summer
and autumn of 1909: she was now 'My darling Miggs'. She promised to
do some drawing for his book. But the conventions of the time were
driving him to the same sort of attitude towards women as young men
had had towards his mother: the taboos on sexuality meant inevitably that

women seemed to become goddesses, and men became guilty and distraught. Julian seems to have made some sort of advance to Marjorie Manners: then –

Dear Marjorie

    Alright, but it's pretty stiff. I suppose I shan't see you again for ages, and in a sort of straight-jacket when I do. But you're right about it – if you had let me see you again now I know I should have broken up again and bored you to distraction. But won't it always be like that? Why should there be much difference between next week or next month or next year? I don't think it is a thing over which I could ever have the least control, and as I get to know you better it will get worse. But I see now that the other thing is impossible, even if you liked me at all – and how you can, from the sample which you have had, is more than I can imagine or believe! Supposing you did like me, supposing a great many other things, and then taking a matter of fact view – what could you do with a man whose charming prospect was to be a junior subaltern in cavalry for at least 12 years?

This was what kept young men in subjection: being forbidden stability with anyone else, they needed their mothers. Julian assured Marjorie Manners that he would always love her: he said he knew this because he was so 'utterly and rootedly selfish there's just room in me for self (including mother) and nobody else and now you have got in not because there was any spare room but because you broke a hole in me'. But still, the best one could hope for conventionally was this hole.

Julian resolved '1. to return to my strong self sufficient self, which will be great fun: 2. to be good; and when you think I've had time to be good enough you'll let me see you again if I wear a really thick pair of green spectacles.' And then '3. We shall live happily ever after as brother and sister, and you will help me in my frantic struggle against falling in love with everyone I meet.'

He was, of course, now writing to his mother again: he told her of his troubles with Marjorie Manners 'because I always tell her everything; she thinks that you have been too wonderfully good about it all, and loves you for it'. But this was when Marjorie was not seeing him. And then, with the silence and scorn coming down about his book, and with his mother's world carrying on with its adoring and adorable friends, Julian began to lose heart. Might it not after all be he, who had attacked his mother's world, and who now had no friends, who was wrong? And if she was still trying to turn him into what she wanted, might not this be loving him? He still tried to defend himself with his old weapon, irony. But now, with his efforts made and rejected, there was in it a touch of despair. He had known he was right – in his book, in his love – but it was as if he were torn between what he knew and the pain of knowing it; between his contempt and the longing to get back into her old false, innocent, but apparently the only comforting world. 'Write and tell me (1) What time you arrive on Sat. (2) What time you meet the Raleighs (I refuse to break your intellectual conversation) . . . (3) Whether you love me . . .'

> Hartham
> Wilts.

Dear Mamma,

I *do* like you; and that is why it grieves me to see you always surrounded by 101 princes of the blood royal. It cuts me off such a centre of interest for us both that you *never* come with me on my visits to Mr Currell (telegraphic address Horseknacking, Hertford) and Brighton Bill (address The Brothels, Brighton). They always ask for her Ladyship – and then I have to say that you are at Buckingham Palace, which makes me feel so degraded. And it isn't as if they weren't nicer than your friends – you just shut yourself off from them and refuse to see them. You do make it pretty hard for me: but I try my best to bear up – and I only ask that you will make things a little easier for me by 'coming along' with me some times – not every week you know but just *sometimes*. I am going to Wonderland on Friday, and I can't tell you how much pleasure it would give me if you came with me. Bill is going to fight Spike Hammerhead, and we have got him pretty fit, I can tell you – and would have got him fitter, if he had not insisted on stout and cockles even when in training. It is no good – one punch in the stomach and down he goes – into the cockles, you know.

I'm staying here along with Anne and I hardly think it's the proper thing you know. There is always the uncomfortable feeling of the brink of the precipice. Leave a letter at Tap telling me of your plans, 'cos I want to see you again.

> I am, Lady Desborough
> Yrs v. truly
> Julian H. F. Grenfell

This letter shows, by parody, something of the style of Ettie's letters to him. But she could find substitutes for her need of Julian in Archie Gordon, in Patrick Shaw Stewart; while he, within the conventions, could find no substitute for her. Also she did not mind hurting him, and he hated hurting her. Though perhaps he had hurt her, with his book. So he began to experience the guilt that was habitual to Ettie's lovers. And he had to ask for forgiveness.

Dear Mother,

It's pretty good being on terms again, isn't it? I'm feeling pleased about it day in and day out. And we shan't have it again like that – only plenty of scarlet arguments, I hope, with all the old fun and none of the old nerves. I've cut all the funny snippets out of my book, as the sign of the birth of a new se.ise of H, and I cure my heartiness now by a rigid use of the flagellum – Disciple for Discipline's sake.

... Write to me and say that you no longer think me a perjured and hardened sinner; it was only a last phase of sin and bloodiness, and I can hardly imagine *how* sinfully bloody it must have been. I am most *frightfully* sorry and apologetic for it, and it weighs heavily upon such as remains of my conscience; I'll take drastic precautions in the future. It's so like the Simple Life to say 'I resolve to be myself' and then straightway to become like a repeating edition of Beelzebub. I'm feeling very 'umble, very rotten indeed (that is one of those new jokes which amuse you so much); it was almost entirely my fault.

Your regenerate
SON

This was a recantation. But it is the pattern of those in power who seek security for their ideals that not only do heretics have to recant, they have to burn.

There are two letters of Julian's to Ettie of this time – most of Julian's letters are undated – which are evidently about his troubles with Marjorie Manners but might almost equally be about his struggle with Ettie herself – so interconnected seems to have become his need to love a girl and his ties with his mother. The letters are from Balliol and are illustrated with drawings: at the top of the first letter is an angel – of mercy or death – hovering above a child sitting as if frightened in a corner with his head in his hands –

Dear Mother,

I want sympathy, I want help. No man can know what I am going through. She will not even write to me. But I know she's doing it all for my own good, God bless her. I shall die if I stay here in this state; I'll come to Taplow

tomorrow morning if you will be there with a little s. and l. (Also to gallop
Buccaneer). If you won't be there, or if your springs of love and sympathy
have dried up, send me a wire, and I'll come Friday. Your poor little son.

J.G.   1909
Hayrick – where I saw her last.

– and then there is a drawing of a hayrick, like a coffin.

The other letter is illustrated with the drawing of a smiling man with a
handlebar moustache like an absurd cavalry officer –

> Dear Mama,
>   I've had a letter.
>   All the girls like me.
>   Cos why?
>   Cos I'm so goodlooking.
>
>   Yrs very sincerely
>   Julian Grenfell

Julian went to and fro – between despair and energy, confidence and
remorse – but it was by this pendulum he was trapped; this was the
rottenness inside him. He saw Marjorie Manners again; he was on terms
with his mother. But a child, to escape from dependence, has to be loved
by those whom it loves: otherwise, it is not freed from fear. But the
conventions were that a child should not be freed.

Julian went back to Oxford in the autumn: by the end of October he
was writing –

> Dear Mother,
>   I've got 'em coming on again, as the song says. It's no b. earthly staying here
> because I can't work 10 mins a day much less 10 hrs; and getting slowly but
> *steadily* worse. I went to Harley about 2 weeks ago and he gave me pills but
> they've done me no good. I'm going to him today; and on to *Brighton*, to see if
> that's any good. Send letters to the Post Office, till I let you know the address.
> I shall stay for a week, and see what happens.   J.
>
> Don't THINK of coming down. I couldn't support life except DEAD ALONE.

He did go to Brighton. But those who feel themselves both tied and
rejected both want and do not want to get away; they try, but they leave

traces, so their lifelines will not be taken from them. They do this even when their lifelines – those able to follow them – are wrapped around their throats –

The Kings Hotel
Brighton
Thurs

Dear Mother,

Here, of all places under the sun! Trying to drive ozone and metaphysics into my stomach which is like a cesspool and my mind which is like a blocked drain. I shall stay 6 days, and if it is successful go back to Oxford: if not, the rubbish heap?

I'm quite happy, and sure it was the only thing to do. I was only curdling at Oxford, and beginning to verge on lunacy.

Don't come down and if you do I shan't speak to you.

All love. J.

But Ettie did come down; and Julian had even sent her a telegram – 'If you're really free come any time before Wednesday' – and she stayed two days, and they went to a performance of *Hedda Gabler* (of all things!) on the pier. And Ettie wrote in her diary that Julian was then much better: and she went back to Taplow, and he to Oxford. But he was not better.

Julian had told Marjorie Manners he was going to Brighton: she had offered to come down: he had written again – 'Miggs thank you *frightfully* for saying you would have come down here. You will go to heaven for it. Of course I should have adored it – but how could I ask you to come this way to see a sort of dead-alive object?' Marjorie would hardly have been able to go through even the pretences of comfort with him: and he knew the battle was with his mother.

Julian did not stay long at Oxford. He came back to Taplow, and then went to stay with the Manners sisters at Belvoir, suffering still (he wrote to Monica) from 'melancholy, brain anaemia, liver rot and nerve collapse'. A doctor forbade him to work or to take exercise. 'I cannot work, and to play I am ashamed.' It was about this time (December 1909) that Archie Gordon had his car smash. The attention of the family became concentrated on Archie's bedside. Ettie continued bravely with her round of social visits: the family and her friends were loud in their praise of her serenity in the face of – what? – her dying lover.

Just before this – perhaps when Julian had returned to Taplow from

Belvoir where he had felt once more without understanding it the violence
of what was battering him inside – he had written to Marjorie –

Dear Marjorie,

. . . I don't know what I am doing, now, I feel as if I had been smashed up
into little bits and put together again very badly with half the bits missing. All
Thursday I felt as if I had something inside my head which was just going to
burst; and then it did burst, and I broke up, and didn't know what I was or
what was going on, except that I had gone right out of myself and become
something quite different; and the agony of it, just the pure physical agony
was like being hammered to death without dying. You see I've always been
utterly selfish – self-sufficient – and all my life has been more or less founded
on my self-sufficiency; so the shock of being driven out of it nearly did for me
altogether . . .

You *have* been good to me, Marjorie, and I do love you, and I know you will
understand. You see you are altogether too marvellous and wonderful to be
seen by anyone all at once; you ought to go about in instalments, carefully
labelled. Thank God I have seen you although I am not yet quite sure whether
it has driven me off my head or not. It is rather pathetic to ask for a photograph
of you, but you see I have only seen you, in my right senses, for one day: and
I *should* like one. I do want to see you soon, because I'm not having much of a
life of it now: still I'll try to bear up. But I *do* think you have been good to
me – and please let me love you properly.

Julian

But he could not love her properly; it was this that was taboo. What had
entered into Julian and made him 'not himself' was just the enemy he
had written about in his book – the power which caused, and was at the
mercy of, guilt and remorse; which depended for consolation not on facts
but on fancies. It was this that made women goddesses – untouchable
except in photographs – and men their helpless devotees. It was the power
over men in thrall to the image of their mothers. For him, his mother was
a reality: but his image of her, and the conventions of her world which
made a young girl desirable but untouchable, had come together; it was
as if they – the girl and the goddess – were invading him, like the dark
god that had invaded the victims of *The Bacchae*. What invaded Julian was
not this god itself because he had not wanted to deny it; but the power of
those around him who had themselves become like a god and had
succeeded in making him deny it – whom he had passionately fought, but

who had defeated him. He had fought with his mind; but he had had no ally in reality. And so he felt himself going out of his mind. Reality, it seemed, was to do with death and madness.

When Ettie was on her round of visits and was waiting for news of Archie Gordon Julian wrote to her – 'I did wish I could have done something to help you when you were at Taplow – I felt more of a broken reed than ever, and you were so awfully good to me'. He could not believe that the love that he felt himself was not felt by others. In the same letter he added, in writing crossed out by savage pen-strokes but still just legible –

O my dear, I've tried your system of playing up, but I'm afraid miserably badly. I've never had such an awful week; I felt utterly plagued and done for under the surface. You can't know what it's like, and I know it's cowardly to say anything about it. But I do feel it's so utterly out of my control, and I know you'd like to help me now if you could – and it does help trying to tell you.   J.

Archie Gordon got worse, and Ettie was summoned to his bedside. Julian was at Taplow, trying to comfort the family. Then Archie Gordon died, and everyone seemed suddenly to say they were radiantly happy. After this, whatever it was that was invading Julian – the chimera of joy and suffering, madness and love – seems to have entered his soul. He wrote to Monica a letter that was indeed 'not himself': it was exactly the sort of letter that his mother would have wanted him to write if it were she who had entered him –

Dear Casie,

I was here when Mother got back from Winchester late last night and she was most frightfully tired: but she had a real good long night, and she is rested today, and so wonderful and happy about it all, *really* happy. It does seem to have been all as perfect and complete and peaceful as anyone could have dreamed of or prayed for – Archie gorgeously and radiantly happy, not knowing (Mother *thinks*) that he was going to die, recognizing everyone round his bed, perfectly conscious most of the time and not in *any* pain, and seeing the one thing he had always wanted – his mother and Violet together. It seems almost too perfect, as if no death can ever have been so marvellous a completion and perfection of a life. He recognized Mother, and was awfully pleased to see her there, and talked quite a lot to her. Mother says she really thinks he never spent a happier day . . .

Then Julian went into his deepest darkness, where he remained for two months; wondering, perhaps, about the connections between happiness and death. He would lie on the sofa of his mother's sitting room with his loaded shot-gun beside him; of which, he wrote to Monica, he 'tentatively fingered the trigger day by day'.

❧ TWENTY–TWO ❧

Severe depressions have to be endured: they are or are not; in either case something may have died – of the person or of that which was plaguing him. Depressions are caused both by conflicts in experience and a person's sensitivity to them: victims are often the most intelligent members of a family. If they do not die, something of their sensitivity may die, to deal with their fears.

Julian lay comatose through December and January: he was seen by a doctor once or twice; he was visited by Tommy Lascelles, whom he treated 'with just as much emotion as if I'd been the footman coming in with his boots'. Ettie was writing her poems in memory of Archie Gordon ('Oh Bird of the Morning, O Spirit of Love/ Are you near? Is it Joy?/ It is Joy') and Billy was writing an appreciation of Archie Gordon ('He knew only the sunlit side of the garden; shame, dishonour, death, to him were but a name'). Life went on at Taplow with its visits, dinners, hunting, shoots. Monica arrived back from Dresden where she had found she could 'really hardly realise all that has happened . . . my thoughts are quite bewildered'. Ettie was writing to Patrick Shaw Stewart – 'Juju isn't a bit better but we won't go into that – and all the dark dispirited words that are a crime of lèse-humanité'. She told Patrick a funny story about how Archie Gordon had used to make jokes about the possibility of his brothers and nephew being killed in a car crash, in which case he, Archie, would have become the Earl of Aberdeen.

Ettie probably could not have avoided her attitude to Julian's depression: with terror of sickness and death instilled into her by her own childhood, these were things that either had to be made glorious or from which she had to turn away. Archie Gordon had been hit by a car; this was fate, so he could be seen as a hero. Julian seemed to have brought disaster upon himself – in his book he had turned on and rent everything that had fostered him – and from this, what was there to do but turn away? Julian probably felt, at moments, much the same himself. His criterion had been happiness; and now did not his family seem happy and was not he sad? It was the cutting-edge of thought that had brought him to such misery; so, might it not be better if there was no thought?

Julian got better in the early spring. He went to join his great-aunt Katie Cowper in Italy and there he lay in the sun, and looked at the landscape, and watched his aunt and her brother painting and quarrelling. He wrote to the people who had been kind to him when he had been ill – to Charles Lister, Edward Horner, Tommy Lascelles. To the latter he wrote thanking him for having been in the worst days the one person who had 'saved his life'. He told him how he, Julian, had asked for help from the people round him – he said he had tried to 'throw himself at their feet' – but they had given him no help: he was out of the depths now, thanks to Tommy and his old aunt Katie Cowper; but he would never ask for help from anyone again.

He began to write home quiet, amusing letters like those of his brother Billy –

I love this country . . . I had never imagined that abroad could be so *different* from anything in England. The people are glorious, they are so poor and dirty and cheerful; and the hill villages simply wonderful, looking as if they were made out of very thin cardboard . . .

The only excitements are the family rows, in which I am made a sort of confidant by either party in order to air their private grievances. But even these are not very serious – about how to make transparent olive green, and salad, and middle distances . . .

Yesterday we had a motor smash; we rammed another motor at a cross-roads, Albert driving, and very nearly boulversed it. As we were both going about $6\frac{1}{2}$ miles an hour very little damage was done. Uncle Willy got out and spoke without a break for just over an hour with rhetorical periods and questionings till a large crowd which had collected in the hopes of excitement dispersed disappointed and the orator was left addressing two small boys in sky blue trousers and bare feet . . .

Thank you awfully for your newsletter, I feel more ashamed than ever of being the only sleeping partner in such an active troupe as the family Grenfell . . .

I honestly feel fit for a plunge into the bosom of my family now. My brain has made surprising strides lately . . . I spelt through three pages of Diana of the Crossways yesterday and understood quite a quarter of it . . . Expect me on Sat next: is that your smart set day? I shall be a perfect rose for the feast . . .

There is a fairy story written by Julian probably a year or so later but which seems to illustrate his state of mind at this time: it is in typescript, and is illustrated with his funny drawings. It tells of a king who had two sons – one called Albert, who was a prig, and the other called Herbert, who was a cad. A series of tests were devised by the old King and the boys' Fairy Godmother to see which son was most suited to succeed to the kingdom. In each of these tests – the first to do with spotting a fraudulent beggar; the second with dealing with a bully in a railway carriage; the third with killing a dragon – it was the cad, Herbert, who by cunning came out best; and it was Albert, with his stiff upper lip, who was worsted and finally eaten by the dragon. Herbert was a racer of greyhounds and a gambler: Albert, in the drawings of him, was like an absurd cavalry officer. At the beginning of the story there had been a third son, a baby called Emmanuel Napoleon Nelson Kitchener – but Herbert had soon got rid of him by throwing him out of a window. The moral of the story was, Julian wrote – 'Do not be an Empire builder until you have built an Empire': or perhaps – Do not think too much until you have built a framework for thought.

He wrote, too, from Italy to Marjorie Manners – 'I made a proposal the other day to the Almighty of a bargain – that I should become the perfect "heygate" on condition of being returned to health and vigour.' 'Heygate' was the code word for everything conventional. Julian added – 'Be careful not to miss the pathos of this letter. All love, J'.

When he returned to England in the spring of 1910 there was much talk about what regiment he should join; it was still assumed without question that he should go into the army. Willy had been making inquiries: he wrote to Ettie –

It is rather a question between a swagger regiment with an 'if' and a steady old fashioned regiment without any great kingly favour . . . I rather incline to the Royals. The Xth are of course more swagger but they have to get over South Africa.

Julian had done his preliminary training from Oxford with the 9th Lancers: he wrote 'But the Royals have only about 2 more years in India and probably don't go to S.A., and the 10th only 3 more in India: so it would hardly be worth changing from the 9th to them'. However, he added to his mother – 'as far as I am concerned I feel the matter is in your hands and the gods' because I know nothing about it and nobody who could tell me. It is very good of you to be taking so much trouble about it, you and his worship Lord D'. The Royals (The Royal Dragoons) were chosen: and Julian was pleased. What he really cared about, it seemed, was that he should get out of the country.

He was back at Oxford in the spring: he worked for a pass degree that would get him into the army rather than for the honours degree for Greats, which he had had to give up after his illness. He took up steeple-chasing again and boxing: though he was losing quite a number of his fights, and Billy was winning his. Billy won the heavyweight championship for Oxford against Cambridge. Julian wrote 'Billy has been wonderful. I've seen more of him than anyone, and we have great tournaments and patters every afternoon. He *is* a good chap, and I feel awfully grateful for my brother, and for those responsible for bringing him into the world.'

Of the rest of the family during the summer of 1910, Willy was in Vienna organizing an exhibition of animals' heads which was the British contribution to an international exhibition; Ettie was in London for the Season which was interrupted by the death of Edward VII (John Revel-stoke had kept her informed of the King's illness by telegrams in the Baring family code – 'Vocative could not be worse personally expect bat today be discreet C.'); Monica was with her mother in London going to classes and suffering from eczema; Ivo was at Summerfields, from which at first he had written to his nanny 'I do hate school, I am so miserable here, I am crying now the days go so slowly they seem like years' but with which he now seemed to have come to terms; and Imogen was left 'reigning supreme at Taplow' (Monica's words) with 'a volunteer labour battalion at her command'. Julian had written of Imogen –

I now see that Mog is the best and greatest thing that ever graced the world: she *was* fun on Sat; gloriously hearty and flinging the cat about; but my word, she used to be a bore – it's the influence of the smart set, competition, display, and social eagerness.

Most of the children showed signs of strain. Monica, when young, had been a thin, pretty, tom-boy girl – a champion diver and swimmer. As she grew up she seemed to become quite suddenly (her friends remembered) large, affected, as if in a dream. Ivo developed a bad stammer. Billy was showing one of Julian's old symptoms, becoming sick just before important contests. Also, this was when he was beginning to have his reputation as a bully. At Taplow, Imogen had a large following of white cats, which she made to sit up and beg at the crack of a whip.

Julian had moved into lodgings at Oxford at 8 Long Wall with Charles Lister, Edward Horner, and Patrick Shaw Stewart. He wrote to Marjorie Manners 'After passing through corruption I want to see you a good deal . . . could not a stunt of some sort be arranged in London?' But he was cautious. He and Edward Horner – who was also fond of Marjorie – used to talk of her now in something of the same way as Bron Lucas and Maurice Baring had once talked of Ettie – as someone untouchable. Julian told Marjorie of one 'real' experience that he had had in London –

I spent one day with Spencer Pryse in Soho on my way back from Italy; he is dirtier than ever, and has done some of the best works of a. I love his style. If he makes a bad shot at a line he just goes on and makes another two or three more, leaving in the misses. By all the laws of nature this should produce something like a finished game of noughts and crosses, but he pulls out a thing like the idea of beauty. He is a good bright grubby little man, and if he is not one of Nature's Noblemen he has the conceit of two.

While Julian was at 8 Long Wall working for his degree for the army in June, Ettie was writing to Patrick Shaw Stewart, who was taking his exam for Greats, at the same address –

June 2nd 1910

Dst,

I do send you such shillions of throbbing wishes and take such pride in knowing what you'll do these days. Shall think of you *all the time* with gallons of wish-transference and hope. It is the next best thing to Julian being in. Go to bed very early, and do all the dodges on earth for preserving a cold steel brain and iced concentration.

Bless you

E.

Ettie's correspondence with Patrick Shaw Stewart which had developed in the autumn of 1908 with the discussion about Hippolytus and. Phaedra had continued lyrically. 'Am sending you some foolish flowers just to remind of out-of-doors and sun and summer and sea and pine-woods and sun-grass-smells and joy' (this was when Patrick Shaw Stewart had mumps). Ettie signed herself, once, 'Matron': and once, 'Little Me'.

They made arrangements to get themselves asked to country houses at the same time ('Would Avon for two nights on actual way to Ox be a possible compromise?'). After Patrick Shaw Stewart had got his First in Greats in the summer of 1910 Ettie encouraged John Revelstoke to give him a job in Baring's Bank – 'Bishopsgate is yours if you want it: over Edom shall you cast your shoe.' Patrick Shaw Stewart replied –

The thanking can only be lived (a) by a beautiful life of dedication in the City, (b) if it were possible, by a tightening and heightening of the dog-like affection which binds me to your feet . . . you are a wonderful person, and wonderful to me, and I do love you ecstatically . . .

Ettie wrote to him when he was away – 'I do miss you dreadfully in London – all our astringent, antiseptic fun . . . No one has ever had less remorse about anything – one of the seven deadly sins of the Persians successfully avoided'.

Julian smashed the new family motor car in the summer – driving it without permission and then putting it into reverse while it was going forward. He wrote to his father 'I could not be more sorry for anything, but being sorry doesn't make the thing any less criminal . . . I hope you will send me the bill for the damages and a charter of pardon'. And to his mother –

It seems such poor gratitude after you have supported me through 6 months rot to go straightly and break your motor. But I know that you will know how miserable it has made me . . . and that you will count it as the last action of one while of unsound mind. Please.

Julian occasionally joined Billy in bouts of rowdyism at Oxford. He wrote to Marjorie Manners – 'all the junior undergraduates at Balliol said to the Master that life in college was impossible because they were afraid of Billy and me – little me and little Billy, mark you!'

He seemed to be getting some confidence back with Marjorie:

I do think our thing is fun, you can say what you like, but I don't believe much in your high-falutin pedestalizations . . . I worship you more than any of your pedestal men, and yet do not expose you to the cold, or strain my own neck.

He was also getting confidence back about his mother. He wrote to Marjorie about a weekend at Taplow:

How very much nicer are we than the older generation who sit in circles and strain at a camel in trying to make better remarks than each other – and succeed only in repeating the remarks of others, and not very good ones at that. They have no idea of fun, or life, or liberty.

Though he added – 'Ld and Lady D and Monica were glorious . . .'

When Willy and Ettie were not together in London or at Taplow now, each often hardly knew where the other was. Willy's laconic letters contained lists of his engagements – committees and dinners – in case Ettie, on her round of visits, might be where their paths might cross. He wrote – 'I haven't the smallest idea where you are: Winnie says you have gone to St Petersburg'. He himself liked to be away – 'Taplow affects my liver I'm sure; I don't know what's to be done'. As British representative on the committee for the Olympic Games he travelled a lot and was entertained by royalty: he wrote from Stockholm – 'Last night I dined at the palace and spent the evening watching the illuminations between two Queens'.

During the summer of 1910 Julian began the one passionate love affair of his life in England: it was perhaps this that gave him back his confidence – with his mother, with Marjorie, with other women. He had been staying with the Manners sisters at Belvoir and there had met Pamela Lytton, the wife of the 3rd Earl of Lytton: as a girl, she had been partly brought up by Violet Rutland, the Manners sisters' mother. Pamela Lytton was somewhat older than Julian: having been married for seven years. She was to her generation something of what Ettie had been to hers – a siren whom men adored – but more of a beauty than Ettie, and more open. (The character of Leila in Maurice Baring's novel *C*, which seems so like Ettie, was believed by Pamela Lytton's contemporaries to have been taken from her.) Ettie had met her and of course did not like her: she had seen her at Winston Churchill's wedding in 1908 and had written of 'Pamela Lytton who looked very nasty and damnably pretty'. (In the same letter, to Arthur Balfour, she remarked on the lack of cabinet ministers at the wedding and had described how Lloyd George had had to be 'marched round and round like the army in the Pantomime'.) Pamela Lytton lived at Knebworth in Hertfordshire, only a short distance from Julian's aunt Katie Cowper at Panshanger. At first Julian did not let Ettie know about himself and Pamela Lytton. Then –

I saw Pamela yesterday. She was utterly *miserable* when I told her that you knew. I couldn't lie to her and not tell her. I've really never seen anyone so broken up.

I *do* like her, frightfully, more than I have ever liked anyone. And of course I should not have said a word about her to anyone – but you – you who knew the moment I came into the room – how could I have lied to you? when you knew, or I knew that you knew, and you knew that I knew that . . . Still, I hate even *seeming* unfaithful to her. Poor thing, she was utterly utterly. She said that you would tell Evan and John: of course I swore on my hope and honour and life that you would sooner cut your throat than tell anyone, just out of loyalty to me – though you knew it before I said a word. I told her that of course I never told you in black and white – but that I knew you knew, and could not lie to her about it. O Mother, be jolly about her just while I like her – because I do like her tremendously! I know you will. It is such fun knowing.

Julian recovered from the worst traumas of the winter. Being loved, and loving, in a way that had touch, substance, he was freed from some fears and dreams. 'Oh Mummie, I had *such* a wonderful two days at Knebs. You will be sorry (or not sorry?) to hear that I love Pamela better every time I see her.' He kept away from London: it was London that 'makes me dog-ill, and miserable, and nervous, and frightened'. And as happens to people in love, he felt he might now love everyone. He wrote to his mother what were almost love letters – ones that he could not write, perhaps, to Pamela Lytton. There was no serious objection that his mother could make about Pamela Lytton; she being married, and thus available, like Ettie herself.

Mother darling,

You *are* wonderful, your wonder is inexhaustible, and keeps coming on me with the shock of newness every time. I've never had such a good ten minutes as on Friday, and never such a good hour as on Saturday. Your dark depths and your surface fun are so perfectly blended that you can laugh at the deepest and weigh the lightest; and it all runs on a connected and continuous line, a perfect picture with its light and shade. And your sympathy, which gives not only meaning, but the half-tone and the shade of the meaning before it is said, sometimes makes it seem silly to talk at all. I want to see you again soon because you are so far better than anyone else. I don't want to see you again ever, because everyone else is like flat soda water after you. Advise me what to do . . .

He made a plan to go to Teneriffe with Pamela Lytton – in the company of Anne Islington, who was going out to New Zealand to join her husband who was Governor General. Julian wrote to Ettie to tell her he

would not be away long – 'I wouldn't go unless I wanted to *most frightfully*
because it will mean missing you for a week . . . I know you won't mind,
you are always so *wonderful* about me: and let me see you all this week
before I go'.

Towards the end of the summer Ettie began to have trouble with her
eyes: this became her symptom of strain during the coming years. Julian
wrote from Knebworth 'It *has* made me miserable about your eyes being
bad . . . I'm sure it's just the after-effects of pink-eye; but . . . *do* take an
"easy" while you are in Scotland – I know you're rather run down though
you look so well. *Please*'.

The time was approaching when Julian was to go out and join his
regiment in India. He had passed his examinations and done the required
preliminary training. He spent the autumn of 1910 between Taplow and
Panshanger and Knebworth. His family hoped to have him to themselves: then, just before he was due to sail, Pamela Lytton became ill and
Julian remained with her at Knebworth. He wrote to Ettie –

My darling Mummie,
    I would have written to you before but Pamela has had a bad relapse and
has been terribly dangerously ill and I've been so wretched about it that I
haven't known what I was doing. But now she is a little better, and the
doctor's accounts are good.
    I'm going away from here now: and I think I shall go to Auntie Ka for a
night: and perhaps they will let me come here for a moment tomorrow.
    Shall you and Dad be at home this Sunday? I'll come home on Saturday
unless –. I know you won't mind me not settling my plans now.
    Goodbye, darling Mummie.
    I feel it will be all right.

J.

This was 27 October. He spent a last weekend at Taplow; went to
say goodbye to Billy at Oxford and Ivo at Summerfields; then went back
to Knebworth. The next day he went to Southampton with Ettie and
Willy and they saw him on board the transport ship *Rewa*.

Ettie wrote in her diary 'Cut in half and bled to death'.

Billy wrote to Ettie 'It must have been too terrible for you today. I
don't think people ought ever to be allowed to say goodbye; they ought
just to fade away silently without these soul-harrowing seconds, and to
leave one to put the past in a frame of gold'.

Pamela Lytton wrote to Katie Cowper to apologize for having taken

Julian away from his family during his last days in England. Katie Cowper replied –

Panshanger
Hertford
Nov 8th 1910

Dear Lady Lytton,

Julian told me how ill you had been. He was glad to be of some little use I think, and has a very capable head on his shoulders.

I feel sure he will like the life he has chosen and will do well in it and he will thoroughly enjoy the picturesque and brilliant glories of the East.

Katie Cowper also wrote to Ettie, enclosing a copy of this letter and of Pamela Lytton's letter to her.

Dearest,

Enclosed will amuse you. Did she write to you I wonder? I also enclose my answer. Rather curt! Intentionally! I suppose he went there again the last week. One of my reasons, if not the chief one, that I did not want him to come here was because I did not like to be an excuse for another visit over there! I hope however Julian did not expect that.

And Pamela Lytton's letter to Katie Cowper had been –

Knebworth House
Knebworth
November 7th 1910

Dear Lady Cowper,

Julian came to say goodbye to us, and I was so thankful that I could see him. He told me he had gone straight to you the night I was taken ill – so I thought I would like to tell you how terribly sorry I am he should have had such an experience here. It haunts me very often. But I can never say how good he was – all who were here have told me of that.

He has gone out into the world with many blessings – a large soul and a simple nature – may he lead a joyous and useful life. I know, with his fine feelings, he will make those who are with him very happy.

I told Julian I should write to you and tell you how wonderful he had been here, and kind.

Yours sincerely,
Pamela Lytton

PART III

Youth
1911—1915

A book depends on what a writer feels. This need not distort objectivity. Feelings can be observed, like that which they are about.

It must be clear to anyone who reads this book that I have some love for Julian Grenfell. He seems to have achieved in a short life a rare authority.

I wanted to understand what made someone so full of life and irony in the end adore war: what was his experience of people, that made him feel closest to horses and dogs.

Julian, in his book, gave some answers to these questions. He saw the society around him based on contradictory premises so that only in death could impossibilities be confuted. What he did not explain was his own failure, having seen this pattern, to escape it.

That I feel this failure had something to do with his mother will also be evident to a reader of this book. It is this feeling that might be misleading.

No one can do much about the processes by which they are brought up: they can perhaps stand back and look at them. Ettie Desborough was brought up in a world in which death was arbitrary and sudden — mothers, fathers, brothers and grand-mothers all went down like flies. A child has to come to terms with death and terror; if these cannot be faced, they have to be made out as something different from what they are.

Ettie's 'stubborn gospel of joy' was an attempt at this, and she gave an enormous amount of joy to many people. The proof of this is in the grateful letters that were sent to her from her childhood to her grave. If she confused her children, this was because more than joy is wanted by a child. Friends can come and go and take what bits of joy they want with them: children are constant, and need reality. Reality includes sickness and terror: if these are not faced, then against depressions there are fantasies.

What Ettie did provide for her children — and this might have been her triumph if she could have seen it — was an upbringing and a love by which her eldest son *could see what she could not. It was Julian who looked at reality, at darkness as well as joy; who could stand back from himself, which she could not. This was Ettie's true achievement as a mother – she passed on something more than she possessed herself. Her tragedy was that her achievement – Julian; together even with the fact that he fought her – was destroyed before he had had a chance of defeating her. But it took the forces of a whole society to defeat him.*

I myself knew Ettie towards the end of her life. I had just come back from the next world war – had loathed it as much as Julian had said he had loved his – had gone to the college at Oxford where Julian had been, where he and his friends had used to sing and shout at night. There I met a girl whom I took out; and who said one Sunday, would I like to visit her old grandmother in Hertfordshire? We drove through country lanes and came to the lodge of what seemed to be a large country house; and a woman came out (I thought – is this her grandmother?) and opened the gates and we drove through a huge park with oak trees to a long low house like a battleship. We went through a back door and along stone passages where all life seemed to have stopped; and then there was a small sitting room and an old lady in a wheelchair. Her grand-daughter introduced me – I still did not know who her grandmother was – and the old lady said 'Ah, I was such a friend of your grandfather's!'

After that I stayed at Panshanger several times: but I was young and perhaps somewhat like Julian with confused feelings about houses like battleships and ladies who had been friends with my grandfather George Curzon. But I liked Ettie Desborough: because out of the world of old gods and goddesses she seemed to be one of the best; her wit, even her gospel of joy, seemed to have some virtue in a world in which expressions of despair were becoming commonplace. It is the business after all, as Julian had said, of each to do his best in his own way. At Panshanger there were the woods where Julian had walked and the lake where he had fished and the room where in 1909 he had slept '21¾ hours out of 24'. And I wondered where indeed a person could go on to from such a place as this; when there might be neither illusions nor battle. Once I was staying at Panshanger with the girl who had brought me there and we were trying to escape from what was expected of us – the talk indoors, the games and the walks in the woods – and we managed to do this for a time: and afterwards Ettie wrote to Monica, the girl's mother – 'The most gorgeous typical hot May day and where do you think they spent the morning? On the filthy roof!'

TOP Taplow in 1902: Willy,
Monica and Ivo.
BOTTOM Julian, Billy and
Monica, Taplow, 1903.

TOP Eton, 1906. Editorial staff of
The Outsider: Patrick Shaw Stewart,
Ronald Knox, Robin Laffan, C. A.
Gold, Edward Horner, Julian Grenfell,
Charles Lister.
BOTTOM LEFT Julian's comment to
his mother on the upbringing of
Imogen, 1907.
RIGHT Julian in Scotland, 1906.

TOP The family in 1905.
BOTTOM The family in 1910, after Julian's illness.

TOP LEFT Sketch by Julian for a
bookplate for Monica.
TOP RIGHT Julian at Balliol in 1908.
BOTTOM Panshanger.

TOP Julian, Marjorie and Letty
Manners, 1909.
BOTTOM Pamela Lytton with
her son Antony, 1905.

TOBY.

Kangaroo' over 5ft 10 in.

TOP LEFT Julian with
Colonel Steele of the
1st Royal Dragoons in
Flanders, 1915.
TOP RIGHT Julian with
his DSO, 1915.
BOTTOM Composite
picture of Ettie, Julian
and Billy, made after
Julian and Billy's deaths.

❧ TWENTY–THREE ❧

The years 1910 and 1911 contained some turning-points in English history; the power of the old landed aristocracy was defeated; workers found that by uniting in strikes they could win more than temporary concessions; women began violently to claim political rights; and the forces of traditional order, in some rage against all this, began to look seriously for a fight, toyed with rebellion, and before long were to find that the First World War had appeared in front of them as if by magic.

The Liberals had come to power in 1906. Asquith had become Prime Minister two years later. Lloyd George's Budget of 1909 had imposed taxes on land. This was seen, correctly, as a challenge to the predominantly Conservative House of Lords. The Lords still had a power of veto, and could wreck any Liberal legislation that the House of Commons put forward. The Lords rejected the Budget, which was an almost unprecedented action, for traditionally it was accepted that the Commons should not be questioned in financial affairs. The debate in the Lords took place on 30 November 1909: this was the day after Archie Gordon's car-smash; when Julian was about to go into his deepest despair. Ettie went to the House of Lords to listen to the debate. A lot of Conservative backwoods peers had come up from the country to vote against the Budget. Ettie wrote of them – 'One *barks* during the speeches; I asked Lord Lovat why he did it, and he said "I think he must be calling to his mate in the gallery" '

A Parliament Bill was prepared by the government which would remove from the Lords all power over finance bills and would limit their delaying and amending powers over other bills to two years. If the Lords did not pass this bill, then the government proposed to ask the King to create enough new Liberal peers to ensure that it would. There were two elections during 1910 to test the feelings of the country – King Edward died in the

middle of the year and the new King had to be reassured – and on each
occasion the Liberals and their allies were returned to power. During the
early part of 1911 the Parliament Bill was pushed through the House of
Commons with the Conservatives delaying it as best they could – there
were over 900 amendments tabled and MPs sat up often all night – then
in May it went to the House of Lords. The Lords cut it, and sent it back
to the Commons. The prospect of several hundred peers being created
was a real one. There were passionate feelings amongst those who took
Parliamentary politics seriously.

Amongst Ettie's entourage Bron Lucas was a Liberal peer, John
Revelstoke was a moderate Conservative, and Willy was becoming
increasingly a die-hard Conservative. One person who did not seem to take
Parliamentary politics too seriously was Arthur Balfour, the leader of the
Conservative Party. He appeared to see the prospect of the defeat of the
landed aristocracy, of which he was one, as of less importance than the
prospects of a European war. Others who did not seem interested in
Parliamentary politics were workers: in 1910 there were large-scale
strikes – a Miners' strike, a Seamen's and Dockers' strike, and a Railwaymen's strike.

In the summer of 1911 there was the coronation of George V. This was
also the summer of Monica's 'coming out'; she went to thirty-eight balls
between Easter and August. Ettie had been made a Lady of the Bedchamber in Waiting to Queen Mary: this meant that she had to be on call
to accompany the Queen on official and unofficial functions. In the spring
the new King and Queen paid a visit to Taplow: in the summer there was
a garden party at Taplow for 150 Colonial Premiers and their wives and
families. At the coronation Ettie was in the Queen's procession and Ivo
was in the Prince of Wales's procession and Willy was amongst the peers.
Ettie told a story of how one peer joked to another as the Guards entered
Westminster Abbey 'Are these the men you are going to turn on us in the
House of Lords next month?' At the height of the political bitterness
there was a big fancy dress ball given by F. E. Smith and Lord Winterton
at Claridge's which both Balfour and Asquith attended. Ettie went as a
Parsee, Monica as a shepherdess, and Billy as Dionysus.

In July Asquith tried to announce in the Commons that the King had
agreed to create enough Liberal peers to get the Parliament Bill through
the Lords but he was shouted down by a group of Conservatives led by
F. E. Smith while Balfour, their nominal leader, sat impassive. Ettie was
watching from the gallery. Margot Asquith, the Prime Minister's wife,

was beside her. Ettie described the scene – 'Margot was hissing in my ear "How I pity Arthur, having to lead a party made up of eunuchs like Linky and cads like F. E. Smith!" ' Linky was Lord Hugh Cecil, another of Ettie's friends, of whose yelling at the Prime Minister a Labour member remarked – 'Many a man has been certified insane for less'. The Speaker had to suspend the sitting – the first time this had had to be done owing to the refusal to let a Prime Minister speak.

Arthur Balfour had expressed his feelings about the attitudes of his own class and party in a memorandum he had prepared but did not publish –

. . . I regard the policy which its advocates call 'fighting to the last' as essentially theatrical, though not on that account necessarily wrong. It does nothing, it can do nothing; it is not even intended to do anything except advertise the situation. The object of those who advocate it is to make people realize what (it is assumed) they will not realize otherwise, namely, the fact that we are victims of a revolution.

Their policy may be a wise one, but there is nothing heroic about it; and all military metaphors which liken the action of the 'fighting' peers to Leonidas at Thermopylae seem to me purely for music-hall consumption.

I grant that the Music Hall attitude of mind is too widespread to be negligible . . .[1]

The Parliament Bill went back to the House of Lords. Diehard Tories like F. E. Smith and George Wyndham were getting ready – Wilfrid Blunt wrote in his diaries – for 'actual armed resistance' if the Lords let the bill through: though there was an alternative – 'George thinks war with Germany quite possible, and he wants it'.[2] The moderate Conservatives were led by George Curzon, who advised peers to abstain from voting so that the defeat could be accepted with dignity. On 10 August most Conservative peers did in fact abstain – Willy had left for Canada the day before – and just enough voted with the government to ensure that the diehards were outnumbered. The first day of the debate – 9 August – was the hottest day ever recorded in England; the temperature reached 100°F. in the shade at Greenwich; roads melted and railway lines became twisted; these seemed like the portents in the streets of Rome at the time of the murder of Caesar.

The Conservatives who had kept their heads were those with the old

[1] Kenneth Young, *Arthur James Balfour* (London, 1963), p. 310.

[2] Wilfred Blunt, op. cit., p. 771.

spirit of the Souls – Balfour, Curzon – who saw that some social change was inevitable but what was required was a continuing thread of sanity. The revolution that Arthur Balfour had observed was to do with the dying of the power of the landed gentry and the emergence of a new power in its place – not yet that of the workers, though this battle was beginning to be fought elsewhere – but the power of money; of men without roots but of energy and ambition who were looking for causes, perhaps, which would seem like roots. There had been an enormous increase in upper-class wealth since the 1890s: this came largely from gold in South Africa. The men who were now the driving force within the Conservative Party were men not necessarily rich themselves but who were circumscribed by riches; they represented a style in the country. Max Beerbohm had an exhibition of cartoons of political figures in the spring of 1911: he wrote to Ettie –

But you are mistaken in envying me the 'fun' I had in doing them. They were born in travail for the most part; are the protests of a too-thin-skinned nature against the coarsenesses and stupidities and pretentiousnesses of mankind at large. That picture of the Tariff Reformer, for example, came out of prolonged writhings against the wretched propaganda that has for the present wrecked the Tory Party (I wonder, by the way, when the Tories will begin to realize that the reason why the country won't have anything to do with them is quite simply that they still feel it their duty to go on hawking around that dismal and so-quickly-seen-through and rejected imposture for the benefit of some few rich people). And the Roosevelt drawing was another instance of my lack of joyous-ness: for weeks I could not open a newspaper without being confronted by the volleyed-out platitudes of that appalling bounder . . . Sargent's pictures of Venice, Shaw's megalomania, the life and works of C. P. Little – these are further instances of the agonies that wrack me, and that compel me to cry out to all who pass by – and the worst of it is that my groans sound just like ripples of rather good-humoured laughter . . .

People who hated the new mood in the country – who had once been patriots – now thought of getting out of England. Willy, from Canada, wrote that he had sold his English investments and was thinking of buying land in Canada. Bron Lucas, earlier, had written from Canada – 'It all makes me wonder whether it's not better to match oneself against nature rather than one's fellow man; whether the great railwaymen and suchlike are not greater than the statesmen.' Arthur Balfour left the country before the crucial vote in the Lords on the Parliament Bill: he went to take the cure at Bad Gastein, and to write an appreciation of Bergson's philosophy. In a few months he was writing to Ettie –

> The Athenaeum
> Pall Mall
> Nov 3rd 1911

My dear Ettie,

I don't want you to learn from any lips (or pens) but mine that I intend to resign the leadership within a few days. I won't attempt to give reasons by letter: when we meet I will do so in full measure, and have no doubt of convincing you that I am right.

Only a few people know, and I am most anxious that the matter should not be talked about or get prematurely into the papers. My life would be even more of a burden than it is if that were to happen!! Please therefore keep a discreet silence.

This decision has nothing to do with the 'ditchers', of whom I reck nothing.

> Yrs. A.J.B.

To which Ettie replied –

> Nov 4th

My dear A.J.B.

I cannot find words to say how touched I am at your finding time and thought to tell me this – in the midst of the extra burdens on life that it must entail at this moment.

I have had a sinking presentiment ever since we last met that you meant to do something of the kind! and of course you *must* be right, and it is presumptuous even to feel unhappy.

But I do feel very miserable. You have turned the tide so magnificently – and you have inspired everyone with fresh life and hope. I do *long* that you should stay another 6 or 8 months and fight the Home Rule Bill – *who can do it but you?* . . .

The Home Rule Bill was the issue over which an embittered class were soon once more to build a barricade: in the meantime, there were the other portents of battle. The increase of wealth amongst the rich had pushed up prices, and miners and dockers and railwaymen were striking for something better than a starvation wage. In the hot and opulent summer of 1911 food rotted and stocks of coal ran short and dockers eventually won their claim to a minimum rate of eightpence an hour. The people at the garden parties and the fancy dress balls did not seem to notice much of this; workers had not been noticed when they were quiet, and people did not have the habit of noticing them when they were in revolt: workers were just not mentioned in polite society, like sex.

A revolt that was determined to get itself noticed was that of the suffragettes. The movement had begun peaceably with marches and demonstrations; but in 1911, after women had been manhandled by police and roughs, it turned nasty. Women smashed windows in shops and offices and set fire to letter boxes; they chased Asquith round a golf course and tried to horsewhip Churchill. They were arrested; and when they would not eat, had pipes forced through their teeth and down their throats. In the hot summer with the coronation jollifications and food rotting in the docks there were scenes of retribution like those in *The Bacchae*.

Ettie did not take much notice of the suffragettes (though Mrs Pankhurst, in a letter to Ethel Smythe, once spoke kindly of Willy). But what could be of interest to Ettie in that area? The suffragettes were fighting for women's power: but had not women like Ettie always had power; had they not been able to treat men like babies? And now women were demanding to become like men – so where would be power? And indeed, what would happen to babies? When men came from the games that they played in the parliaments of the world, who would be at home to give them strength? Would they cease to be like babies; or would they tear themselves to pieces?

❦ TWENTY–FOUR ❦

Julian had longed to get out of England. His choice of regiment had been influenced by the length of time he could stay abroad. Of the passengers on board the boat to India he wrote –

there are the violently social who try to drown the noise of the water with constant conversation and the violently anti-social who sit in deck chairs and try to drown the conversation by sheer savagery of expression. I belong to the latter class.

He arrived in India at the end of November 1910 and went to Muttra, south of Delhi, near the Taj Mahal. He wrote –

I love India and the sun and the cold (which is penetrating) and the Royal Dragoons (who are magnificent and yet friendly) and my clothes, especially my boots, and rice, and curry, and the entire lack of privacy – three men black as your hat sitting on your doorstep all day – and vultures, and those bloody little birds which look like moorhens and are apparently doves, and the Taj, which takes my breath away . . .

The Royal Dragoons were a heavy cavalry regiment and their military activity in India consisted mainly in drill: when they were not drilling they were usually pigsticking or playing polo.

It is horse and saddle and boots (Field Boots, Polo Boots, Gaiters, Wellingtons, Undress Wellingtons, Mess Wellingtons, Dress Wellingtons) all day and every day . . . riding to riding school, riding in riding school, riding back from riding school, changing into very tight black trousers with a yellow stripe and a very tight red tunic, riding to stables, riding back from stables, riding to luncheon, riding back from luncheon, changing into riding breeches, riding to foot drill, foot drill on FOOT, riding back from foot drill, polo (on horse back) or stalking (on or behind a horse), then tea, dinner and bed.

He told his mother that he loved the life and felt very well; which was not true, as he told her later. He did say that he had had very bad toothache on the boat, and that he had had to go to an American dentist in Agra who had pulled out the two nerves of a back tooth 'with a corkscrew and no gas'.

About his fellow officers in the Royals he said – 'I like these people better than the Oxford people: I thought it would be the reverse.' He shared a hut with a man 'who is called Sclater Booth and looks it; he is very ugly and very nice'. Sclater Booth had a piano which he played all day. Julian had gone with him to a silent film at Port Said, which –

Booth could not understand, the words being by the nature of the performance left for the intelligence of the audience to supply. So I kept up a running commentary: Booth – What are they doing now, eh? Self – Well you see, they are trying to kill him; the cowboys are not sitting on him to try to keep him warm. Booth – Why have they put that rope round his neck, eh what? Self – They are going to *hang* him with the rope. That is why they have put it round his *neck*.

In the afternoons at Muttra there were games and sport. 'I played cricket today for B Squadron v The Band; I bowled rather fast, with a long run, getting six wickets, the second drum on the head, and the bassoon just above the instep.'

Also –

I go out on a pony with Auntie Ka's rifle and a most villainous man that I have engaged, and if buck are out in the open we all three walk up to them pretending to be natives or turnips, and if there is any cover the man holds the horse and waits while I advance on my stomach. The first day I got a black buck and a chinkara which is a little buck – both good ones.

The sport however was restricted by the arrival of the Crown Prince of Germany on an official visit (the German Emperor was the Colonel-in-Chief of the Royals) and for a time the only permitted activities were those in which

old and cunning pigstickers ride and drive the pigs towards him and old and cunning polo players edge the ball gently up to him . . . We are all quite weary with bowing and scraping . . . my democratic feelings arouse themselves at 11 pm; by 12 I am a socialist and by 1 am an anarchist.

He wrote a poem at the time of the visit of the Crown Prince and his entourage –

LINES TO A FRIEND
I came from afar to a tropical land
But never I hoped to meet
A man with five thumbs on each hand
And ten big toes on his feet . . .

of which the *Envoi* was –

Prince, much as I esteem you and your friends,
Much as I value you as my allies,
There is a limit which this man transcends,
For he is gross, with large extremities.

The sport which Julian liked best was pigsticking, which was done on horseback 'like coursing with human greyhounds'.

You get up alongside the brute and wait till he turns in and goes at you; then if you are lucky he runs on to the spear and if you are unlucky he runs on to you. It is no good prodding at him; you just hold out the spear and say your prayer and the pig does the rest with great gusto.

He said he loved the animals of India: 'You've no idea what a paradise Muttra is to the unsoshal . . . I saw on my evening ride the other day 2 real live crocodiles, 18 pigs, 3 black buck, 1 wild cat, 2 foxes, 6 jackal and a bird of paradise'.

He wrote another poem –

HYMN TO THE FIGHTING BOAR
God gave the horse for man to ride
And steel wherewith to fight,
And wine to swell his soul with pride
And women for delight:
But a better gift than all these four
Was when he made the fighting boar . . .

What made young men like Julian long to leave England for India was some such desire for recklessness, for freedom from constraint, even if to achieve this they had to join the cavalry and dress up in tight trousers. There was little else for a fashionable young man to do if he wanted to get away from artificiality and yet did not want to be almost totally alone. The army in India had become a sort of club providing formalities for would-be eccentrics. Young men could also learn; but in this they would probably be alone.

Julian wrote – 'I move at present like a blind man in a dark room: there is so much to learn that the little one learns makes no impression on the bulk of the unlearnt.'

He read Shakespeare ('all') and Arnold Bennett, and the plays of Synge, and Hardy's *Jude the Obscure*, and Shelley, and 'Emerson and Job, which are rather good antidotes to each other'. He asked his mother to send him more books. He wrote – 'What is Post Impressionism and the Post Impressionists? I see vague things about it in the papers but never a word explaining what it is. And I feel so strongly that I am a Post Impressionist.' This was the time of the first big exhibition in London of Cézanne, Gauguin and Van Gogh. Later Julian wrote

I'm awfully sorry to have missed the Post Impressionist movement: it's the right movement got on to the wrong lines – e.g. the *treeness* of a tree is what you want to paint, you don't want to copy a tree because there's no use in a worse copy of a better original; but on the other hand you don't get treeness any better by painting a brickbat like the P-I's do.

Soon after arriving in India he had had a bad fall from his horse: 'The horse, who is called The Hawk, wanted to go one side of the bush and I wanted to go the other; we neither of us pulled quite hard enough and he ended by taking to his native element and flying it. Unluckily there were two more bushes on the landing side . . .' Julian had concussion, and was ordered to bed where he remained for six weeks, with an abnormally low pulse.

He tried to explain to his mother something of whatever had been said or not said between them the previous summer when he had been in love with Pamela Lytton –

I believe so utterly and so immoderately in the complete and absolute liberty of the individual that I know I often don't realize what the effort and the strain is to leave a person alone in what you think is wrong. But I *have* known what it cost you not to say more to me and I am grateful to you for it. I believe you did as near exactly right as anyone can ever do. *Of course* I knew what you thought; how can you 'shirk expression' when there is no need to express? And of course you knew that I knew what you thought; and there it was, black and white, with nothing more to be done – except that you might have worried me or not worried me and you did not worry me; and for that I shall be grateful to you for ever and ever . . . As for me, I am utterly happy and at peace which indeed I have been ever since I finally made up my own mind about it . . . I miss, terribly, of course, and constantly, every day; but each time I offer up thanks for all that came to me, all the new breadth and knowledge of tenderness; and my gratitude to the given almost kills the bitterness of separation. But to write this to you is as if you were to 'worry' me: it must be a locked subject – in these two aspects I mean.

He was better in early March and went back to regimental duties; and to pigsticking and polo. The Royals were due to go to South Africa in the autumn and Julian was sad at having been out of action for so much of his short time in India. He wrote to his mother – 'Can't you use your influence with the Queen when she is putting on her stays and persuade her to let us stay?'

He had been outraged when he had heard of his mother's appointment as Lady of the Bedchamber in Waiting to Queen Mary: he had written –

It really is too disgusting for words, and so ridiculous; one looks on all those things as dead and gone like 'Chop off her head' or as only belonging to panto-mime. But I suppose you have simply *got* to do it, which makes it all a very grim joke. And now that Casie is 'coming out' it really makes things pretty impossible. Shan't you be able to resign it soon? It does make me angry.

He continued to snipe at her from time to time – 'Have you begun your Bottle-washing yet?' 'In waiting – what a good word!'

In April he was unwell again, this time with jaundice. 'I became bright yellow all over like God's gift to loneliness.' He was sent to convalesce in the hills. He went riding, but felt dizzy. He sat on a terrace from where he could see the foothills of the Himalayas. He wrote a poem –

> Mussoorie and Chakrata Hill
>   The Jumna flows between;
> And from Chakrata's hills afar
>   Mussoorie's vale is seen.
> The mountains sing together
> In cloud or sunny weather
> The Jumna, through their tether
>   Foams white, or plunges green. . . .
>
> They are as changeless as the rock
>   And changeful as the sea;
> They rest, but as a lover rests
>   After love's ecstasy.

> They watch, as a true lover
> Watches the quick lights hover
> About the lids that cover
> His eyes so wearily . . .

Ettie did not mention Julian's illnesses when writing to family or friends: he was well, and happy, and enjoying soldiering in India. For much of the time this was the impression that Julian gave himself: 'I simply worship all the Royal Dragoons who have been charming to me on my bed of sickness'; 'the Colonel is the nicest man in the world'. When he was back at Muttra he was 'frightfully well and as strong as two lions, and having a great success with the regiment who think I am quite mad but "good value" '. Then suddenly at the end of June he was writing –

I have had an awful six months; worse than ever before, almost, because it came just at the one time I wanted to be fit and able to render a decent account of myself. I got rotten on the voyage; then, just as I thought I had collared it and was on the mend – after a month of praying for the end of each hour I was in; struggling through riding school and polo and stables – I got concussion, which put me right back again. You *can't* fight nerves alone in bed in a bungalow; and of course it's the nerves that matter. I never mind the physical illness part without them. Then I started at the beginning again and just as I was coming out on top my liver went phut and for three weeks I ate nothing and then came out bright yellow with jaundice. But it's over now, and I feel very fit, and I've beat it . . .

Julian always thought that he could beat it; just as he never said he had had it till after it was over. Ettie wrote in her Family Journal that Julian suffered no more from depression after 1910. In August 1911 he was writing – after time for letters to get to England and back –

Yes I agree about nerves; but I think that after a certain point is passed you have *got* to slump: not on principle, but simply to get enough energy into your empty system to fight them with. At that point you are just existing, and all your energy is wanted to exist; attempting to do anything more is poisoning yourself . . .

He had a confused correspondence at this time with his parents about the allowance that they were paying him. At Oxford he had been getting £400 a year on which 'I think one ought to live fairly comfortably without riding; I really don't think it is possible to hunt on that here now'. He had in fact managed to hunt, with extra help from his father in buying horses. When he joined the army his allowance was raised to £600. During the change-over Julian thought he had been overpaid £100 and pointed this out: his father and mother were under the impression at first that he was complaining he had been underpaid. He always tried to be scrupulous about money; at Oxford he had overspent at first and had written to his mother

I know that I have got into a sloppy way of looking at money just lately – partly because I loathe ever thinking of it, and partly because everyone else here lives on the opposite system . . . But you've *absolutely* convinced me, and I'm going to set my face and take a most tremendous pull . . .

In the army, his basic pay as a cavalry subaltern was 7/8d a day; there were additions of a Colonial Allowance of 4/– a day and a 'Customs Rebate' of 1/2d: this made a total of about £230 a year. His mess bill in the regiment (everyday living expenses) came to about £280 a year. He later added to his allowance and pay by clever dealing in the buying and selling of horses, and by backing himself in races.

In the summer the temperature at Muttra went up to 117°F. in the shade: 'I *love* it, punkahs, and a swimming bath, and a streaming face all day; and getting up at 4 and sleeping in the middle of the day . . . I am going to settle at Muttra with a dusky harem when the regiment leaves for South Africa'. He told how he was avoiding the advances of a fellow officer's wife; he had had to tell his servant not to let her into his bungalow. He himself would lie out at night 'in a great ravine, in the moon, armed to the teeth (2 rifles and a hog spear) waiting for panther; but they decline combat'. He had become 'thin as a skeleton' or 'like a post and rails'. He had a photograph taken of himself standing untidily in front of his hut with his horses; his mother did not like it. He wrote 'I always did say that you have a degraded taste in art; that you mistake smartness for true and inherent beauty'. He promised her 'a photograph in full kit, holding a tin hat and looking a B.F. – exactly as you approve'.

In September he went on leave to Simla – the fashionable resort of the British when the rains came at the end of the heat. From Muttra, in spite of the attentions of the fellow-officer's wife, he had written – 'You have no idea how turbulent one becomes after six months in the hot wilderness without the sight of a single fair face'. At Simla there were fair faces but –

they are immoral in speech only and lead irreproachable lives. Do you know Bron's word for a woman who is a teaser? they are all classic examples of that.

Tired of doing nothing for five years, the poor girls adopt a superior attitude and are above dancing and puss-in-the-corner and such childish sport, surveying life from a giddy height. But give them another two years, when they are up against the serious business of matrimony, and they become as playful as kittens again.

He moved on to Kashmir, where he shot deer and bear; but – 'the beautiful dark-eyed maidens of Kashmir are a myth, they are all exactly like Auntie Mabel only neither so tall nor so aristocratic . . . I am reserving myself for Miss Barney Barnato of Johannesburg'. He was thinking a lot about girls. When not doing this, or riding, or shooting, he was doing 'a lot of post-impressionist works of art. The contrast is so extraordinary – the peaceful sleepy sunny misty valley surrounded by the great grim angry blue hills; like love in the middle of war'.

The Royal Dragoons left India in October and Julian looked forward to 'a new country and hard soldiering'. He had loved the landscape, the animals, the heat, of India; but what had he been up to? India was a place to which young men went to get out of England: to which mothers perhaps pushed them out like seaside landladies. But Empire, when the games were over, was like a street corner on Sundays. It was a bone-headed life, looking round for something to happen. An intelligent young man perhaps should find something different; but this was not easy with your mother's world so glamorous and your father's world so stupid. In killing pigs, you at least got rid of some of your feelings.

❦ TWENTY–FIVE ❦

In the England that Julian had left, Ettie was 'bringing out' Monica and from time to time was with the Queen. She was more than ever beset by a rush of engagements. Her diaries record with increasing frequency how she was 'dead' at the end of a day; how for a few minutes on her own she would be 'at peace'.

Monica described what it was like to be a debutante in 1911.

We saw all our girl-friends constantly, but our young men friends only in group settings. These were the dancing years, and at first I thought of all the balls as glorified children's parties ... All the girls collected after the previous dance and the sitting-out interval in a cluster to be claimed by their next partner; so our mothers knew who we were dancing with, and who we were dancing with too often. There were people of all ages at these huge balls, so our chaperones met all their greatest friends.

Monica fell in love with a young man called Montie Bertie of whom her mother did not approve: or rather she did not approve so long as he seemed to be fond of Monica. And if a mother did not approve, there was not much that a conventional girl could do about it; 'because, owing to the custom of the day, we could not see our young men friends except at parties'. Other customs of the day were that young girls did not drink wine, read newspapers, or 'reverse' when waltzing if royalty were present. Mothers and daughters were in a curiously symbiotic relationship: 'when we got back from the balls Mummie and I had to unhook each others' elaborate evening gowns for we could not pull these clothes off over our heads'. And mothers, of course, could see as much as they wanted to of the young men ostensibly provided for their daughters.

Ettie's relationship with Patrick Shaw Stewart seemed to become more unreserved after Julian had left England. In May 1911 Patrick Shaw

Stewart was writing – '. . . Will you be my partner at the Cotillon on Monday? *Please*. Tell me quickly at All Souls. I shan't sleep till I know. And will the Derby's ball next night be very good – good enough to stay for without a dinner party?' And Ettie replied – '*Yes* – with joy – Cotillon – Your letter made my bed rock this a.m. – even after three balls running – and how I *adore* laughing. E. Yes *certainly* Derby's.'

Ettie's letters to Patrick Shaw Stewart are the only ones of hers to a passionate admirer that survive. They have an almost schoolgirlish (or schoolmistressy) physical quality that perhaps illustrates the kind of excitement that she transmitted –

> Villa le Foret
> Paramé
> Bretagne
> Aug 31 1911

Dst,

I did love getting your letter, and you made me laugh immeasurably about all the silly old Floater. You do know that at my Heygatest I only classified your ill-doing in the breaking wine-glasses (or Panshanger papercutters!) category – i.e. as tiresome rather than evil. I rocked at the thought of poor darling F's midnight walk with you round and round and round the garden – she is the most generous and forgiving being *on earth* (oh how I *wish* I had her breadth of magnanimity) and I am perfectly certain you made all well. I do love thinking of you getting off for such a glorious and gloriously planned holiday – and rejoice in our tigsy overlap at Inverness. Do remind the Gisburnites how joyfully Casie and I hope that they will really let us come there mid-October? – Oh, on the way to *England and Winter!* It sends a shudder through all this sunshine. The Divineness here I never could tell or you guess. I have never been ½ so well or 2½ so happy. And the Rest and Peace make great overflowing restoration for all the London nights with only 3 hours Indian shut-eye. This house is *in* the sea – all windows and balconies – and big overhanging stone terrace, and steps down into hot peacock-blue water and acres of sands, and looking over limitless irridescent sun-striped summer sea – it is *fearfully* hot, you can't move between 12 and 4 – but wholly blissfully ideally delicious . . .

In January 1912 there was a big fancy-dress ball at Taplow, to which Patrick Shaw Stewart came 'in the full regalia of a pseudo double Earl'. Billy was a Roman centurion, Willy a Cavalier ancestor called Sir Bevil Grenville, and Ettie again a Parsee. A party from Cliveden next door came as monks and nuns with (in Monica's description) 'sham cardboard hands and enormous bare cardboard feet'. 'A photographer was set up in one of the bathrooms and took flashlight photographs all night.'

Billy had still been doing well scholastically – he had won a Craven scholarship at Oxford – but he was ill ('overgrown') in the spring of 1911 and was stopped by doctors from running in the University sports. He was boxing, and had won the Oxford heavyweight title; he had also won with his partner John Manners the real tennis match against Cambridge. But he was finding it increasingly difficult to work. The life in which he had been brought up seemed less and less serious. He wrote to Ettie –

Balliol College
Oxford

Darling,

    . . . I am glad to hear from Pat you are making the best possible out of quick fun in London. Uncle Evan is here in the most splendid form; he has left behind his years, his principles, his restraint in vocabulary, ethics, and manners, and appears in this exhilarating atmosphere with a new glossy wig, as fresh as Aegeus from Medea's cauldron. How I love him; he has an uncanny fascination for me. We all had dinner at Micklem last night, and they were all furious with me for leaving at 10 partly to read Homer and partly to escape Patrick's post-prandial embraces – both motives worthy of St Anthony. How hard that the good should be perpetually misunderstood!

From time to time, when he wanted to escape, he moved into what had been Julian's world: he seemed to fall in love with Marjorie Manners. He also went into Julian's underworld –

    . . . On Sat night Trowsers and I stole out unbeknown and went to wonderland, Whitechapel, returning with the cold meat train. A marvellously orderly crowd of tramps, murderers and aliens, in desperate prize-fighting. A detective was told off to be our guard. I find I must have *one* bust a week . . .

At the end of the summer of 1912 he was sent down from Oxford for three terms: his reputation for rowdyism had come to a head. Ettie described the culminating incident in her Family Journal: 'there was a great bear-fight one evening in the Balliol Quad and all the furniture in one man's room was thrown out of the window'. There was also a charge of assault: but Billy explained to his mother – 'the assault accusation was quashed by most delicate wire-pulling and a brazen front'. However – 'later there were secret meetings among dons, and open deputations from non-conformist Balliol, all because M. Baring and I had wished to speak about Walt Whitman, our favourite author . . .' Billy alternated between heartfelt apologies to his parents – 'I am bitterly sorry to have pained you in this way' – and a refusal to take any of it seriously, for – 'you know what a real sin I think it is to be unhappy'. He was lectured by the Dean of Balliol, but – 'I could not hear what he said as he has so few teeth now and the traffic in Holywell was so uproarious'. Billy retired to Sandwich to work for yet another scholarship. 'Hurray, what fun not to be going back to that material and clerical swamp!'

It was difficult, in 1912, to know what was or was not serious. Seventy-eight dockers and six policemen had been injured in East London; the Prime Minister was being accused of torturing innocent women; soldiers and miners were confronting each other in South Wales; the first threats of revolution were being uttered by Tories over Northern Ireland. Willy had become Chancellor of the Primrose League – an organization with the support of over a million people dedicated to the upholding of 'religion, constitution, empire'. Ettie was moving in and out of Waiting: her old friend Charty Ribblesdale wrote to her – 'I hope you find it a good bedchamber to frolic in: Mary III seems to be such a dull woman, but I daresay her *surrounders* interest you . . . I suppose you like this thought, for there is always a way out is there not?' Julian was writing to Monica – 'When are you presented at Court? Or aren't you presented at Court? Are you presented first, and then go to balls, or do you go to balls first, and then if you do well, get presented?'

Ettie had shown her own attitude to court life a few years earlier when she had written to Archie Gordon from Sandringham –

The air is lurid here with Royal Blood . . . the greatest difficulty is to know where to place one's back . . . I play very strange bridge with the Queen, the K of Spain, and the Duke of Alba. We never finish anything, and there are usually only 3 cards in the trick.

H. G. Wells, who spent a weekend at Taplow at this time, wrote to Ettie –

If a social revolution should occur – in this wrath nothing is impossible – and I should be Dictator – a trying position for a modest man but one for which all the rest of my gifts fit me – Taplow Court shall be sacred and one delightful family at least secure from the guillotine.

The house at Sandwich to which Billy had retired to work (he did not get the scholarship he had hoped for; nor did he get his First in Greats later) belonged to Nancy Astor, recently married to Waldorf Astor, who had come to live at Cliveden, the huge house next door to Taplow. Billy had become a friend of the Astors: Ettie, at first, did not. There had been a time when John Revelstoke had begun to write to Nancy his quiet, adoring letters: there had even been talk of their marrying. But these plans had fallen through – presumably, it was said, after pressure from Ettie. Ettie of course denied this: and she would not have had to apply much pressure. In 1908 John Revelstoke was writing to her –

It *kills* me to have the least cloud with you, you are all to me, and I do so lean on you and count on you and it *finishes* me to see you sad or displeased. So, my dear, do not be angry with me, for it is hard to bear and it takes all the heart out of my life and you do help me so much in everything and are so golden and strong.

Billy in England became something like Julian might have been if he had not been determined to get away from home – in his bursts of violence and his guilt; in his feelings of futility, and his efforts to laugh at these –

I wish I was not so passionately addicted to pleasure; I find myself plotting for it at every moment of the day, especially when I ought to be thinking of that solemn humbug Aristotle or the amelioration of Lost Dogs and Destitute Prostitutes. Nancy came down on Saturday bringing a moth-eaten wormy wordy little Tory called Maurice Woods . . . We had lunch in John's room which contained a hospitable fire. I was in the *most awful* state of wallop after five minutes, and had to take off my coat after fish, and my waistcoat between cutlets and roast fowl. Nancy spent half her time in calling attention to the course taken by the drops down my puffed visage, and divided the remainder about equally between noisy platitudes on the political situation and directions to Waldorf on the best way to force spinach down William's throat . . . Why are political discussions so b...y dull? I think it is because Liberals are never admitted to our houses. So one only hears denunciations ad nauseam. A little more amusement now that they slang A.J.B. – what does he think about it?

Few of the boys who had seemed so glorious at Eton and during their first years at Oxford seemed to have found much worth living or working for after they had left. Charles Lister had joined the Diplomatic Corps: he had given up socialism; he was in the Embassy in Rome where –

I feel I'm looked on as a pleasant but sometimes rather tiresome child who *will* leave the chancery safe open and is apt to get run over by trams and to have rows with cabmen etc; who is always asking to be taken to the cinematograph in

the evening and who generally wants looking after – I explore music-halls etc
solus as I can never get anyone to go out in the evenings.

He asked Ettie if she could use her influence with Lord Kitchener to get
him transferred to Egypt; but he assured her, as Julian did, that of course,
in spite of appearances, he was very well and happy.

Even Patrick Shaw Stewart, for whom Ettie had got the job in Baring's
Bank and who had always been ambitious in the ways of social advancement and money, was finding life difficult. Billy wrote from Taplow –

Patrick came down here last night and was charming, but infinitely depressed,
poor old Shylock, at the thought of banking during the dog days and the autumn
equinox, and till the end of all time. However I was a good Job's comforter, and
heartened him with the prospect of being a merchant prince, which is surely as
good or better than most things in this untidy and monotonous world. My own
wants are simple; so long as I have the use of my exquisite body and moderate
brain, the lave may go by me. Conduct does not interest me v. much, and other
people's comments on it not at all. Patrick is more complicated, and wants
friends and society and other luxuries; he is going to spend his one fortnight's
holiday at the Inverness Gathering under a northern pseudonym I guess, and in a
kilt. I am off to Sandwich tomorrow to tramp the sea-links with darling Nancy . . .

The only member of the Eton-and-Oxford group who seemed to be
making much of a life for himself was Denys Finch-Hatton, who had
gone to East Africa and there – as Julian described it later – 'made a lot
of money by shipping timber from his place in Norway, and bought a
palace from an American millionaire where he entertains the countryside
on champagne and caviare'. Julian planned to join him there in the
summer of 1914. 'He's such a tonic after all the dead-beats.'

In 1912 it was still the dream of young men to get out of England; but
they carried their patterns of mind around with them. Neither Julian nor
Denys Finch-Hatton quite escaped these. Finch-Hatton survived the war,
but was killed in an aeroplane crash in 1931. He was, like Julian, an
individualist; and often haunted by depression. He is described, beautifully,
in Karen Blixen's *Out of Africa*.

Billy, who did not get out of England, wrote to his mother – 'I can have
provided little but a series of shattering disappointments to you for Lord
knows how many years past now': and – 'I preach nothing, but have a
glimpse every now and then of what a roaring joke we must present from
the bird's-eye point of view'.

❧ TWENTY–SIX ❧

The anger that was in Julian and that had been directed largely against himself began to find objects on which to vent itself in South Africa. The regiment arrived there at the end of 1911 and went into camp at Robert's Heights near Pretoria.

Dear Mother,

We have just arrived here and it is a filthy place, great grass downs studded with rocks and no trees and tin huts everywhere . . . The mess is made of tin and the quarters are made of tin and everything else is grass and sky. We have one little room to live in and a sort of box joining it where we sleep all made of tin: and everything is numbered FO6a and RQ21 and even the bath and chamber utensils are Army Form X something . . . The whole thing seems clean and orderly and ticketed after India, I am sure I like dirt and disorderliness in the long run . . . As for the climate being good it is the grossest lie. It thunders every day . . . A man went mad here the other day from sheer boredom; he ran along the kops and dorps and spruits and poorts simply playing with 2 infantry regiments and 1 cavalry regiment who were sent out to bring him in. They did not find him for two days and eventually came upon him asleep on the high road to Johannesburg. He got up and said good morning to them, and asked them what they wanted; and since then he has been perfectly sane . . .

Julian began to talk of wanting to get out of the army; or at least to change the sort of job he was doing in it. 'I am going to strike shortly as I want to learn French and mule-driving and signalling and short-hand and Hegel.' These desires were usually put in the form of jokes – 'I am going to desert and join the Irregular Sind Horse as a vet' – but he made his feelings evident. There was no more talk of his love of his fellow officers – 'Here everything and everybody is stereotyped and devitalised and flat' – nor even of himself – 'I cannot draw, or write, or think or breathe, and I am disgusting to my fellow men. I am going to buy a cat and a canary for company and learn to do a little knitting'. The fellow-officer's wife who had tried to get into his bungalow in India was now no longer a subject for funny stories but 'more boring and like a street walker then ever; she ought never to be allowed about except in Piccadilly after 11 pm on very rainy nights'. Even Sclater Booth was now unpleasantly made a scapegoat.

He got intoxicated at the Sergeants' Ball and we had a temperance orgy with him afterwards; we gave him 5 of my tabloid cascara, 1 tea-spoonful of castor oil, 1 glass Kutnow, 10 grains quinine, 1 port glass 'Honey and Flowers' hair oil, a sleeping draught, a small glass Kutnow and Eno mixed, and some Aspirin and Phenacetin in case he got a headache. How he did not die of it, I cannot guess.

Julian found some sanity in reading. He loved *Ethan Frome*, Masefield's *The Everlasting Mercy*, and *Kim*: however about 'a book of M. Corelli's called *The Life Everlasting* – if it is like that, I am not going to enter'. In order to try to exercise his mind he took over the editorship of the regimental magazine, *The Eagle*, for which he wrote leading articles and comic plays and songs. He ran out of books – 'I feel a sort of terrible emptiness and dryness inside my head from reading so few good things'. His mother had sent him a few fashionable books but, he explained,

I hate material books where the whole interest is centred on whether people are successful or not, successful in the most worldly sense. I like books about artists and philosophers and dreamers and anybody who is a little bit off his dot. I can't explain to you, being in S.A., and we should certainly quarrel about it if I did explain to you. Indeed we *will* in the future. All love to the happy family. J.

He began to write the almost straight-faced mocking letters that he had used to write to her during his third year at Oxford.

About Revolt against Environment, Injudicious, how true what you say is! How do you think of it all? Did it come in a blinding flash, or as the result of a practical process of reasoning? The great truths that come to mankind come sometimes in one way, sometimes in the other.

And –

Do you see that England has been doing very well in the Test Matches? Clem Hill must have been caught on an off-day, even the greatest batsmen have off-days like the rest of us, and certainly the light was none too good when that fast ball took his leg bails from the off stump. It appears that an earthquake took place in Java at the identical moment. Clem Hill is not a Javan, but his uncle is.

He complained to his mother – 'You talk for me as well as for yourself: like the child's guide to Knowledge'.

He also attacked people at home. He commented on the aristocratic young men who were being paraded at Taplow as eligible suitors for the eighteen-year-old Monica: 'I love your lists of the Viscount parties; and oh, I do love the photographs of Geordie like a Satyr cleaned up for the occasion with that monstrously sensual face empty except for its vice and low cunning'. He again broke a taboo by criticizing the adored youngest member of the family, Imogen. 'About Mog's "nice nature" I feel deeply sceptical; she is a poisoner at heart, and only a fairly successful hypocrite.' He repeated to his mother his images of poisoning – 'Why don't you poison Bonar Law about disclaiming your acquaintance? It would liven things up to return to the times of the Borgias; and you are admirably fitted by nature to the role of poisoner, don't you think?'

He attacked Patrick Shaw Stewart. They had been close friends at first at Oxford; but even then Julian had wished he 'had not taken such a mellow turn . . . he was unsurpassed as the mandrill pure and simple, the "rough" man without any of the human-pity milk'. Now Julian wrote to his mother (this was at the time when she and Patrick were dancing cotillons together) – 'I wish you didn't like Patrick S–S; I have come to the conclusion that he is a really *nasty* character'. And when letters had had time to go between South Africa and England –

About Patrick I don't know. But I look back with growing animosity on his memory. I hated him so when he was wallopy. I hated him in the mornings. I didn't like him much when he was drunk. I liked him very much sometimes when he was a long way off, and I liked being told the things he said. But I didn't like the way he walked, even when he was walking away. I didn't like his hands or his feet or his streaky hair, or his love of money, or his dislike of dogs. Animals always edged away from him, and the more intelligent they were the further they edged. I think there is something rather obscene about him, like the electric eel at the zoo.

One of the few people in his mother's world of whom Julian did have a good word to say was Harry Cust – of whom Ettie had seemed to be in awe ever since the time of her story about him in Venice in 1890. Julian had once called him 'an old bore with vulgar hair and disgusting habits': he now wrote – 'Do you know, I believe he will wear you down in the end yet! I do dislike him; he is like Patrick in many ways; but I admire the way he has stood up to you, don't you?'

Julian sent his mother the photograph of himself in full dress uniform that he had promised her from India –

You will notice the proud mien of the soldier combined with the slightly and gracefully bowed legs of the *Cavalry* Soldier, who cannot discard the attitude of the pigskin even when in rest – the feet elongated by the continual pressure of the stirrup iron, the alert pose with fingers resting lightly on the covered menace of the sword, the graceful inclination of the figure similar to that of the Tower of Pisa and other notable pieces of architecture, but due in this case to the photographic artist having cut out the photograph crooked. I feel sure that you will like it. I 'ates that sort of fing myself.

His rage was partly against the place – 'Life goes on as usual in this utterly abominable country; Jews and Dutch doing each other in all day': partly against his work which was at the moment musketry – 'It is very dull, living in continual noise for so long: you stand at the firing point to see that they don't shoot each other or you sit in the butts to see the markers don't cheat': and partly against his fellow officers, who provided no stimulus to imagination or thought. 'The soldier sits in a large chair in the mess room and enjoys a state which is half sleeping, a quarter reading the paper, and a quarter laughing when he hears someone else laughing or saying "By Jove" when someone else makes a remark.' The average Sandhurst officer was someone who was 'put into one end of the machine a bloody puppy and who comes out the other end a bloody soldier. Do you know, we have got three people in the regiment who believe in the Apostle's Creed from end to end and most of the Nicene Creed, and the Fire Everlasting for such as you and I'. Compared with this even Johannesburg was preferable. 'It is a wild place, with Jews and Boers and Africans drinking themselves silly in bars all day long, and a lot of soldiers, and ladies of uncertain morality and gigantic hats. Everybody comes here for a fling. It is a good change for a day or two, but a week would leave you dead.'

His solace, apart from reading, was, as usual, animals. He bought three polo ponies and tried, with only spasmodic success, to love polo. But he did love his ponies which were 'like Greek sculptures only with a neater style of galloping; just think how tired it would make you to play 8 chukkas on a horse which always had all four legs in the air at once'. He more and more loved his dogs. He wrote a poem to, and did a drawing of, his favourite greyhound, Toby. This is his best poem, apart from his last.

TO A BLACK GREYHOUND

Shining black in the shining light,
  Inky black in the golden sun,
Graceful as the swallow's flight,
  Light as swallow, winged one;
Swift as driven hurricane –
  Double sinewed stretch and spring,
Muffled thus of flying feet,
  See the black dog galloping
  Hear his wild foot-beat.

See him lie when the day is dead,
  Black curves curled on the boarded floor.
Sleepy eyes, my sleepy-head –
  Eyes that were aflame before.
Gentle now, they burn no more;
  Gentle now, and softly warm,
With the fire that made them bright
  Hidden – as when after storm
  Softly falls the night.

God of Speed, who makes the fire –
  God of Peace, who lulls the same –
God who gives the fierce desire,
  Lust for blood as fierce as flame –
God who stands in Pity's name –
  Many may ye be or less,
Ye who rule the earth and sun:
  Gods of strength and gentleness
  Ye are ever one.

He tried to be gentle to his mother – 'Poor Mama, you are in waiting now, how long does it go on for at a time?' He continued to worry about her eyes which were again suffering from strain – 'I do hope and trust and pray that they will get all right directly'. Ettie had told him that, with the extra costs of entertaining in 1911 and 1912, they were short of money. He wrote – 'I *am* sorry and worried. I can always sell two ponies if it is a norful hustle. *Do* tell me. I could do it tomorrow. *Please* tell me'. He ended some letters – 'This takes you tons and tons of love and blessings'; and then would become ironical again – 'Make me a good boy, Amen'.

He tried to find more poetry to read. He read Marlowe, and Ovid's *Amores*. He liked Ovid because he 'never tried to make out what a fearful dog he was like the modern erotics do; he just states his fun quite naturally and without surprise'. Also – 'How I love the Rupert Brooke poems, who is Rupert B? Don't you like the one called The Voice? The "Fish" poem is good, isn't it, the most poetical of the lot, and metaphysical and weird . . . Who is Rupert, what is he?' Then –

I saw some pictures in Jo'burg yesterday – John, Orpen, Sargent: and it suddenly carried one away into a land with things in it, and warmth in it, and burning interest; out of the sordid, mercenary, ugly, inhuman sham that this country is. Did you ever see a picture by Orpen called 'The Fairy Ring'? I did so like it. Aug. John must be a raving lunatic – is he dead yet or have his habits toned down? He is the sort of man who might kill himself or turn round and become a religious maniac.

About success – 'I like the people best who take it as it comes, or doesn't come, and are busy about impractical and ideal things in their heart of hearts all the time'.

He went on a fishing holiday to Natal; but still disliked the country and most of the people –

Three drunken farmers came in and wanted me to drink with them and I told them that I took the pledge in New York in '98. The Basutos are going to make war, and I don't blame them, living in a country like this. If you burnt the whole country it would look just the same in a fortnight, houses and all, if you imported a few dozen Scotch settlers. There are no trees. Think of it, no trees!

And back with the Regiment –

Robert's Heights is a small corrugated iron facsimile of Purgatory. It would not be so bad if there were some place near it you could go from Sat-Mon and drink Veuve Clicquot with glorious women in green dresses, and talk to them about art and literature and religion; or even a decent jungle with a pig. But the only relaxation is to see Mrs Steele, very much overdressed, driving a lame troop-horse in a second-hand buggy.

He asked his mother more seriously if she could help him to get out. 'Can you find out from the War Office or political nuts whether we are likely to stay on long in this country? because I really *can't* face coming back here if it is to be for too long. I would sooner go and do first footman to someone in India if they would have me – or Java, or New Zealand'. And – 'Can you get me a job? Black Rod, or Minister of Agriculture, or Envoy Plenipotentiary to the King of Barbados?'

Ettie seemed to make no response to his pleas. Once, she even actively discouraged him. In a letter to Arthur Balfour of a slightly later date when discussing an offer which had been made to Julian to stand for Parliament as a candidate for Hertford, she wrote – 'He is very far from politics at present and *absorbed* in soldiering'.

In England, Marjorie Manners became engaged to the Marquis of Anglesey. Julian had always kept her photograph and four of her paintings in his room. He wrote –

> Bivouac. De Tweel Spruit
> nr Premier Mine
> Sunday July 29th

My darling Marjorie,

I've just heard of your engagement! Just in time to send you one line of blessing, which may or may not catch the mail. I don't know him; but he is a damn lucky man – and I always think that he looks a ripper. I hope you will be *tremendously tremendously* happy – and I'm quite sure that you will. God bless you, many many times. My dear, I haven't got time to say anything that I want to say: but you know that anything that can be wished for or prayed for, I wish and pray for you. You have been the best friend that I've ever had, or ever shall have: and I think you've given me more good and blessing than anyone else. I hope you'll go on being friends with me. Thank you, my darling, for all you have been: I shall never forget. Goodbye. Shall I see you in Sept or Oct? J.

And to Ettie –

He is a damn lucky fellow. If I could only have got leave this year I might have had a try to short head him. If not, I would have done him down with a knife or perished in the attempt. As it is, I can only bide here all ineffective. But I am consumed with envy and malice and all evil, and I shall die a bachelor unless I can marry a Totty Lightfoot at 55 to cheer my old age. There has never been and never will be anyone like M.M.: and he is nice, isn't he?

Julian went into training for boxing again. He took some of his men to Johannesburg for the Army Championships, but found he was the only officer entered at his weight. So he got the promoters to offer a cup for a four-round contest between himself and any challenger –

. . . and a man who was in training for the Amateur Championship said he would come and fight me. He was a fireman called Tye; he used to be a sailor, and he looked as hard as a hammer. I quaked in my shoes when I saw him, and quaked more when I heard he was 2-1 on favourite for the Championships; and quaked most when my trainer went to see him box and returned with word that he had knocked out two men in $\frac{1}{4}$ of an hour. We went into the ring on the night and he came straight for me like a tiger and hit left and right; I stopped his left but it knocked my guard aside and he crashed with his right clean on to the point of my jaw. I was clean knocked out; but by the fluke of God I recovered and came to and got on to my feet again by the time they had counted six. I could hardly stand, and I could only see a white blur in front of me; but I just had sense to keep my guard up, and hit hard at the blur whenever it came in range. He knocked me down twice more, but my head was clearing every moment, and I felt a strange sort of confidence that I was master of him. I put him down in the 2nd round with a right counter, which shook him; he took a count of 8. In the third round I went into him and beat his guard down – then crossed again with the right and felt it go right home, with all my arm and body behind it. I knew it was the end when I hit; and he never moved for 20 seconds. They said it was the best fight they had seen for years in Jo'burg; and my boxing men went clean off their heads with delight and carried me twice round the hall. I was 11st 4 and he was 11st 3; and I think it was the best fight I shall ever have.

It is noticeable that when Julian wrote about his exploits in boxing or in war his writing became – and these were the only times that it did – almost platitudinous.

In July his regiment went on manoeuvres and he was happier: 'the great empty veld has a sort of charm when one is living on it and in it'. But – 'I am not popular with my fellow officers'. He was trying to befriend a man whom the regiment were trying to get rid of – not for being a bad officer, but for being not a gentleman. Julian said he was longing to come home on leave, which had been promised to him in the autumn. The prospect of this made him retract, though hesitantly, some of the suggestions he had made about changing his work: 'I would liefer be a lieutenant in Africa than odd man to a general in heaven – I think'. For – 'I do so much better in the wilds than in England where there are so many more conventions to gird against . . . and girding is so bad'. He seemed to be both longing for England; yet perhaps afraid of what he might find there.

❧ TWENTY–SEVEN ❧

His family had been looking forward to Julian's return. He had been abroad for two years. In the summer of 1912 Ettie was in Normandy with the three younger children. Evan Charteris and John Revelstoke had both been to stay. Willy had returned to Taplow from the Olympic Games in Stockholm but Ettie had discouraged him from coming to Normandy; she said he would not like the bad weather. Willy stayed at home and saw to the installation of a new laundry and a new kitchen range. Ettie had put herself on a more exact routine than ever during the summer: she tabulated this in her diary.

Breakfast 8.30; Household 9–10; Times 10–10.30; Write 10.30–12; Out till 12.45; Read with Monica 12.45–1.45; Luncheon 1.45; Rest till 2.45; Out 2.45–4.45; Read or Try-on 4.45–5.30; Tea with Babes 5.30; Baba 6–7; Sleep 7–7.45; Read Monica 7.45–8.30; Dinner 8.30; Bed 10.30. No nerves. Sleep 10 hrs if at all tired. Punctual. *No hurry.* Pink tonic 3 weeks. B. Dawson's 3 weeks. Olive oil. *Eat.* Spare eyes when tired.

Julian arrived in England on 21 September. The family had returned to Taplow. Ettie wrote apologetically to Patrick Shaw Stewart –

Pat Dst, It was glorious to hear from you. I can't think why we've had such a pen-par, for I've thought towards you a lot and am overcrowded with things to say. We got back from a cold France – yet touched by sunny enchantment at the end – to a colder England, to meet Julian last Sat. And the joy of that could never be said in rhyme. I do really feel as if I've been cut in half for two years, and joined together again.

He is more the nth power of himself than ever before – utterly unchanged – you couldn't believe in two years having worked so little alteration but just intensified. And wildly, romantically well – and happy. And more than ever like

Hipporax – 'Take my coat, and I will hit Butos in the eye, for I am ambidextrous, and never miss my aim'. He has now gone to the Tower of London to hit a Butos in the Scots Guards, in preparation for Army Boxing. (Hasn't this a familiar ring?) He does look delightful. But enough of this dotage . . .

Ettie liked Julian when he was fighting: then, she appeared to know where she was. It was the other sides of his character that upset her; that she herself had to fight. She wrote in her Family Journal about Julian's leave during 1912–13 –

Julian's great absorption that winter, besides hunting, was in pictures and art; he had a very great love of them, and a really remarkable talent for drawing. He one day announced quite gravely a project of giving up the army and going to work at painting in Paris – but this idea was received with such irrepressible laughter by Billy and Bron that it was not mentioned much more . . .

There is no record of the laughter from Billy and Bron; Billy himself stayed in Paris the following summer and led something of a bohemian life and loved it; Bron Lucas might have laughed, for much of him was like Ettie. But it was Ettie herself who recorded with approval the mocking of Julian out of his desire to get out of the army; and she did this in 1916, after two of her sons had been killed. It was inconceivable to Ettie that a son of hers might truly want to be a painter or a writer rather than a soldier. In 1913, Patrick Shaw Stewart wrote that Julian was still saying 'quite definitely that he hated the army'. This was when Ettie was writing to Arthur Balfour insisting that Julian was 'absorbed in soldiering'.

Ettie's obstinacy and philistinism (which Julian recognized) is perhaps hard to understand in someone who had been a founder member of the Souls – those characters dedicated mythically to intelligence and sensitivity. But the sensitivity of the Souls had been mainly towards jokers, satirists, parodists, toyers with words and ideas; the literary world in which Ettie moved was that of Chesterton, Belloc, Maurice Baring, Edmund Gosse; she did not seem to know any of the truly original writers of the time – though Evan Charteris was a friend of Henry James and Cynthia Asquith was soon to become a friend of D. H. Lawrence. The list of books that she had read and that she noted at the end of her engagement diaries each year gives the impression of trophies won and then put away in an attic – 'Les Frères Karamazov: 850 pages!' Ettie never had much interest in painting, and she hated music. Julian's drawings, which he had begun to do more and more in the army, were considered amusing –

embellishments to family letters. But the real objection to the idea of Julian's becoming a painter or a writer was just snobbish: artists, if respectable, might be patronized; but they were not the sort of people whom one would want one's daughter to marry. And with her son a soldier, a mother might actually feel safe. Soldiers sometimes got killed; but they could not make – as an artist could – one's whole life seem ridiculous.

Julian's father Willy was held up as the perfect type of Englishman – a man honest and brave, with fine manners, but who had renounced all pretensions to imagination or inquiry. As a young man Willy had seemed to try to exercise his mind as he exercised his body: but then he and those like him had handed over processes of mind to women. Willy now moved from committee to committee, from the killing of birds to the killing of stags, without much more mental originality being required of him than that to deal with railway timetables. During all these years he never corresponded with Julian about ideas or books. He sometimes mentioned politics, but briefly and superficially, as if it was inconceivable that opinions would have to be argued between gentlemen. In his later life people remembered Willy as having little conversation except about Bimetallism, or horses, or rowing; he would sometimes seem to give up speech altogether and converse with startled friends in sporting mime – the casting of a fly, or a lunge with an épée. After Julian's death, when an inquirer wrote (as many did) to Willy asking for information about Julian as a poet, Willy replied –

He did not look on himself as a poet, but essentially as a fighting man, boxer, steeplechase rider and lover of animals . . . He used to write verses when the spirit moved him, and very often threw them away. Whether he would have taken up writing seriously when he grew older and less absorbed in outdoor pursuits it is impossible to say. He wrote with very great facility, and was very fond of the Classics and all imaginative writers.

Julian did not spend much of the time at Taplow during the winter of 1912–13; he stayed with Bron Lucas in Yorkshire and in London, and his family did not seem to notice much of what he did when he was away. He would sometimes appear at London parties together with Billy and they would both seem to be 'possessed by the same controlled restlessness as though they were keyed up to the same moment of departure, each one with a toe on the line impatient to be off'.[1] He went

[1] Sonia Keppel, *Edwardian Daughter* (London, 1958), p. 115.

to parties now in pursuit of girls: he chased Violet Keppel 'alternately with poetry and pugilism; sometimes he came to see her with a sheaf of verses in his hand, sometimes with an eye closed in a sparring bout. Always he looked wonderfully fit, like a Roman gladiator'.[1] Once he caught, and was caught with, Violet Keppel in a housemaid's cupboard and there was a slight scandal: Julian asked his mother to straighten things out with Mrs Keppel. There is no record of his seeing Pamela Lytton during his leave, though he sent one telegram from Knebworth station. In October, he wrote to Marjorie Anglesey from Taplow –

I *was* pleased to get your letter my darling, and to think of the gigantic fun of seeing you soon. I can't bear your being married, but that is just one of the things that one has to put up with . . . when you come to London on the 20th can't you just pop down here for the inside of *one* day – or is it too much to ask of you? I will come up to Paddington and fetch you – and it will only take $\frac{1}{2}$ an hour; and we'll walk in the woods and *talk* and *talk*. I've got oceans to hear from you: and to tell you. And I've got an ostrich feather, white, ten feet long. Write to me. J.

– but it seems that he did not see her that winter, for he was writing to her in 1914 – 'I didn't want to see you last year because I thought I should frizzle up with jealousy, and I never have the least control over what goes on inside me'. Also – 'I couldn't do England last year, I got melancholy mad'.

He did go in for the army boxing championships, as a middle-weight, but was beaten in the second round. He hunted a lot. Even his old friends did not see much of him that winter: he seemed an elusive and somewhat magical figure – 'a rather refined Botticelli Mars – leaner, harder and more forceful' (Tommy Lascelles).

Once when I and another man were dining in Brooks' Julian was late, and we started, and in a minute or two he rushed in across that solemn room beaming all over absolutely like the sun in a comic picture; and sat down, and seized his napkin and brandished it over his head shouting 'Hurrah!' – the funny old demure correct waiters beaming too all around us.

(Edward Marsh)

He was of course always letting things happen to him; perhaps he scarcely realized how his personality made at least some things happen to him which others would have to seek out with labour.

(Patrick Shaw Stewart)

[1] op. cit., p. 115.

He did not quarrel with his mother much now. She went on with her life of 'establishing the nearest English approach to the great Parisian salons . . . collecting at Taplow – an ugly, overgrown villa furnished like a hotel – the cream of the political and literary intelligentsia, with a constant leaven of brilliant young men whose mother she might have been' (Tommy Lascelles). And Julian went – where? – perhaps somewhere with his greyhound-racers, his boxing-partners, his 'artist' friends with 'cockney genius'. It is difficult to imagine a group in 1913 with whom Julian would have felt at home. Bloomsbury, for instance, would have seemed listless to him. He moved around, and was himself, and came back to Taplow. What he had once written to his mother probably remained true – 'things people say and do, and things in books, often seem absolutely incomprehensible to me: I've no standard within myself by which to know or judge them'.

Nineteen hundred and thirteen was the year when senior army officers were considering mutiny; when leading lawyers were encouraging illegality; when Sir Edward Carson QC said about the prospect of Ulster being included in Irish Home Rule – 'We have pledges and promises from some of the greatest generals in the army that when the time comes and if necessary they will come over to help us keep the old flag flying and to defy those who dare to invade our liberties'.[1] It was the time of Yeats's 'the best lack all conviction, and the worst are full of a passionate intensity'. Amongst Julian's generation the best were supposed to be the Coterie – the children of the Souls – who had 'an insidiously corruptive poison in their midst'; whose 'anti-cant is really suicidal to happiness'. From senseless passions or cynicism people had begun to look round for an escape; to some condition in which feelings might be clean again. In 1911 there had almost been war when the Germans had sent a gunboat to the Moroccan port of Agadir: Ettie had written 'John writes from Balmoral (Sir Edward Grey and A.J.B. there) that they do *not* think it will come *now* but are nervous about *next Spring*.' From South Africa in 1912 Julian had written 'I suppose we really aren't going to fight Germany yet from what Haldane told you'. War with Germany was being spoken about as if it would certainly come, but would contain none of the characteristics of war, would be simply a contest like polo. There was a fashionable excitement about flying: Ettie wrote from a Berlin air-show where she had gone with John Revelstoke 'I have become the *Flying*

[1] Quoted in George Dangerfield, *The Strange Death of Liberal England* (London, 1972), p. 129.

Machine Bore for life.' Monica fell in love with a French airman, Gustav Hamel. In the spring of 1913 mysterious airships began to be seen over the English coast; these were thought to be German; but they did not exist; they were projections on to an external enemy from internal fears and confusions. For the first time people at the very top of public life – the remnants of the Souls – ceased to speak to one another. Margot Asquith wrote to Ettie in January 1913 – 'I cried when you never sent me one line for Xmas: since life divided into deep devotion for 20 years and impatient hate for these last years, I have quite lost my nerve'. Willy, a year later, was writing –

I hope the troops will fraternize with the Ulstermen . . . the whole thing is a great blow to government of any sort in this country; but if one is governed by liars and swindlers it is only what should be expected . . . Asquith will go down in history as a drunken time-server, with no moral qualities and prostituted abilities.

What struck people about Julian during his leave of 1912–13 was his gentleness – when he was not boxing, or hunting, or charming girls. Patrick Shaw Stewart wrote – 'Was there ever a man who had such perfect manners by nature and who was occasionally so rude on principle?' Charles Lister, later, wrote –

I suppose everyone noticed dear Julian's vitality, but I don't think they were so conscious of that great tenderness of heart that underlay it. With women generally it was his special charm. I think of the way he used to take my hand if he had felt disappointed with anything I had done, and then find out why I'd done it. I remember the time when he was under the impression that I had chucked Socialism for the 'loaves and fishes' etc – and of course that sort of thing he couldn't abide. And he thought this for a longish while; then found out that it wasn't that after all, and took my hand in the most loving way . . .

What stopped Julian from trying seriously to get out of the army in 1913 seems to have been, besides the mockery of his family, the know-ledge that by staying in, he could at least be out of England. And this is what he found imperative – to get away from hypocrisies and animosities. It was when he had been in England for some time that the army did not seem too bad; it was when he was back in South Africa that he felt his situation there again to be hopeless. He did make up his own mind, finally, to get out – without the help of his mother. But by then it was too late.

While he was still on leave in 1913 Ettie and Willy and Monica went to Egypt to stay with Lord Kitchener. After his mother had gone, Julian found that he missed her – 'We haven't yet half thrashed things out, have we?' In Cairo Monica caught measles, but within a day or two was up and about and with Ettie doing the round of officers and balls. She and Ettie went to Luxor with a young officer called Major Fitzgerald: there Monica recorded – 'I disgraced myself all over again by having influenza and a very high temperature', while Ettie exhibited her 'zest both for new friendships and sightseeing' in the company of Major Fitzgerald. Monica commented, unimaginatively – 'What a wrecker I was and a hindrance!' Willy had moved on to shoot hippopotami in the Southern Sudan.

Ettie's Aunt Katie Cowper died before the end of Julian's leave and Ettie inherited her vast house Panshanger with its collection of beautiful pictures. Julian had a parting shot at Ettie before he left – 'I've decided to give up my military career in favour of dentistry, and I'm just starting with a friend of mine who has a good practice in London'. Then Ettie, back from Egypt, went to Southampton to see him off; 'in a tangle of greyhounds and their leashes'.

✖ TWENTY–EIGHT ✖

On the boat between England and South Africa Julian began a poem –

> . . . The ordered Past behind us lies –
> The Past with ordered argosies
> Of memory's abiding treasure,
> Of pains and joys and driving pleasure.
> Passion, a burning fiery sword,
> Swooping, the Angel of the Lord,
> Has struck the soul with fire and rout,
> Has cut a flaming way about,
> Has struck, and cleansed, and wandered out.
> And lust, the son of Storm and Thunder,
> Has seized the empty souls for plunder:
> Lust, that Red Mimic, jagged light,
> Who deadens sense, and sears the sight . . .

– and then screwed it up and threw it away, but it was picked up and preserved by a fellow passenger.

On the boat, he told his mother, were

three delicious Swedes in the 2nd class, sisters; also their mother. Good old Swedish name of Bergstroom; one of the oldest families in Scandinavia and very rich. I hope you will like them. I am engaged to the second sister, whose name is Inez. She is about 5 ft 6½ in in height, with brown hair turning to gold and a lovely complexion. She is not so pretty as her elder sister, Seagull; but Seagull has red hair, is very vivacious, and dances the Grizzly Bear all day – so I thought she would not make such a good wife as Inez.

In his next letter all this had changed into –

the bevy of beautiful Dutch sisters in the second class whom you spotted with such extraordinary quickness the moment you came on the boat. Their chief idea in life is to 'have a bit of fun'. They generally manage to get it, and it is not a bad philosophy . . . I have got to be a tremendous dab at the Turkey Trot . . . I also won the bucket quoits, defeating Israel in the semifinal and Solomon in the final (this is true).

Julian rejoined his regiment at Potchefstroom southwest of Johannesburg, which was 'not at all a bad place after the Heights of Despair'. Potchefstroom was also within easy reach of Johannesburg, so Julian could continue his pursuit of girls.

The Potchefstroom season is over, having lasted just one week; a bevy of beautiful fairies was imported from Johannesburg and planted out in a spare bungalow – 6 of them. All our looking-glasses, sponges, etc. were borrowed for them and a kaffir hired to cook. They must have had great fun with the undivided attention of the male garrison.

He could also follow them to Johannesburg where

they all dress like chorus girls on a holiday and behave with much less hypocrisy. It is a very good town in which to see life for a little with a smile on one's face and a revolver in one's pocket. I had great fun going round some of the suburbs with the detective fellows. The opium dens are extraordinary; and I actually saw men playing poker with their pistols loaded on the table which I thought only occurred in wild west novels. Jews and Dutch and Indians and Greeks and Russians and Chinamen and white women and black women all chock-a-block: it must be the most cosmopolitan town in the world.

For the festivities at Potchefstroom he wrote a pantomime which was performed by his men.

It is called 'The Wicked Count . . . To Say Nothing Of The Countess'. It is terribly improp, and I shall probably lose my commission over it, but the men laugh so much while they are doing it that I think it will have a great success. It opens with the Countess (a man 6 ft 4 with large boots) in bed. Enter 1st lover: business. Knock at the door: enter 2nd lover: first lover disappears under bed. When there are 3 lovers under the bed enter Count. Placard: Count – What is it? Countess – It must be an earthquake darling.

His enjoyment of the pursuit of girls dissolved part of his hatred of army life: he became a dashing young cavalry officer, gallant and admired.

He also found something serious to turn his attention to. In the summer of 1913 there were widespread strikes in the mines around Johannesburg, and the army were called in to keep order.

We got to Jo'burg at about 2 o'clock on Friday and got a feed – the men had had nothing since 7 the night before – and then we were hurried straight off to the Market Square where we met our other 2 squadrons. There were tremendous crowds and a good deal of shouting; the Government had stopped a big meeting which was to have been held. But the actual miners seemed quite peaceable and good-natured even when they were walking about in processions with banners: the people who looked like trouble were the real Jo'burg roughs who are rougher and dirtier and less human than any other roughs in the world. We stayed on the Market Square till about 5 in the afternoon; then galloped off to the big station, Park Station, which they said they were going to burn. We went through this and cleared all the people out with loaded rifles and revolvers; but everyone went away at once after a little chaff. One old lady in the Refreshment Room was terrified and fell into my arms with about 20 brown paper parcels imploring me to save her which I did . . .

When we left the station we got into the thick of the hooligans, everyone yelling, and bottles and stones flying and roughs upsetting the horses with whips – led by a woman who was trying to pull the men off their horses. It looked very ugly; they were the dirtiest of the crowd – not the strikers themselves – and angry. However we did not even draw swords, but just grinned and bore it. It's very hard to know what to do, especially when one's men are getting cut about with bottles and one's temper getting worse every moment. As things turned out, I believe it would have been better if we had got off and fired. Eventually the shooting was the only thing which stopped them, and I believe that if we had shot before they would have stopped before . . .

The strikes reached a stalemate – 'the Government cannot possibly grant the men's demands and the men cannot possibly declare a general strike or they would starve'. What struck Julian about the strikes was, firstly, 'the utter beastliness of both sides – the Jews at the Rand Club who loaf about and drink all day, and the Dutch and Dagos who curse and shoot in the streets'. Neither of these seemed to have much to do with the miners themselves, who were orderly.

Secondly –

I think that the oddest thing of the strike was the entire unconcern of quite half the crowd, who were casually looking on in the streets while their friends were shot down next to them. A lot of people came out of a matinée while the firing was going strong, looked on for a bit, and then walked back into the theatre again and finished their play. Think what would happen if you fired a few shots down a street in London!

But in London, in fact, his mother did not seem very interested in his news of the strike. He wrote –

I was longing for letters full of anxiety, sympathy and admiration for the little 'ero's facing undaunted the bullets of the fierce and alien mob; and all you ask is 'How did the strike strike you?' I *do* call it a bit hard; and I always thought you disliked puns.

With the rioting over he found he was having his 'usual temptation to plunge straight into La Vie Orageuse for which Jo'burg offers ample opportunity with the added excitement of being a marked man among the roughs'. However – 'all the fairies have now followed us to Potch, which makes life most exciting, as you never know round which corner you are going to run into the General, Mrs General, and Miss General, with one of the same fairies upon your arm'.

Back at regimental duties – polo, steeplechasing, showjumping, editing *The Eagle* – he said that he had decided, for the time being, that 'my job is the profession of arms. I love my fellow officers now, and my dogs, and horses. Isn't it funny that the more one loves one's fellow officers the more one loves one's dogs, instead of less?' For he was having 'the success of my life with the Gaiety company, in spite of a bloody nose'. He wrote to his father to congratulate him on the stand he was taking with the die-hard conservatives about Ulster: 'It makes me prouder than ever of having you for a father, but it always makes me terribly jealous and envious too; and it's strictly contrary to the Christian religion to be jealous of one's father.' He wrote commiseratingly about Billy when he heard of his achieving only a Second in Greats: 'I am so awfully sad about poor Billy-boy . . . he had almost too much insolence and confidence'. And about his mother's taking over Panshanger – 'Did you ever get the misgiving that big houses are a thing of the past?'

With Julian in good spirits (at Oxford a friend had once remarked 'I think I like you better when you are melancholy') Ettie was going through a period of depression. Julian wrote 'I'm so sorry you had a bit of a slump . . . are you getting any rest now? . . . no more nonsense about failure of courage, please'.

He went on a three-week trek to Basutoland with the regimental scouts, which he loved:

My long dogs go with us and we practically live off what they kill. The camps are just like gypsy camps: all the men round the fire watching the dinner being cooked and all the horses round outside, watching too. They are jolly men, all the wild spirits, and they love being out. One gets to know them very well, living with them – more than one would in years of barrack life.

He told his mother –

Yes, I'm now very glad that we had such a good fight, although I feel that it has taken years off my life. But I wish that I had been a little older: I should have put up such a much better fight for you. And I am afraid I shall never have another chance, because I shall always laugh too soon in any future conflict.

What grief one comes to, through trying to get things straight and exact and altogether! But how rotten one would be, if one didn't start by trying that way!

Back in Johannesburg there was the 'Rag-time ball last night, it was really wonderful, everyone out for blood, and the time spent in lightning changes from the ball-room to the bed-room'. There was a lady called Mrs Dale Lace who wore a monocle and who gave 'a moonlight romp at her farm with chinese lanterns and bottles of fizz under every bush. In the middle of it she came up and drew me aside and said "Look here old *chap*, if you want a bed, it's the first room round on the right, and safe as houses"'. His only complaint was of the Tango –' A beastly dance . . . like a Platonic friendship'.

He teased his mother by telling her he had settled down with a girl and family on the outskirts of Potchefstroom: 'When shall I bring home my colonial-born family? My girl is very well and sends you and Poppa her best respects. We are to be married in February. She is the loveliest, gentlest, best, and most loving little darling I have ever met. Gee, but I am happy!' He did in fact have a steady girl-friend at the time because the following year he was telling his mother, from the heart, how she had left him to marry a rich stockbroker. 'In a stupid mood of desperation I wrote to her that I had only got to wait till the lure and glamour of filthy lucre wore off.' He seemed to tease his mother about girls partly as a continuation of his battle with her; partly as a defence against his own misgivings about his ability to settle down and love anyone else. In the Johannesburg summer (this was Christmas, 1913) he was still in good spirits:

I always think the biggest nonsense in the world is when people like Wells talk about women tempting men and leading them on to destruction, poor fellows, when the poor fellows are using whatever brains God has given them in a fervid gallop to the one end. And what harm, when the women are as independent and anxious as the men?

He was lectured by his Colonel about the girls who came to see him: he parodied this –

They would come down here and make scenes on the platform which is undignified and degrading for a gentleman and an officer; besides, you see, when you are in command of men you *must* consider what they are thinking, you can't think only of yourself, it is the Responsibility that is so sacred.

For a time he was forbidden to go into Johannesburg or to receive visitors. He commented 'This is a mistake.' He was becoming rebellious again. He found in the regimental orderly room a list of recommendations about dress and deportment for officers: he made up his own list –

Don't dress if you feel more natural naked. Don't go naked if it's cold, wear a bathing dress. Don't draw class distinctions, it's against the Spirit of the Age and the Spirit of the New Testament – and besides, it's almost impossible to draw the line. Don't salute your superior officers if you feel that your individuality is on a higher grade than theirs.

Again, he began to think of getting out of the army. The summer had been fun, but fun was ephemeral: he began again to take his irritation out on people at home for whom parties never seemed to pall. Ettie had described to him a weekend at Hackwood, George Curzon's house in Hampshire, where there had been a gathering of the literary and political establishment. Julian wrote –

Isn't it funny how drunk all the savants get? I believe that this is the real distinction between the brain and the body – if you want to have a brain you *must* get drunk the oftener the better; if, on the other hand, you want to have a body, you must not get drunk more than, say, twice a week.

About his mother's efforts to attach Monica to the eldest sons of peers he wrote –

Have you managed to lure John Manners and Jack Althorp to the altar yet, or have you had to resort to locking them in the Tennis Court in the early hours of the morning? I always thought your choice of the Tennis Court gallery so odd;

it seems to be a place calculated to damp the most ardent lover, with its vault-like atmosphere and acid smell and the scattered symbolic remnants of the dry wings of dead moths. (Taplow had an indoor tennis court.)

As for his own feelings about marriage –

What a far better thing it is not to get married! Marriage is such a short odds gamble, and the funny thing is that the real gamblers and chancers have the sense to leave it alone knowing that it's a bad bet; while the careful ones, who know neither the form nor the odds, plunge and go down.

He heard that his mother had sold a Raphael painting from Panshanger for £70,000 in order to pay estate duty and to be able to install central heating; he joked – 'I believe the Raphael was entailed, and I am getting up a lawsuit'.

He seemed to be turning most things into a joke; this was part of the conventions that he had once hated. But in the army, in South Africa, even with the Johannesburg girls, what else was there to do? It was a life of a certain style, but still no content. Even about the things he loved, he joked; though here there seemed to be some longing too. He was reading

The Brothers Karamavitchskofponskinremya – It *is* good, isn't it? I love it. I got muddled up between the names of the brothers and uncles and lady-friends at first, so I made a list; then they all have three names, used alternately, so I made a new list, at greater length, with imaginary sketches . . . Oh I *do* love *The Brothers Pavvalofitchkop*, more and more, every page that I read! It makes me love the Russians too. I believe they really *are* like that, aren't they?

There was another strike in Johannesburg in 1914 but the government declared martial law and the town quickly filled with 'tall grim Boers with long hair and short stubbly beards only opening their mouths to spit, slung with rifle and cartridges and spare boots and socks and bread and biltong. You could see what a tough lot they must have been to fight'. Around them was 'the new Dutch generation – the "jongs" – weedy, flashy, pale-faced, chattering wasters, mostly drunk'. The strike again collapsed, but – 'one can't help thinking that the violent section will refuse to take it lying down and that, next time they do anything, they will start straight away by blowing things up before the burghers arrive'.

At this time he was having his great successes in steeplechasing and showjumping: 'When one practices and thinks of nothing else for years one is whacked; when one rushes in at the last moment with a yell and a grin one wins'. He cleared a jump which was a record for height in South Africa – 6 ft 5 in – though his horse was carrying 13 stone. About his ponies –

O Mummy, I can't tell you the daily joy of my glorious thorobred polo-ponies – new every morning like the sun. They are fierce and fit and beautiful. I let them loose in the mornings and they gallop and play about with the greyhounds. Sorry for being a bore . . .

He began to think again about coming home on leave. But he was undecided about this. There were rumours that the regiment might return to England in the autumn of 1914. Or he might use his leave 'taking the greyhounds up to hunt the wily lion, and some hog-spears and ghurka knives for close quarters'. Or he might apply to go to the Flying School in England. This was the time, too, when he had his plan to join Denys Finch-Hatton in Kenya. Finch-Hatton had been on a trip to Arabia where, reputedly, he had bought a million cattle at half a crown a head and was about to drive them, presumably miraculously, across the Red Sea and sell them for £150 a head in Nairobi. Then he was going to grow cotton. Julian wrote 'Don't you think it would be great fun? They have never grown any cotton there yet, and the soil is most unfavourable to the growth of the same, but that really only makes the experiment more interesting'.

But there seemed to be something stopping him making up his mind – he was like Hamlet – he wrote lovingly to his mother saying he was longing to see her; then – 'Do you think we shall get on this time, or shall I still be frightened of your watchfulness, craftiness, and intellect-ualism?' He asked – 'Have you been working any big ramps lately, Mummy?' Then – 'I'm in a terribly bad temper tonight, it's all so silly'.

It was difficult to know what would be running away, or what would be going forward. Of course, he could hunt lions or grow cotton in Kenya: or stay in the army and have fun with girls and snipe at his mother: but still, it seemed that he wanted none of these things; he wanted to pick up his own life where it had been broken four years before and to mend it. His life had been broken in battles at home. Now, suddenly, he seemed to know what he should do –

I've quite settled up about my leave now. I'm going to hunt lions in Rhodesia (not British East) in August, very soon; and then I'm coming home (in October or January) by British East and the Red Sea. Then I'm going to the Flying School at Netheravon, and up to the Staff College exam in June 1915. In March I am going to the Polo at the Panama Exhibition; and next year I will stand for Parliament.

The date of this letter was 15 July 1914.

❧ TWENTY–NINE ❧

The Great War crept up almost unnoticed by English people perhaps because they had got so used to its apparition – talk in dining rooms had been for so long about when, rather than whether, it would come – that when it did they still could not believe it would have substance; it was a relief from present confusions – from Ulster, from the strikes, perhaps even from women – but as for its own terrors, these were unknown. Germans dreamed of war because they could not get what they thought they deserved without it; they were like unfavoured sons with hopes of fratricide. Frenchmen dreamed of war as revenge for their defeat in 1870; they were nostalgic for the days when they too had been like Cain in Europe. Englishmen, sitting on an Empire, had no problems like these: but they seemed to suffer from some surfeit: the strikes, the class-hatreds, the threats of rebellion – these were symptoms of people who had got what they thought they wanted and were disturbed that dissatisfactions remained as strong as ever. There was a longing for simplicity; for a return to the old days when the view of an enemy had been clear.

In 1914 there seemed to be nothing atrocious about war: war was a story: life was a vale of tears and war was perhaps a sponge to mop it. These were potent images; as was that of another life in which there would be no strikes, no rebellions, but rewards for deserts with each man his own prize-giver and pupil. Julian's analysis of the patterns of mind in which he grew up was based on the observation that contradictory ideals – those of competitiveness and self-sacrifice – produced fantasy: people were taken over by a plethora of images like those of a witches' sabbath. The prospect of killing was clean, because it would cut out complexity.

For thousands of years young Europeans had been brought up to think that war was proper – a way by which a man could 'prove' himself; by which a nation could exercise itself and maintain fitness. This 'proof' of a man, or of a nation, seemed like an exercise of reason: you are dead, I am alive; *quod erat demonstrandum*. And women could prove their love by sending men out to die: how else could there be competitiveness and sacrifice?

A readiness to fight had once been necessary: circumstances had changed, but patterns of mind had not. In 1914 there were few real dangers that demanded physical valour and sacrifice: the dangers were from the ideas that demanded these apart from the context. It might be possible to think that such states of mind were in fact so moribund that some violent breaking up and re-arrangement might be necessary. But few people – even Julian – got round to saying this.

In 1914 'France' or 'Germany' were images like heraldic animals – or Cain and Abel. The horrors of war were not imagined because these were not in the story-books. The stories were – that the war could not last too long because this was not financially possible: together with the pheasant-shooting, it would be over soon after Christmas. Such stories were in fantasy; there was no evidence for them in fact. From 1899 to 1901 a few thousand Boer farmers had kept occupied and inflicted heavy casualties on the best regiments of the British Army: they had done this by not sticking to the rules of the game or of the season, and by using modern weapons, notably machine guns. In 1914 it was known that the German Army was the most powerful in the world. There was the chance, of course, that the Germans might win the war quickly. But this was not considered by Englishmen. The slogan was – that the English and French would win by Christmas.

The stories about war that people loved concerned young men with plumes in their hair and white gloves and moustaches: about honour, and the necessity to react – the prerogative of the amoeba. There seemed to be no honour in thought, because thinking was difficult. But it was thinking that had produced the modern weapons that were so complex: and it was these that honour was to come up against.

The superficial story of events leading up to the outbreak of war in August 1914 is one of crossed telegrams and of unalterable railway time-tables. The Austrian Archduke Ferdinand was assassinated on 28 June: the Russians mobilized; the Germans mobilized; messages passed to and fro between Chancelleries and Embassies in such bulk that staffs broke down. Movements of troops towards frontiers that had been started by a word could not be stopped by a word because there had been no words practised to do this. Foreign secretaries and prime ministers wept, because machinery had run away with them. England made no warlike moves until, on 4 August, the Germans invaded Belgium. Such inactivity might or might not have been a fault: in an infantile world, disaster is sometimes averted by a statement of intention.

Julian had seen and had objected to the underlying fantasies leading to war: when war came, he seemed to welome it. It is not clear whether he himself had been defeated by the fantasies that he had once fought, or whether he had come to glimpse that the war might be part of a process of defeating them. Probably, he did not know this himself. Or, he felt both.

Julian was only twenty-six when the war started: he had just made up his mind to get out of the army and to stand for Parliament. So far, in spite of reverses, his life had followed a pattern in which he did not seem to be defeated. But there was perhaps always something in him of the old style which would have welcomed war. He wrote from South Africa in August 1914 –

It must be wonderful to be in England now: I suppose the excitement is beyond all words . . . It reinforces one's failing belief in the Old Flag and the Mother Country and the Heavy Brigade and the Thin Red Line and the Imperial Idea which gets rather shadowy in peace time, don't you think?

The Old Flag and the Mother Country (his use of capital letters shows some shame) were representations of the world of his mother and father – whom he loved and disapproved of, because they dealt in contradictions; and seemed to feel no shame. He could try to get away from them – to South Africa, to Kenya – but that which he was tied to was in his mind. Lovers of the Mother Country – such as himself, such as lovers of his mother – seemed to be people perpetually with their arms out; prisoners, or children in front of sustenance. A country's lovers had not grown up – had not been taught to grow up – by the Mother Country. But in war – one could be close to the mother again – there would be no quarrel!

In the years leading up to 1914 there had been an idealization of death which affluence and technical accomplishment had not altered – perhaps had even exacerbated; a pattern of mind can become more virulent if circumstances mock it. In the nineteenth century there had been the romantic praise of death – 'he hath awakened from the dream of life . . . *We* decay like corpses in a charnel' (Shelley). This had been extended logically at the time of the Great War into a belief such as that expressed by the Dadaists that because death was preferable to life then it was proper not just to die but to kill – in order to be charitable. Europeans had always toyed with this idea: Greek tragedians had repeatedly suggested it – better even than to die young is never to have been born at all. At the back of much of European imagination there seems to have been the hope that men might outwit the fact of death by getting in as it were first: if death was welcomed, it could not have power. This had been one of Ettie's accomplishments.

When Julian and Billy were killed in 1915 this is what her friends insisted on to Ettie – for comfort, but then they held their comfort to be true. 'I feel as if all of us were dead and only they were alive (Sydney Herbert); 'They are in peace: it is only for ourselves that we have to be sorry' (Hugh Cecil). As a step from this, there was the pride that the living took that they had contributed to the dead – 'None of us who give our sons in this war are so much to be pitied as those who have no sons to give' (Lord Grey); 'It was the Civil War Duke of Ormonde who said . . . that he preferred his dead son to any living son in Christendom' (Walter Raleigh). 'I have only one longing – that my son may enter the navy next year and be ready to lay down his life as yours laid their lives down.' There was the idea that in this way the living, especially mothers, could partake of the pleasures of death – this was their comfort. 'There is something very wonderful in motherhood today; we were given our children at a time when they would be ready to fight the good fight . . . and it is given us to know that what we have given of ourselves has done its duty' (Frances Balfour). 'How truly the English Aristocracy has proved itself in these past and glorious days; there has been nothing like it since the French Aristocracy went so gaily to the guillotine' (Katherine Tynan Hinkson). This was what people assured Ettie – that she was almost as lucky as her dead sons – for it was in her name that they had been fighting. 'They were indeed your "jewels" and you have given them' (Ellen Garnett). 'In all that he did he had you on his heart, it was for you he won and wore his honours, it was through you he triumphed to the very end' (Evan Charteris). There was, her friends explained, the Christian pattern for all this – that of Him who 'is asking you to drink of that battered cup which His own mother, the thing dearest to Him upon earth, drained to the very dregs when He willed that she should stand by His cross and see Him die' (Lord Halifax – forgetting the ways in which Christ has so bleakly ignored his mother). There was also the Greek pattern – 'Sometimes one gets a little involved and tangled, even a little doubting, about country, freedom, sacrifice – but were there nothing else to straighten out one's ideas one has only to turn back to Greece and learn again and see all the values adjusted' (Evan Charteris). It was in an ideal world that these were the values that mattered; not in the world of experience. 'It seems that the vital affections are built upon a scale quite other than that of this world and outlast it; like a palace standing out from the waters of a lake or the music which transcends the instrument' (Hilaire Belloc); 'I cannot express how passionately I admire and reverence those who give themselves to suffer or die in a good cause; it is just the finest thing except martyrdom so to die' (Hugh Cecil). With the weight of all this tradition, was it not reasonable to think that young men were better dead? Better, in that they might not experience the growing up and the confusions of the living?

With ideas about this world in such despair it might indeed seem reasonable to want loved ones to get out – to a world where suffering had a simple point, where happiness could be dreamed of and self-indulgence need not lead to guilt. A mother could, by death, seem to possess her sons for ever; in what other way could a mother's love seem fruitful? In 1918 Ettie wrote to Mary Wemyss, who herself had lost two sons – 'As these agonising days go on one can feel *almost* glad that Ego and Ivo and Julian and Billy are safe in the dream of peace'.

Julian had written his book in 1909: in it, he had hoped that men's primitive instincts might be exercised in areas that were primitive – in sport, in relationships with animals – not with sophisticated weapons in war. To act primitively when power was no longer primitive was to court self-destruction. What was required was discrimination between those parts of a man that were childish and those which were grown up. Like this, destruction need not be disastrous.

When five years later the war broke out Julian did not feel there was anything he could do about it – how could he? – it was the world of which he had disapproved that was blowing itself up. He also did not want to escape it – where was there to go? But it is true his feelings were more positive than this. It was characteristic of him perhaps that in the self-destruction of much of what he hated he, as its child, seemed to feel himself part of it: he knew that children do not wholly escape from their parents. And there might even be a pleasure in this; for were not such processes inevitable? Here, at least, was irony. There is a sense in which Julian, in 1914, was acting as, according to a Marxist, a good aristocrat should – he was being an energetic member of his class's self-destruction. Irony is traditionally the prerogative of aristocrats – if not of Marxists. Wagner's old gods stand back and see themselves going down: they even help those who will supplant them. And if this is so – then why not, as part of one's own audience and one's own opera, get pleasure?

Julian loved war. He made no secret of this. 'You were not surprised when you were told he was the only man on either side who did not wish the war was over' (Ronald Knox). His love of war is not explicable simply in terms of his being able at last to free himself from the restraints of the conventions which he hated – though this is how he himself explained it. It seems more to do with an opposite emotion – that for the first time he felt that he had some proper function within a society – within a conventional society doing what a conventional society should – that is, dissolving itself. For European society in 1914 was behaving in some sort of accord with evolutionary theory; having grown sick, and having felt itself sick, not through failure, but through the successful completion of some cycle, it was now seeing to its own breaking-up with a view perhaps to some possible re-arrangement. Human beings were not just behaving like lemmings: they were able to see that they were behaving like lemmings, and so were exhibiting characteristics that might be encouraged afterwards. One of these characteristics might be just the ability to get pleasure from what was inevitable – inevitability being terrible, but often ridiculous.

Julian's love of war is shocking to modern taste. Taste approves of young men who went starry-eyed to war and then were knocked all-of-a-heap by it; who picked up their guns and fired and then were amazed at killing; who did not think that the dead would have so much blood in them. There is comfort in guilt – and in the prolongation of innocence. Julian had no illusions about war: he was not surprised when killing was killing. The war in 1914 was probably unavoidable: Europeans would have gone on till they got it; and when Germans marched through Belgium it would not have been easy for Englishmen to stay aloof. This was important: if there is to be any point let alone pleasure in violence (this is indeed shocking) the occasion has to be fitting. Julian got excitement from war probably for the same primitive reasons as those of the conventionalists who for the most part he hated: but part of his pleasure was in war's ironies.

Young men who wrote poetry about the war often were in close relationship with their mothers: it was this that gave them their desire for sacrifice (mother has done so much for me) and their heroism (what can I do for her?) and their acceptance of death (what better gift than my sacrifice being eternal?). Most poets were trapped within their need to

make, by their poetry, death acceptable. They were going back to childhood; and what further consummations can there be – other than poetry
and sacrifice – in the love between a son and a mother? This love was
traditionally held to be the highest; perhaps because it was inescapable.

Julian wrote his best poem about war; it was a poem full of joy, such as
was acceptable to his mother. But it was also representative of himself,
because it was written not in fantasy but from experience. 'If anyone else
had written "Into Battle" you would have said that it was an astonishing
poem but that the man couldn't really have felt like that; in Julian, you
knew it was sincere' (Ronald Knox). This was Julian's other achievement –
to be not only ironic, but sincere. What way other than that of irony was
there of being sincere – in a great war, and thinking it proper?

The pattern of mind which can see both that it is the child of a society
that is destroying itself and, growing up, because it sees that all this may
be worthwhile, enjoys itself – this state of mind is difficult to comprehend
in a society that still believes, against all the evidence, that what is
destructive can be neither profitable nor enjoyable; and when it is, has to
call these experiences by other names – sacrifice, duty. But it is the ironic
state of mind that fits the facts. The childish parts of men land Europeans
in wars and the childish parts of people, including Julian, for the most
part enjoy them: but what is not childish is that part of men that observes
this. It is unlikely that wars can be fought without some childishness:
for growing-up, what is required is recognition of complexity.

To feel oneself within the processes of destruction and yet to love life
because these are the processes out of which life continually comes – this is
dangerous, because destruction can thus be encouraged. This was Ettie's
predicament: she wanted to make war holy. But then Ettie, ashamed of
childish feelings, had to call war by grandiose names; her dangerousness
was in the delusion. Julian saw war for what it was – its childishness and
terror – and he did not want to describe it otherwise. And so, in spite of
his pleasure, he does not seem an encourager of war; pleasure did not
involve approbation. That he did not seem to want to go on living was
perhaps the sign of Ettie's victory over him: the growing-up part of him
had been too much alone. As a dying hero he could be a child in his
mother's arms again. But part of him would still be amused by this. He
could see both the scene and himself in relation to it: this 'he' that saw
being neither victim nor killer; but codifier, artist.

❦ THIRTY ❦

Julian's regiment left South Africa on 25 August; there were rumours
that they might be going to India or Egypt; they arrived in England on
10 September. In the six weeks of war the Germans had advanced almost
to Paris, had been defeated at the battle of the Marne, and had retreated
to the area near the Belgian and French borders where the Western Front
was to be dug in for the next four years.

On the day on which war had been declared, 4 August, Ettie had dined
with John Revelstoke and Arthur Balfour, and Lord Kitchener had called
in before dinner: he had been told he was to be made Minister for War.
On 7 August Billy went to the War Office and applied for a commission
in the Rifle Brigade. Monica went to the London Hospital and applied
to be taken on as a probationer nurse. During the first month of the war
several of their friends were killed – John Manners, who had played real
tennis with Billy for Oxford; and Percy Wyndham, the son of George
Wyndham.

When Julian arrived in England he went to a camp on Salisbury Plain.
His mother visited him and they spent an afternoon on the downs. In her
Family Journal Ettie quoted a letter as if from Julian the next day –
'Did you love our day on the hill tops? You looked so exactly the same as
when I was a likka boy. I have never been so much in love with any woman
as I have been and always shall be with you'. This letter is not amongst
the other carefully preserved letters of Julian's, and it is less in Julian's
style than in the style of the insertions which Ettie was accustomed to
make in his letters in her Journal. But faced with war, it is possible that
he might have said something of the kind to her.

He went to London to buy equipment. There he ran into Patrick Shaw
Stewart, who was just off to Belgium with the Naval Division, and they
helped each other to pack roaring with laughter. He spent a day at
Panshanger, shooting partridges.

He sailed for France on 6 October. Ettie wrote to Monica: 'the anguish of this – and yet the *uplift*'. The First Royal Dragoons were part of the Third Cavalry Division of the Fourth Army Corps – one of the four Corps comprising the British Expeditionary Force. The Royals were kept behind the lines for two weeks: the Allied and German armies were still trying to outflank each other in moves towards the sea. These were the last battles for four years in which there was some freedom of movement – and a hope that cavalry might be used.

Oct 11th 1914

. . . it's all the best fun one ever dreamed of, and up to now it has only wanted a few shells and a little noise to supply the necessary element of excitement. The uncertainty of it is so good, like a picnic when you don't know where you're going to; and the rush and the hustle of trying to settle things in the whole confusion, unpacking and packing up again, and dumping down men and horses in strange fields or houses or towns, and fighting to get food and water and beds for the men and oneself, when one knows that probably another start will be made long before anything is got. There are really so many things to do at the same moment that one does not bother about things one has forgotten or not done, because there is only time to go on with the actual thing of the moment. And the extraordinary thing is that everything does seem to get done . . .

The people are quite frantic about us and they line the roads giving beer and fruit and cakes to us as we ride by. They shout IP IP WHERRAY and OLAPP (hold up) when a horse stumbles. They have got some of the London motor buses out here carting about supplies and wounded: a great fat London driver passed us the other day and shouted 'Oxford Street, Bank'. The buses have still got all the London playbills and advertisements on them. The roads are chock-a-block with troops and guns and supplies and transport and wounded; and aeroplanes always in the air. It is a wonderfully peaceful looking country . . .

The country was on the French side of Ypres, near the Belgian border, twenty miles from the sea. Julian reported that the comment of one of his corporals was – 'What tires me in this bloody country is Jesus Christ and all his relatives in glass cases at every bloody corner.'

Oct 15th

. . . The guns go on all day and most of the night. Of course it is very hard to follow what is going on; even the squadron leaders know nothing; and one marches and counter marches without end, backwards and forwards, nearer and further, apparently without object. Only the Christian virtue of faith emerges triumphant. It is all the most *wonderful* fun; better fun than one could ever imagine. I hope it goes on a nice long time; but pigsticking will be the only tolerable pursuit after this or one will die of sheer ennui . . .

He asked his mother to send him a raincoat, a map-case, a pipe-lighter, a sou'wester, a compass, torch batteries, field glasses, toothpaste, a hold-all, candles, methylated spirits, and a daily paper – *The Times*, not the *Daily Mail*, which was 'loathsome'. Ettie sent all these: also comforts for his men – cigarettes, tobacco, chocolate, whisky. Parcels and letters arrived promptly, even in the confusion.

Oct 17th
. . . It's still marching and counter marching with everything in the entirely vague and non-committal stage of the start. Only patrol and outpost fighting. We've knocked into one or two of their patrols – only 2 horses and one man of ours wounded. None of us know anything. The Germans seem to be all over the place, and our different allied armies all mixed up. We are going to clear up a forest tomorrow where there are Germans and three different varieties of allies so we hope for a fair mixed bag. The worst of this is that when one is coming in or going out on advance patrols in the fog and rain one is just as likely to get shot by the allied forces as by the Huns. This has happened rather too often . . . It's a great war whatever. Isn't it luck for me to have been born so as to be just the right age and just in the right place – not too high up to be worried – to enjoy it the most?

This was still war as people had dreamed about it – shooting without much bloodshed. But already there is the question – what sort of lives could such young men as Julian have had, that this life should seem so 'real' and so enjoyable?

18th. We are living like fighting cocks. The Machonochie tin ration (meat and vegetables) is delicious when you heat it up. And they give us very good bread and butter in the houses, and also their beds and everything, without worrying much whether they get paid or not. The only thing is that we are eating and resting too much and doing too little just at present. It has been the same lately with all the other cavalry fellows who have been out here all the time. Most of them have got very fat and lazy . . .

The first Battle of Ypres began the next day, 19 October, and was the end of the two sides' efforts to outflank each other to the sea. They turned and met: the British and French forces were outnumbered at first by two to one. Julian's cavalry division was brought in as infantry and fought near the road to Menin, south-west of Ypres.

Oct 24th 1914

We've had it pretty hot this last day or two in the *trenches*. We take to it like ducks to water and dig much better trenches than the infantry, and far quicker. We're all awfully well, except those who have stopped something. We've been fighting night and day – first rest today – for about four days. The worst of it is *no* sleep practically. I can't tell you how wonderful all our men were, going straight for the first time into a fierce fire. They surpassed my utmost expectations. I've never been so fit or nearly so happy in my life before; I adore the fighting and the continual interest which compensates for every disadvantage. We've only had cavalry these days in this part of the line and I imagine it's rather critical; but all goes well. The German guns are terribly good, they have spies everywhere, signalling to them by night and day; and they pick you up wherever you go . . . *Oct. 27th.* We've been in the trenches for two days and nights since I started this . . . I've got my half troop, 12 men, in a trench in a root field with the rest of the squadron about 100 yards each side of us and a farm half knocked down by shells just behind. We get our rations sent up once a day in the dark and two men creep out to cook us tea in the quiet intervals. Tea is the great mainstay on service, as it was on manoeuvres and treks. The men are *splendid* and as happy as schoolboys. We've got plenty of straw in the bottom of the trench, which is better than any feather-bed. We only had one bad night, when it pelted with rain for 6 hrs. It's not *very* cold yet, and we've had 2 or 3 fine days . . .

Our first day's real close-up fighting was Monday 19th. We cavalry went on about a day and a half in front of the infantry. We got into a village and our advance patrols started fighting hard, with a certain amount of fire from everywhere in front of us. Our advanced patrols gained the first groups of houses, and we joined them. Firing came from a farm in front of us, and then a man came out and waved a white flag. I yelled '200 – white flag – rapid fire'; but Hardwick stopped me shooting. Then the squadron advanced across the root fields towards the farm (dismounted, in open order) and they opened a sharp fire on us from the farm and the next fields. We took three prisoners in the roots, and retired to the houses again. That was our first experience of them – the white flag dodge. We lost 2 men and 1 wounded.

Then I got leave to make a dash across a field for another farm, where they were sniping at us. I could only get half way, my sergeant was killed, and my corporal hit. We lay down; luckily it was high roots and we were out of sight. But they had fairly got our range and the bullets kept knocking the dirt into one's face and all around. We just lay doggo for about ½ hour, and then the firing slackened, and we crawled back to the houses and the rest of the squadron.

I *was* pleased with my troop under bad fire. They used the most filthy language, talking quite quietly and laughing all the time, even after men were knocked over within a yard of them. I longed to be able to say that I liked it, after all one has heard of being under fire for the first time. But it's bloody. I pretended to myself for a bit that I liked it; but it was no good; it only made one careless and unwatchful and self-absorbed. But when one acknowledged to oneself that it *was* bloody, one became all right again, and cool.

After the firing had slackened we advanced again a bit into the next group of houses which were the edge of the village proper. I can't tell you how *muddling* it is. We did not know which was our front: we did not know whether our own troops had come round us on the flanks or whether they had stopped behind and were firing into us. And besides, a lot of German snipers were left in the houses we had come through, and every now and then bullets came singing by from God knows where. Four of us were talking and laughing in the road when about a dozen bullets came with a whistle. We all dived for the nearest door, which happened to be a lav, and fell over each other, *yelling* with laughter . . .

I *adore* war. It is like a big picnic without the objectlessness of a picnic. I've never been so well or so happy. No one grumbles at one for being dirty. I've only had my boots off once in the last ten days, and only washed twice. We are up and standing to our rifles by 5 a.m. when doing this infantry work, and saddled up by 4.30 a.m. when with our horses. Our poor horses don't get their saddles off when we are in the trenches.

The wretched inhabitants here have got practically no food left. It is miserable to see them leaving their houses and trekking away with great bundles and children in their hands. And the dogs and cats left in the deserted villages are piteous.

I got today your letter of the 23rd; also Dad's and Casie's. Yes, you are a really great War Mother. All emotion is fatal now . . .

Julian's love of war he himself explained in terms of his being allowed to be dirty: he meant this physically, but psychologically it was relevant too. For the first time a generation brought up to be clean and bright and obedient could, without guilt, be fierce and babyish and vile. Such behaviour had been forbidden them when such attitudes might have been natural: the relief when it was allowed them later was overwhelming.

And with an enemy in front, all childish rage and violence could be projected. This was the joy – there were no more self-inflicted wounds:

with one's own side there could just be laughter. The relief was orgiastic: there could be hurting without the responsibility of hurting.

Julian's men felt the 'reality' of war too: this curse was not just aristocratic. It was evidence of the falsities over the whole range of society. War was a freedom both from society and from social fantasies: it was one area in which there were standards of excellence other than those of snobbishness, bitchiness or money.

Julian did not take part in any of the massed mechanical slaughters that were later characteristic of the war. In the conditions of 1914 and early 1915 he seemed to be able to see war as a matter of almost personal performance. He thought the Germans had to be beaten, but he did not dream of a better world. He seemed to feel that in war he could at last do what was expected of him without being false. He became something of a legend. Billy's Colonel wrote of him 'Julian has set an example of light-hearted courage which is famous all through the Army in France.' He seemed to walk about battlefields as if on his own; like one of the army's visionary angels.

The long and happy descriptions of war he wrote to his mother seemed to be saying – Here I am; is not this the hero that you wanted? Also – If I tell you enough, will this still be the hero that you want? This is what I want: and if heroes die, then –

Then, at the same time, he could both be received into, and have made a nonsense of, the world in which he had been brought up by his mother.

There was no language in 1914 in which people could talk about these things: they could demonstrate them through fighting and disaster. A child, to be loved, sometimes has to say – Look, you have killed me. Only if it grasps some of the connections, does it not want to die.

Julian had learned to talk with humour about his personal predicaments. In war, he was up against an almost universal simplicity.

It was when he was not fighting that he was confused. The Royals were taken out of the line for a time during the first battle of Ypres and Julian lamented 'It is horrible to think one might as well be in Piccadilly Circus for all the good one is doing and much better for all the pleasure one is getting'. But then, again, he was from time to time more human –

We've been doing all shelled trench work lately and it's horrible: you just lie there, hunched up, and all day long the shells burst – just outside the trench if you're lucky and just inside if you're unlucky. Anyhow the noise is appalling and one's head is rocking with it by the end of the day . . . one's nerves are really absolutely beaten down. I can understand now why our infantry *have* to retreat sometimes – a sight which came as a shock to one at first, after having been brought up in the belief that the English infantry cannot retreat.

And –

We took a German officer and some men prisoners in a wood the other day. I felt hatred for them, after our dead, and as the officer came by I scowled at him – and the men were cursing at them. The officer looked me in the face and saluted me as I passed; and I've never seen a man look so proud and resolute and smart and confident in his hour of bitterness. He made me feel terribly ashamed.

His view of other people's attitudes to the war became confused: 'One hears that the Germans are retiring in train-loads, and the next minute there is a vicious night attack'. 'Can you make out why the people in England (and the generals here) say the war is going to end directly? I can't for the life of me make out how or why, can you?' Sorrow for the local people became inescapable; 'they are lucky however not to have been eaten up by the Germans or shelled down or burned by either side'. He wanted to get back into the fight where emotions would be simple again. 'The fighting excitement revitalises everything – every sight and word and action. One loves one's fellow man so much more when one is bent on killing him.'

Julian said things that other people might have felt but did not say. It is the unspoken fact of war that, simply, people enjoy killing. By this they know where they are – by other people being dead – even by the chance of themselves being killed or wounded. By this – by a placement in life or death – people are given identity. This is not to say that this is not deplorable.

Before the end of the battle of Ypres the Royals were back in the trenches and Julian performed the feat that was to win him the conventional renown that had been required of him and that now he wanted. His description of this feat, like that of his famous boxing match in Johannesburg, is almost unique in his writings because it is somewhat platitudinous.

We had been awfully worried by their snipers all along; and I had always been asking for leave to go out and have a try myself. Well on Tuesday 16th, day before yesterday, they gave me leave. Only after great difficulty. They told me to take a section with me, and I said I would sooner cut my throat and have done with it. So they let me go alone. Off I crawled, through the sodden clay and branches, going about a yard a minute and listening and looking as I thought it was not possible to look and listen. I went out to the right of our lines, where the 10th were and where the Germans were nearest. I took about 30 minutes to do 30 yards. Then I saw the Hun trench, and I waited for a long time, but could see or hear nothing. It was about 10 yards from me. Then I heard some Germans talking, and saw one put his head up over some bushes about 10 yards behind the trench. I could not get a shot at him; I was too low down; and of course I couldn't get up. So I crawled on again very slowly to the parapet of their trench. It was very exciting. I was not *sure* that there might not have been someone there – or a little further along the trench. I peered through their loophole, and saw nobody in the trench. Then the German behind put his head up again. He was laughing and talking. I saw his teeth glisten against my foresight, and I pulled the trigger very steady. He just gave a grunt and crumpled up. The others got up and whispered to each other. I don't know which were most frightened, they or me. I think there were 4 or 5 of them. They couldn't place the shot. I was flat behind their parapet and hidden. I just had the nerve not to move a muscle and stay there. My heart was fairly hammering. They did not come forward, and I could not see them, as they were behind some bushes and trees. So I crept back, inch by inch.

I went out again in the afternoon, in front of our bit of the line. About 60 yards off I found their trench again. I waited there for an hour, but saw nobody. Then I went back, because I did not want to get inside some of their patrols . . .

The next day just before dawn I crawled out there again and found the trench empty. Then a single German came through the wood towards the trench. I saw him 50 yards off. He was coming along upright quite carelessly, making a great noise. I let him get within 25 yards and then shot him in the heart. He never made a sound. Nothing for 10 minutes; then there was noise and talking and a lot of them came along through the wood behind the trench about 40 yards from me. I counted about 20, and there were more coming. They halted in front, and I picked out the one I thought was the officer or sergeant. He stood facing the other way, and I had a steady shot at him behind the shoulders. He went down, and that was all I saw – I went back at a sort of galloping crawl to our lines and sent a message to the 10th that the Germans were moving up their way in some numbers. Half an hour later they attacked the 10th and our right in massed formation, advancing slowly to within 10 yards of the trenches. We simply mowed them down; it was rather horrible . . .

They have made quite a ridiculous fuss about my stalking and getting the message through; I believe they are going to send me up to the General, and all sorts. It was only up to someone to do it – instead of leaving it all to the Germans and losing 2 officers a day through snipers. All our men have started it now, it's the popular amusement . . .

For this exploit – the style of which, like that of its description, is almost Homeric – Julian was given the DSO. He made two entries in his game book – after that of '105 partridges' at Panshanger in early October – 'November 16th: 1 Pomeranian'; – 'November 17th: 2 Pomeranians'.

❧ THIRTY–ONE ❧

In England Billy was training with the Rifle Brigade, Ivo was with the Eton Volunteers, Monica was nursing at the London Hospital, Ettie was organizing working parties for the Maidenhead Red Cross, and Willy had started the Taplow Defence Force and was later to become President of the Volunteer Defence Force for the whole country.

Monica, just twenty-one, having been brought up in a world in which it was held that no girl could be in intimate relationship with a man for five minutes, suddenly found herself, with the approval of that world, dealing with masculine pain and dirt and death for fourteen hours a day: and for a while –

a nausea for the whole thing quite overcame me . . . I felt strongly that it would be far better to let people just die, either slowly or quickly, than that they should be submitted to all this, or that other living people should be called on to give the treatments. I even felt resentful that I had not been warned about it by my friends who knew, and I felt I could not think in the same way about anyone I knew who had nursed.

Monica later became an expert and much-loved nurse, as letters from patients to her testify. She, too, came to look back on the war as a time in which for once she had been in contact with reality.

Ettie continued her correspondence with Patrick Shaw Stewart, who had returned from Belgium and was in training with the Naval Division for the expedition to the Dardanelles which took place the following year. Ettie was from time to time still in Waiting to the Queen. She kept Patrick Shaw Stewart up to date with gossip about friends in and around London –

. . . I hear a sad account of Windsor Castle 'on the water wagon'. Tempers were but little improved by temperance, and a crêpe wreath was fastened to the cellar door and Charlie Cust fainted the first night after dinner; the only cheerful person being Margot, who took copious swigs out of a medicine bottle and talked a great deal, but no one else spoke except to contradict her.

Talking of Margot, you know they were playing the game one night of who they would like to see best come into the room and Nancy Cunard said in that high voice 'Lady Cunard *dead*'. So Margot sent for her to lecture her but of course Nancy was sharp enough to absolutely deny the *mot* and Margot was left in an abject situation of apology . . .

I asked Bron what he thought Maurice really did at the front and he said 'Oh I suppose he is just led about with the Flying Corps like the Welsh Fusiliers' goat' which I suspect is exactly the state of the case . . .

Maurice Baring, at the age of forty, had gone out to France as a staff officer with the Royal Flying Corps; Evan Charteris, at forty-nine, joined him. Bron Lucas, thirty-nine, was in 1914 Minister for Agriculture with a seat in the Cabinet; he joined the Flying Corps in 1915 and became a pilot and was killed over the German lines the following year.

In the winter of 1914–15 Ettie sent some of Julian's letters to the Editor of *The Times*, who printed them as an anonymous young cavalry officer's impressions of the front. Julian's sentence – 'Isn't it luck for me to have been born so as to be just the right age and just in the right place?' was quoted at the head of a *Times* leading article, which declared on the strength of it that the trivialities of recent politics now seemed to have been left behind, and 'conscience and faith has suddenly and splendidly revived'.

Ettie must have repeated to Julian her stories about life at Windsor Castle because he commented 'I loved your story about Nancy Cunard, is she a good girl? . . . Margot seems to be in terrific form; I should think she is just one of the people who are at their best in war, and try to raise a state of war even in peace time, just to help themselves out'.

He came home for three days' leave at the end of November, and again in December and January. The fighting around Ypres had settled down. He saw Marjorie Anglesey in London; she now had a baby: he had written to her – 'It must be a wonderful thing having something all your own like that; more your own than a greyhound or a racing horse, which is the nearest I can get to it as a standard of comparison'. The news of his DSO came through and there were telegrams of congratulation. When he went back to France at the end of January, he took with him his three greyhounds.

He had been offered a job as ADC to General Pulteney, who had been one of Ettie's admirers in her 'golden' year of 1891 when the horses of young Guards officers at Windsor had been said automatically to turn their heads towards Taplow. Julian refused the job, saying his regiment was short of officers. However during the winter the cavalry were used only once in the line and he got bored: 'everyone here seems to think we are going to wait here till the spring . . . if this is so, I quite agree with you that the ratepayers ought to raise tallywhack and tandem.' But he was put in charge of the training of the regimental Scouts, which cheered him.

Ettie supplied him and the Scouts with a map-measurer, a magnifying glass, a compass, magnesium wire, torches, mittens and warm under-clothes. Willy sent out fishing lines and reels, to which snipers could attach themselves and so send back messages to their own front line. The staffs at Taplow and Panshanger contributed to a fund which was used to send out cigarettes and cakes. When the Scouts were trained and he had nothing further to do Julian went coursing with his dogs, and tried to organize steeplechases. 'It feels so wrong to be comfortable when others are in the trenches.' One night there was an alarm and the regiment moved towards the front and he got 'a "right" feeling again'. He was promoted Captain. He wrote 'I hate being a Captain; I would like to be either God or a General or a Lieutenant. I had *such* fun as a Lieutenant'.

Early in 1915 and still bored ('one would not mind waiting in the least if only one could feel sure that there would be a good *fat* piece of work at the end') he went to a boxing exhibition in a local town hall and there he issued a challenge, as was his custom, to all comers. The challenge was accepted by –

a *very* large private in the Army Service Corps . . . imagine my chagrin and horror! Especially when I was told that the man was a boxing pro . . . He closed my left eye right up in the first round and they wanted to stop the fight because it was bad. But I told them I was right, and in the second round I caught him a beauty and they had to carry him out to hospital . . . My eye is all right now, and a glorious colour – purple shot with green – and the man is all right too.

The regiment went to Ypres for a few days.

Every other house has a shell through it, and they put about 20 shells through it every night while we were there. It was the most lovely town in the world before they battered it . . . But the people, the townspeople, were as happy as grigs; charging 500% for everything and enjoying themselves hugely. Many of them had stopped in the town the whole time. The girls – some of them really lovely – were splendid about it. One of them said to me 'Oui, c'est terrible la guerre! Maar ek het ne jamais en autant de plaisir que pendant cette guerre!'

Then we went into the trenches for 5 days, in our same old wood where I got into the Bosches. Very good trenches, with the German trenches 15 yards off at one or two places and generally about 50 yards. The drawback to our trenches was that in odd places in the parapet there were buried very shallow poor dead Huns and French and English whose bodies were periodically resurrected by the rain and bombs and bullets. We took over at dead of night as usual. We had a quiet time; but every night the Germans dug and dug and every morning one saw a new German trench a little nearer our own. We did nothing – but I will reserve criticism till I see you again. One afternoon they fired five bombs at us out of a trench mortar. I was off duty and asleep when the first arrived. I did not know what in Hell it was. I rushed out with your mackintosh bed-roll round my feet like a man in a sack race, and found the men all roaring with laughter because the bomb had landed near old Sammy Smith's dug-out and had pretty near buried old Sammy. Old Sammy was pulled out by the feet uninjured except in self respect. Then they all shouted 'Look out boys' and we looked up and saw the next bomb coming: that just missed the trench too. Then I got our rifle bombs and started shooting back at them. They sent 3 more close to the trench but not into it. I shot three at them. I must have been on my lucky day because I burst all three slap into their trench, and then they stopped and left us in peace ever afterwards . . . The nights were the best, flares going up from each side all the time and lighting up the pines like a wood in a pantomime . . . It rained and snowed and froze, but we had whale-oil for our feet, which is a great thing. It was very good to get an experience of this sedentary non-aggressive fighting; but what nonsense it is, I want to talk to you about it . . .

You should have seen our men setting out from here for the trenches – absolutely radiant with excitement and joy to be getting back to the fight . . .

I've got a real 'Spring Running' on me. I wish they'd let me go and fight the Bosches on my own . . .

The 'nonsense' about which Julian wanted to talk to his mother was the realization, probably, that at the back of war was not so much a desire to get it over – to achieve the aims of politicians – but a liking by many people, himself included, of war's rituals.

He asked his father to send out his .303 rifle with a telescopic sight; 'it is just what one wants for shooting at their loopholes'. He tried to get

himself involved in a scheme for transferring officers from the cavalry to
the infantry, but this fell through. He asked his mother to send out two
footballs. He saw in the *Daily Telegraph* his description of his sniping
exploit reputedly written by 'a Canadian officer': he cut it out and sent it
to Ettie asking 'Mummy, who is your Canadian friend?' Ettie did not
reply and this irked him: he repeated – 'Did you send the "Canadian
Officer's" letter to the *Daily Telegraph*? Did you get that letter of mine
enclosing it?'

The cigarettes and food that were being sent out to him were not getting
through and Julian discovered they were being held up by the Colonel.

He seems rather to resent the men getting things at all, or else why should he
stack them in a room? And why should he take up the attitude 'they've got
plenty of things and they should not have more'? (O Christ, I hope this letter is
not opened by the regimental censor.)

He wrote a poem –

PRAYER FOR THOSE ON THE STAFF

Fighting in mud, we turn to Thee
    In these dread times of battle, Lord,
To keep us safe, if so may be,
    From shrapnel, snipers, shell and sword.

Yet not on us – (for we are men
    Of meaner clay, who fight in clay) –
But on the Staff, the Upper Ten,
    Depends the issue of the day.

The Staff is working with its brains
    While we are sitting in the trench;
The Staff the universe ordains
    (Subject to Thee and General French).

God, help the Staff – especially
    The young ones, many of them sprung
From our high aristocracy;
    Their task is hard, and they are young.

O Lord, who mad'st all things to be
    And madest some things very good
Please keep the extra ADC.
    From horrid scenes, and sights of blood . . .

He was visited by the Duchess of Sutherland, who ran a hospital in France, and who took him out in her car with her entourage –

all the picture-postcard people were there . . . apparently they go anywhere and do anything, which I suppose is possible when anybody has got that absolutely natural and unconscious amount of nerve, cheek and face . . . I spent the day with them; it was rather amusing . . . Millie looking *too* lovely . . . and tremendously in love with Fitz, who treats her in rather a cavalier manner. Fitz rather too too, don't you think? . . .

His impatience was going into mockery again, as it had done at times at Oxford and in South Africa:

I was talking to a man here the other day who really seems to know about such things and he said the great idea was to disguise the Cavalry Corps as reindeer and to send them up by Norway.

Philip said we should get so much quicker to the Rhine by train, when also the restaurant cars would do away with the difficulty about supplies.

Moggie's good letter arrived about the new guinea-pigs – 'two white ones and a black, that makes seven' – she ought to be in the Army Intelligence department for estimating German casualties.

He got himself involved in another boxing match –

We had a boxing show on Saturday and another ASC volunteered to fight me, called Hay. When we went into the ring and stripped, in deadly silence, a loud voice suddenly came from the back of the room from one of his friends –
                    'PORE OLD 'AY!'
It was rather a good omen for me, and I landed him a terrific thump with my second punch, which shook him up so that I outed him in the second round. The same voice came again –
                    'OO'S THE NEXT?'
I wish I could find out who it was; he would be a very good man to hire as a bravo to give me moral support whenever I fight.

There were rumours of a big attack in the spring; but the papers told lies ('don't you hate the hysteria of the newspapers, it makes me mad') and the talk of soldiers seemed mostly of fantasy. 'I don't think myself that we shall ever make a hole through their line – simply because of the impossibility of attack under these conditions. If they could not get

through our line at Wipers, how shall we get through theirs now?' Also –
'I wish I could have any optimism about your Dardanelles theory; or did
you only put that forward as "argumentum ad hominem"?'

The Dardanelles expedition sailed in March 1915; it was an attempt
to get round the impasse in France by going so far behind it as to be almost
back at the walls of Troy. Patrick Shaw Stewart sailed with Charles Lister
and Rupert Brooke: they had all been classical scholars; Patrick Shaw
Stewart wrote to Billy on the journey out of – 'the fun of cruising about
among these ridiculous classic scenes . . . redolent of thyme and balsam
and thickly covered with Theocritan lizards and Homeric-hymnary
tortoises'. They hung about the Islands from which the myths of their
education had sprung: Rupert Brooke died of a blood infection before they
landed on the Turkish coast. Patrick Shaw Stewart was in the fighting at
Gallipoli: during a period of rest, he wrote –

> I saw a man this morning
>   Who did not wish to die;
> I ask, and cannot answer
>   If otherwise wish I . . .
>
> Oh hell of ships and cities,
>   Hell of men like me;
> Fatal second Helen,
>   Why must I follow thee?
>
> Achilles came to Troyland
>   And I to Chersonese;
> He turned from wrath to battle
>   And I from three days' peace.
>
> Was it so hard, Achilles?
>   So very hard to die?
> Thou knowest and I know not –
>   So much the happier I.
>
> I will go back this morning
>   From Imbros over the sea;
> Stand in the trench, Achilles,
>   Flame-capped, and shout for me.

Patrick Shaw Stewart becomes a greatly sympathetic figure in the war: he lived longer than most of his contemporaries from Eton and Oxford: he would have wanted to live, having no quarrel with the society around him. He continued to write to Ettie letters which were now grave and gentle; letting her know that he loved her. In 1915, after both Julian and Billy had been killed, he wrote 'Darling, if I could only give up my life to you and be a thousandth part of what you have lost'. About Julian he wrote – 'His physical splendour was so great . . . He was the most magnificent human thing I have ever seen'. Patrick Shaw Stewart survived Gallipoli, fought in France, and was killed there at the end of 1917.

Charles Lister, the other of Julian's friends from Eton and Oxford who had played a large part in his life, was wounded three times at Gallipoli and died after the third wound in August 1915. He was recovering from the second when he heard of Julian's death. He wrote to Ettie from the Blue Sisters Convent in Malta –

Julian in his search for truth and in his search for what he believed to be his true Self caused himself no end of worry and unhappiness . . . Surely the Lady he sought with such tireless faith, the Lady for whom he did and dared so much on lonely paths, will now reward him?

❦ THIRTY–TWO ❦

Julian began to keep a diary in 1915 – a small pocket-book in which he wrote spasmodically. This is his only piece of writing that has survived which was not written to be seen by others. It shows a more gentle (and probably truer) attitude to war than the one he showed to his mother.

February 6th. Funny how tired the war feeling and the sound of guns makes one. Nerves? No, just strain of excitement . . .

Sunday 7th. Very hot day for me in Ypres. All these people take Free Love as a matter of course and habit. The daughter says – Ask mother if she will give us a bed . . .

Friday 12th. Thrush singing in wood every morning. Poor mating season. Cat along our trenches at night. Lucky so far.

Saturday 13th. Huns dug new trench last night. They have now got about 4 diff. lines of trench. Hear our billets last week in Ypres were shelled last night with 20 casualties to 1 L.G. who are in them now. Hope I get a chance to do some damage to the Huns before I get killed in some stray way like that.

Monday 15th. Wonderful to get back to rest out of bullets. Bath, 7 days beard off. Even five days (not fighting) a great strain. Even the moderate Estaminet civilization a wonderful change. People who like being dirty best like being clean best. Although I like trenches, I love getting back. Slept 9 a.m.– 6 p.m.

NB Night when I heard noise of bomb dropping on top of dug-out. Petrified. Lost self-control – lay still, clenching my hands, for 20 secs. Asked what it was. 'Rum jar thrown away'.

NB Germans only hold front line trenches with 2 men and a boy, snipers and machine guns. Best way. Can avoid shells – *if* we ever shell them. Means less casualties than us when they are not attacking, in ordinary trench warfare.

Wednesday 24th. Rode over to Lynde with the dogs and had a run after a hare which got up very wide and beat them.

Tuesday 9th March. In evening news arrived that we are to stand in readiness during attack by British near La Bassée.

Thursday 11th. Marched to La Motte and waited there till late afternoon. News that the La Bassée attack is going well but 2000 casualties yesterday. Filthy dull cold day on edge of wood. Coffee and omelette in little farm. In evening marched on through Merville.

Friday 12th. Standing to all day. News of 100 prisoners in a.m.: 600, p.m. Saw about 30 marched along road into Merville. News that attack goes well. Lovely sunny morning. Rumour that we have taken La Bassée. Subsequently confirmed that we have not taken La B. and 4,000 casualties. Bad to wait doing nothing while all friends killed.

In letters to his mother Julian kept up jauntiness and propriety: 'I *do* love the warm spring brown of the trees, don't you?' 'We have had such a *boiling* hot spring week, with all the birds shouting.' And – 'We have moved billets again but only a little way into rather a good village but off the hill where we were before . . . I am billeted with a *lovely* girl (and her Mother) and we sit solemnly for hours (with the Mother) kicking each other under the table.'

In April 1915 he went to Paris on leave – his first visit. It was a revelation of what life could be – a life supported, not strangled, by convention.

Paris! I can't imagine how I have lived so long without being there. I was absolutely fascinated by the *whole* thing. I had four divine spring days there. Isn't it gloriously light and gay and beautiful? The view from the Arc de Triomphe down the Champs Elysées is as good as anything in the world, isn't it? I loved Versailles too, but not frightfully: I think it is just a little blatant, just a little vulgar in its 'grand-seigneur'ishness. What do you think? What I liked most about Paris was the light-heartedness of it all, the complete joie-de-vivre of the place and the people. They are so much lighter of heart than anything of ours, and really much more natural. And such *artists* in fun.

Isn't the Sunday crowd in the Jardins des Tuileries good, walking about and watching each other and enjoying each other? Aren't the Revues witty and amusing and unlike ours? And the tremendous tension of war running through all the gaiety and throwing it into relief. I saw a bit of everything – 'igh society, and the artists, and the racing set (not the Lord Derbys, but the real racing push); the boxers too, and the nuts, and the actresses, and the mannequins, and all the different very strictly defined classes of girls all in their own particular places . . .

It was the biggest experience of New Things I've ever had in my life, bigger than India, because it's more like our things and more comparable – but really how much further removed from anything of ours!

While he was in Paris he met a girl who wrote to him c/o the Ritz Hotel –

Mercredi

21 Avril 15

Petit Ami,

   Voila deux fois que je telephone et vous etes absent. Quand partez vous? Dites le moi, et si vous le voulez on pourrait diner ce soir ensemble.

Bons baisers

Peggy

This letter was found in Julian's wallet when he was wounded: also a photograph of Peggy, a round-faced girl with fair hair. The photograph had an inscription – 'A un brave Anglais. Peggy. 20.4.15. Souvenir'.

Also in Julian's wallet was a photograph of another round-faced girl, on a horse, jumping a post-and-rails – from the look of the landscape, probably in South Africa.

The vision that Julian had of Paris a month before his death was one in which he might have lived if he had been able to carry out his wish to be an artist: if he had not been mocked, nor listened to mockery. He left Paris on 21 April: he did not have dinner with Peggy. On his way back to the front he called in briefly on his sister Monica who was now nursing at Wimereux near Boulogne – 'I've never seen her looking so well and radiant and *pretty* . . . She was so good with the wounded Tommies who all seem to *love* her; she was just exactly "right there" with them'. Then he rejoined his regiment.

On 22 April, the first gas attack in war was launched by the Germans north of Ypres: the French, taken by surprise, fled. For a month there were the attacks and the counter-attacks of the Second Battle of Ypres: the Germans continued to use gas against the British and the Canadians; but, as the soldiers became accustomed to it, with less effect. For a time they only had improvised protection – handkerchiefs and linen soaked in liquid – before gas-masks were issued. Ettie sent out makeshift masks: Harriet, Julian's old nurserymaid, became skilled at making them. Monica wrote of her hospital – 'The soldiers came pouring in with discoloured darkened faces gasping painfully for breath and some of them burned and blinded . . . There were patients in every bed and lying on the floor too, on stretchers, wherever it was possible to put them'.

In the Second Battle of Ypres the Germans tried to dislodge the British and Canadians and French by gas and then to break up the counter-attacks by enormous weight of artillery fire; they had far more guns and shells than the Allies. Within the salient east of Ypres which the Allies had won the previous autumn – a semi-circle of about four miles' radius – there were British casualties within a month of over 2,000 officers and 50,000 other ranks with 10,500 dead; German losses were 860 officers and 34,000 other ranks.

On 24 April, after the second gas attack, Julian's regiment moved closer to the front. Julian wrote in his diary –

Saturday 24th. Moved off 10 a.m. and marched to place E of Poperinghe. Lots of French troops moving up. Turcos in motors, rough men, cheered by our troops. Tremendous choc-a-bloc on roads. We had moved without our Echelon B and so without our rations. Men had no rations with them when we started yesterday (no time or means of carrying them) and none today, and no prospect of getting them apparently. Back to billets at Boeschoote 10.30 p.m. Bitterly cold these first 2 days: then, warm and lovely.

Sunday 25th. Rations at last arrived. Moved at 9.30 to field S of Poperinghe. Waited – moved on in afternoon N.W. of Poperinghe. Went into billets at Ourkerke Houtkerke. Refugees flying on all the roads. Slept in barn, men in field.

Monday 26th. Stood to 5.30 a.m. and moved to Brigade rendezvous soon after 6. Waited there till 10 a.m. and moved to field S.W. of Poperinghe. Waited till 11 p.m. Tremendous gunning. News good and bad. Looks as if they must get Ypres. Shells into Poperinghe. We went up 2 miles on the horses, tied them up, left one man to 4 and walked through Pop to Vlamertinghe, arriving 2 a.m. Slept in loft 3 a.m. and men in barn of factory.

Tuesday 27th. Slept till 8. All sorts in this house: Canadians, Yeomanry, Scots Greys, and us. Quiet morning. Shells started 5 p.m. About 2 dozen. Stampede of Greys' horses in field next road. 12 killed. 2 men – Greys in trenches. Men wonderful. Collected horses and moved them all down road. Wagons, wounded, galloping, refugees running and crying, man knocked 10 yards by loose Grey horse. Our men collected, waited quietly outside factory. Road scene amusing. Battledore and shuttlecock between Pop and Vlam. French supply column coming up. English mule jibbed. French white horse bit him, and he ran away. Aeroplane bomb into garden hit 2 Canadians. 2 of our men hit by shell. Mil police gallop back, walk forward. Turned out about 9 p.m. to go and help Turcos on Iser. But as you were after $\frac{1}{4}$ hour.

Wednesday 28th. Rodgered last night. Quiet day. No shelling. 12 noon long walk back to horses. Then back into billets farm near Watou at 9 p.m. Kindness to refugees. Always given best place, not to be disturbed. Lots of boys selling chocolate to troops. Horses, their patience. Mule instead of our lost (shelled) horse, running with horses in limber.

Tuesday 29th. Moved off 8 a.m. towards Pop. Brigade rested in field. Rested all day, and got back to our farm at 7.30 p.m. Pork chops for dinner. Wonderful sunny lazy days – but longing to be up and doing something. Slept out. Wrote poem – 'Into Battle'.

The poem that Julian wrote – two weeks before he was wounded and four weeks before he died, against the above background of confusion and randomness and waiting – is almost unique amongst poems of the First World War in that it shows no outrage against war and yet its luminousness and serenity do not seem false. Because it is a poem about love of life in time of war, it was once much loved; later, when there was peace and life was again loved less, it was loved less too.

INTO BATTLE

The naked earth is warm with spring,
And with green grass and bursting trees
Leans to the sun's kiss glorying,
And quivers in the loving breeze;
And Life is Colour and Warmth and Light
And a striving evermore for these;
And he is dead who will not fight;
And who dies fighting has increase.

The fighting man shall from the sun
Take warmth, and life from the glowing earth;
Speed with the light-foot winds to run,
And with the trees a newer birth;
And when his fighting shall be done,
Great rest, and fulness after dearth.

All the bright company of Heaven
Hold him in their high comradeship –
The Dog-star and the Sisters Seven,
Orion's belt and sworded hip.

The woodland trees that stand together,
They stand to him each one a friend;
They gently speak in the windy weather,
They guide to valley and ridge's end.

The kestrel hovering by day,
And the little owls that call by night,
Bid him be swift and keen as they –
As keen of sound, as swift of sight.

The blackbird sings to him 'Brother, brother,
If this be the last song you shall sing,
Sing well, for you will not sing another;
Brother, sing!'

In dreary doubtful waiting hours,
Before the brazen frenzy starts,
The horses show him nobler powers;
O patient eyes, courageous hearts!

And when the burning moment breaks,
And all things else are out of mind,
And Joy of Battle only takes
Him by the throat, and makes him blind –

Through joy and blindness he shall know,
Not caring much to know, that still
Nor lead nor steel shall reach him so
That it be not the Destined Will.

The thundering line of battle stands,
And in the air Death moans and sings;
And Day shall clasp him with strong hands,
And Night shall fold him in soft wings.

Julian copied out this poem, signed it 'J.G. Belgium – April 1915' and
sent it to his mother. He wrote 'I rather like it'. He told her she could
try to get it published if she liked.

For another week Julian and his regiment waited in the fields occasionally being shelled and occasionally moving closer to the fighting and then away. He saw gas casualties coming into a dressing station – the 'shattered' look both of 'the wounded and the men going back'. He did shadow-boxing and exercises to keep himself fit. In the beautiful weather he slept out and listened to the nightingales. One of his greyhounds was run over by a bus and he had to shoot it. The rifle with the telescopic sight arrived from his father and he tried it out on a target. He wrote in his diary – 'Plato's idea of happiness realised – no personal property or ties, just as ready to move or to stay'.

On 8 May he wrote to his mother –

Thank you awfully for your letters, you will be finishing your fortnight's Waiting now? . . . The men *did* love the things so much – the lighters and the lamps and the chocolate and the cigarettes. I just had time to throw them to the troop as we were starting off somewhere loaded up with every kind of weapon and ammunition; they said 'Ho Lord, we'll 'ave to put this in our mouths'; but always managed to stow them away somewhere.

There had been a plan that his mother and father should come out to France and visit Monica at her hospital near Boulogne; also possibly get up to see General Pulteney at his headquarters of the Third Division. Julian wrote –

It will be the greatest fun if you get up to Putty or if I can get down to Boulogne. But I imagine it will be difficult to get leave from now onwards. But we *must* fix it somehow. Poor Casie, I expect she is working plenty just now . . .

I'm so glad you liked the verses, because I liked them a lot; although I thought afterwards that they were slightly meretricious, due no doubt to a recent visit to Paris and the earlier influences of other people; but 'good meretricious', which is after all no bad quality. Yes, send them to *The Times* . . .

The long dogs were very good when I got back here. A kind woman at the farm kept them and fed them for me. We arrived in the middle of the night, and when they heard my voice they came out into the yard like shrapnel bursting. *Comrade* jumped up on to the horse's shoulder; and when he fell back they all started fighting like hell from sheer joy.

The next day the regiment moved towards the line again.

Sunday May 9th. Standing to at ½ hour's notice, saddled up from 8 a.m. At 10.30 ordered to turn out at once, dismounted. Buses arrived. Moved off 12 noon. 21 men per troop. 150 rounds. No news. Thought we were last hope of Empire, being last reserve. 'Iron Ration' – Houses of Parliament. Thought certain to fight. Joy. Summer day but bitter cold – summer clothes. Arrived Vlamertinghe 3.30 p.m. and marched ½ mile up Brielen road. Billeted in wooden huts. Men under coats and blankets all right always. No food, but what matter.

Monday 10th. Rations arrived 2.15 a.m. Too cold to sleep. 75s in field next us. German shells not very close. Dug dug-outs for ourselves in morning in case of shell fire. Heard of French v. successful attack at Arras, our unsuccessful attack at Aubers Ridge. Our Ypres troops going back slowly but holding Huns. 5 Hun attacks yesterday. Aeroplanes all day. Huns better than ours. How we lie. 2nd Cav Brigade sent up to trenches for counter-attack. Good omen. Cav shld be used like that.

Tuesday 11th. Aeroplanes all day. Huns better than ours. Ours do not go forward much. Moved off 7.30 to support trenches 27th Division wood next railway E of H in Halte, next field where we lost horses shelled. Walked through outskirts of Ypres *blazing* in summer night; stink, rotting horses and men. Drew rations on road and got into trench 11.30 p.m. Detachments of Argyll and S's and Royal Fusiliers, dead beat, in our trench.

Wednesday 12th. *Wandering* infantry. Say that front trenches shelled v. badly. Hardly any of our guns fire up here.

This was the last entry in Julian's diary. The story of what happened that day, and the next, was discovered by Ettie and Willy from the accounts of friends.

By 12 May the Allied line had withdrawn to within two miles of Ypres. The Sixth Cavalry Brigade, in which were Julian's First Royal Dragoons, were in the second line of trenches between Hooge Lake and a railway line half a mile to the north. There was a small rise in the ground, called Railway Hill, and which Julian called 'the little hill of death'. At 4 am on 13 May, which was Ascension Day, the Germans started a heavy bombardment of the trenches and the hill; there was no counter-fire from the Allied guns, and the troops to the north of the Cavalry Brigade retreated. The Royals were told to keep a watch from Railway Hill to see if the Germans were advancing round their flank. At noon Julian went up on the hill – it was on this sort of occasion that he used to 'stroll around', as General Pulteney said, 'as if he were on a river' – and he was knocked down by a shell, but only his coat was torn. He brought back information that the Germans were coming round the flank. He volunteered to take a message through to the Somerset Yeomanry in the trenches in front. A company commander in the Somerset Yeomanry remembered

Julian walking up to him under heavy fire and introducing himself – 'You once gave me a mount with the Belvoir Hounds'. Julian brought back further messages; then went up Railway Hill again with the General in command of the Brigade. A shell landed a few yards from them, and both Julian and the General were hit. Julian said 'Go on down, I'm done'. But the General, who was only slightly wounded, helped Julian down the hill. Julian had a splinter of shell in his head.

He was so cheerful that people did not think his wound was serious. He said 'I think I shall die'. When a friend remonstrated with him he said 'You see if I don't!' He was taken to a dressing station, and it was still thought that his wound was not serious enough to prevent him being sent to England. He wrote a letter to his mother while at the Casualty Clearing Station: it is strongly written in pencil, and stained with blood. It was forwarded to Ettie by the chaplain at the Clearing Station, who explained that in the condition in which the envelope had been given to him it had not been safe to post.

May 14th 1915

Darling Mother,

Isn't it wonderful and glorious that at last after long waiting the Cavalry have put it across the Boches on their flat feet and have pulled the frying pan out of the fire for the second time. Good old 'iron ration'! We are practically wiped out, but we charged and took the Hun trenches yesterday. I stopped a Jack Johnson with my head, and my skull is slightly cracked. But I'm getting on splendidly. I did awfully well. Today I go down to Wimereux, to hospital, shall you be there? *All all* love.

Julian of the 'Ard 'Ead.
Longing to see you and *talk!!*
Bless you!

❧ THIRTY–THREE ❧

Julian was sent to a hospital at Boulogne, and Monica came to see him from Wimereux next door. She sent a telegram to her father and mother on 15 May saying that Julian had been wounded but there was no cause for anxiety: they should cancel the arrangements that had now been made for them to embark for Boulogne, because Julian would be sent back to England. On the morning of the 16th they got Julian's letter written from the Casualty Clearing Station: they waited at Taplow to hear news of his return. On the same day, in Boulogne, Julian was X-rayed, and it was discovered that his wound was far more serious than had been supposed. The shell splinter had gone one and a half inches through his skull, and there was damage to the brain. An operation was performed, which was successful, but it was said that it would not be known for eleven days whether he would live or die.

Monica sent another telegram to her father and mother telling them to come at once as had been planned. They got permission from the Admiralty to cross the Channel that same night on an ammunition boat. They arrived at Boulogne at 5 am and went to the hospital and found Monica with Julian. It pleased Julian that his father and mother had reached him half a day before anyone had thought it possible that they could.

Julian was in a room with three other badly wounded officers. Ettie and Willy stayed in lodgings in the town. Ettie found herself in the position that she had been in before, and would be in again, of having to wait a number of days before she knew whether or not someone she loved was dying.

Julian was conscious, but he was told he should not speak much. He wanted to talk of the fighting. It was not true, as he had imagined, that the Royals had charged and taken the German trenches: but they had held on, and in fact the Germans made no more advances around Ypres that year.

The Royals had suffered great casualties; only three officers were left out of fifteen. It had been a battle of gas and gunfire against men; and no one had won.

Julian's cheerfulness continued to give the impression that he could not be as ill as he was. One of his doctors wrote later of his being 'extraordinary good company even on his death bed'. But Julian told Ettie, privately, that his journey from the front to the hospital had been terrible.

On 20 May Billy arrived at Boulogne with his battalion of the Rifle Brigade and was given a day's leave to visit Julian. He said he thought that it looked as if Julian might die. When Billy left to go to the front, Julian said 'I'm glad there was no gap'. That evening Billy wrote the first of his happy, absorbed letters on active service that were like Julian's – 'It has been such glorious golden weather: Hobbemas on every side as we march along!'

Ettie had a bulletin about Julian's progress typed to send to her friends: 'He is *quite sensible* when he speaks, and very quiet. His temperature and pulse are very good. There is no paralysis at present, and he has not been sick . . .' She wrote to Maurice Baring who was with the Flying Corps – 'Julian is terribly wounded . . . come to me if you can' – and she signed it S, which stood for his old name for her, Sottise. People in England rang up Taplow for the latest news: the Queen telegraphed 'Trust Julian's condition is satisfactory so far'; and Winston Churchill – 'Deeply sorry for your anxiety'. George Curzon sent, with his messages of sympathy, news of the political crisis at home: Winston Churchill was having to leave the Cabinet after the failure of the Dardanelles expedition and a Coalition Government was being formed. Evan Charteris and John Revelstoke wrote to Ettie every day. Imogen wrote 'Do try and make Juju well': and Ivo 'I'm sure Julian's wonderful bravery and calmness will pull him through'. Betty Montgomery reminded Ettie of a 'terrible presentiment of danger' that Ettie had had about Julian and Billy the day before Julian had been wounded: Betty described this scene later as –

the morning in May when I was with you in the London Hotel and you suddenly burst into tears and cried out 'Oh! I am so frightened about them!' and then a few minutes later with wondrous courage you lifted up your head, dried your eyes, and with a strange wonderful smile said 'Well, they could not do more than die for their country – since the days of Athens.'

Marjorie Anglesey wrote to Ettie –

I crave if you, or any of yours, have a minute, to send me news of Julian's progress?

and if he is well enough, will you give him my love? I think of your mortal anxiety every minute, and pray on my knees for his dear curly head to be well and out of pain.

For a time Julian did seem to be better: he sat up in bed and ate brioches and ice creams. Being fed by his mother, he remarked – 'the right way to eat is to swallow enormous mouthfuls of food washed down by huge gulps of liquid'. And when she did not contradict him, he said – 'Why don't you *argue*, Mummy?' One morning when Monica came into the room, he said – 'Here is the girl with sunshine in her hair, the sunshine lingering in her hair'.

On the morning of 23 May, which was Whit Sunday, he said he was much better, and he took Holy Communion with his mother and father. Just after this the doctors discovered he had further inflammation of the brain, and they operated on him again immediately. Then he was in pain. He lay still, and would sometimes say his father's name, and when Willy replied he would say 'Good'. On Monday the pain was less and he said to his mother – 'Did they really think I was going off my rocker?' He said to Monica – 'That second operation was very nearly the end of I'.

During the next three days one or other of his family were always with him – he was now in a room on his own – and they told him of how well he had fought, and how they would take him to get well in the forests by the sea in Normandy. They talked to him of old holidays, in Scotland or at Panshanger; of an enormous fish he had once caught. He once clasped his mother's hand and she said to him 'That is what you do when you are asleep and you think I am going away' and he said 'No, it is only affection'. He said to his father when one of his arms began to be paralysed 'Take my hand in your two strong hands and rub my poor arm'; and when his father did this and he groaned, he explained – 'It is only contentment'.

He liked to have poetry read to him, and sometimes said poetry to himself. Of his own poems he liked to say 'The Fighting Boar'. He also said his favourite speech from Euripides' *Hippolytus*, in which Phaedra laments that she cannot be like her stepson. He prayed, mostly childhood prayers – those about which he had sometimes been ironical.

It was Ettie who wrote the day-to-day account of Julian's time in hospital; and it was Ettie's way to insist that there was no sadness nor fear about death. She insisted on this now – 'The thought that he was dying seemed to go and come but he always seemed radiantly happy and he never saw any of the people he loved look sad'. But it is likely that

Julian did in fact, when dying, behave and feel as his mother had always so much hoped he would behave and feel. He now had no quarrel with her.

In Julian's wallet when he had been wounded, together with the letter from Peggy and the two photographs, was an extract from a poem of George Meredith's; typewritten on flimsy paper, and smeared with blood –

> Oh, Mother Earth, teach me like thee
> To kiss the season and shun regrets.
>   Teach me to blot regrets
>   Great Mother! me inspire
>   With faith that forward sets
> But feeds the living fire,
>   Faith that never frets
>   For vagueness in the form.
>   In life, O keep me warm!
>   For, what is human grief?
>   And what do men desire?
> Teach me to feel myself the tree,
>   And not the withered leaf.
>
> Fixed am I and await the dark to-be.
>   And O, green bounteous Earth
> Bacchante Mother! stern to those
> Who live not in thy heart of mirth;
> Death shall I shrink from, loving thee?
> Into the breast that gives the rose,
>   Shall I with shuddering fall?
>
> She can lead us, only she,
> Unto God's footstool, whither she reaches:
> Loved, enjoyed, her gifts must be,
> Reverenced the truths she teaches,
> Ere a man may hope that he
> Ever can attain the glee
> Of things without a destiny!

On 25 May Julian said to Monica 'Goodbye Casie'; and to his mother – 'Hold my hand till I go'. Ettie saw how 'a shaft of sunlight came in at the darkened window and fell across his feet'. He smiled at her and said 'Phoebus Apollo'. After that – 'He did not speak again, except once, to say his father's name'.

He lived on during the day of 26 May, his mother and father and sister staying with him. Then – 'at twenty minutes to four in the afternoon . . . he moved his mother's hand to his lips. At the moment that he died, he opened his eyes a little with the most radiant smile that they had ever seen even on his face'.

The next day, together with the news of his death, there was published in *The Times* his poem, 'Into Battle'.

Julian was buried in the soldiers' cemetery on the hill above Boulogne. No one wore mourning for him. His mother covered his grave with wild flowers and oak leaves.

Billy came to Boulogne on 29 May and spent the afternoon with his family. Monica met him and he asked her how their mother was and Monica said she had been very weak, but now was stronger. Billy, climbing a sand dune, said 'She must be strong if she got up here'. Billy went back to the trenches that day, and his family never saw him again.

Ivo, from Eton, wrote 'God bless Julian for all his wonderful life on earth and for the joy he has been to us all'. Imogen, aged ten, wrote 'I am glad that he is at peace and did his duty'.

Maurice Baring wrote a sonnet for Julian, which was published in *The Times*: and other people wrote poems in honour of Julian's poem: and there were hundreds of letters to Ettie saying how terrible Julian's death was but there was nothing finer to be hoped for: 'To live greatly and to die soon is a lot which all must admire and some of us envy: indeed to my thinking it cannot be bettered' (Arthur Balfour); 'He was all that you could have desired and all that our race needs to keep its honour fair and bright . . . He at any rate lived and died as he would have wished' (Winston Churchill).

Pamela Lytton wrote 'I loved him deeply, honoured him, admired him. I loved him for my children too, and his sweetness to them. I looked forward to him always'. Marjorie Anglesey wrote 'I feel so *tired*, Ettie, that's what life has done for me, just tired me out. Can you sleep?'

Ettie was ill for a time with a poisoned eye: she alternated between her resolute cheerfulness, and despair. It was at this time that people wrote of her as being like a heroine in tragedy – 'and one does not offer consolation to heroines of Greek Tragedy' (Raymond Asquith). She gave the impression both of helplessness, and of the determination that this should not be so.

Billy was killed on 30 July, leading a charge near Hooge, within a mile of where Julian had been wounded. He had written – 'I pray that one tenth of his gay spirit may descend on me'. He was killed in one of the mass attacks which he, and indeed everyone, his Colonel said, 'knew was almost certain death'. Billy wrote – 'Death is such a frail barrier out here that men cross it smilingly and gallantly every day'. In two months' fighting he had achieved a reputation something like Julian's; also for his own 'humour, his original views on all subjects, and his quaint ways'. His body, in the carnage around Ypres, was buried, lost, and never re-discovered.

Ettie began to write the Family Journal which was to be her memorial to Julian and Billy; and her assurance to others and herself that in spite of appearances there was still no darkness nor sorrow. The sentences that she added to Julian's letters were usually to do with what he might have remembered of her when he had loved her as a boy; in the woods at Taplow, or on the road to Eton.

Ettie's Family Journal was privately circulated and was of great comfort to most of her friends. Maurice Baring wrote 'It sums up all that is best of England, and English things, like a Constable landscape or a speech in Shakespeare'. Evan Charteris wrote 'You have done with your sons what no one has ever done before, and raised to them with your own hands a memorial of perpetual beauty'.

Marjorie Anglesey wrote to her own mother – '*I*, of course, don't like it *at all*, in any sense or way. It is so pathetic the way parents see their children in quite a different character from what the rest of the world – or at least *some* of the rest of the world – see them'.

Ettie altered two or three words in Julian's poem 'Into Battle'; putting 'ear' instead of 'sound' in the fifth stanza; 'may' instead of 'will' in the sixth; and replacing 'loving' by 'sunny', which Julian had crossed out, in the first.

Julian's poem made him loved by many people who had never known him. Henry James wrote of

those extraordinarily living and breathing, ringing and stinging, verses . . . I seem almost to have known your splendid son even though that ravaged felicity hadn't come my way . . . What great and terrible and unspeakable things! but out of which, round his sublime young image, a noble and exquisite legend will flower.

In the poem by George Meredith which was found in Julian's wallet when he was wounded, two lines had been left out when it had been typed, probably by Ettie. These were –

> And am I more than the mother who bore,
> Mock me not with thy harmony!

The last words that Julian spoke to Ettie – 'Phoebus Apollo' – were recorded by Ettie with delight. But Phoebus Apollo is the god, though of the sun, whose irradiating powers have not yet separated from destructiveness; whom mortals still use for justification.

Ettie's third son, Ivo, died after a motor accident in 1926. He was driving home to the farm where he lived late one night and the steering of his car seemed to fail, and his head, as he leaned over the side of the car, was struck against a wall. He lay in hospital for thirteen days, with his family round him. Ettie wrote of 'the exact replica of the Boulogne days eleven years ago'; of 'every wound torn open and bleeding together'; of Ivo's 'smiling back with his lovely look of love and trust, undismayed to the end'. There were also memories, she wrote to a friend, of the death of Archie Gordon.

Willy lived to the age of eighty-nine and died in 1945. People wrote of him – 'He was the only man whose actual appearance had the quality of ennobling those with him'; and 'I do not believe that in his own chosen way there has ever been a greater Englishman'.

Ettie lived till 1952 and died at the age of eighty-four. An obituary letter in *The Times* spoke of 'the years before 1914 when she held a position in the world of wit and fashion that nobody has occupied since'; also of her as 'a lady of great age, lying half paralysed in a huge empty house, and saying with the heart-rending ghost of a gay smile "We did have fun, didn't we?" '

Ettie had carefully preserved all Julian's letters to her, even the ones she had not liked. She, like he, had known that life was a battle.

☙ INDEX ☙

Bradley, F. H., 117
Brooke, Rupert, 208, 250
Buller, General Sir Redvers Henry, 66

Campbell, Mrs Patrick, 56
Carson, Sir Edward, 216
Cavendish, Lord Frederick, 69
Cecil, Lord Hugh, 'Linky', 1869–1956.
Fifth son of third Marquess of Salisbury.
Conservative M.P. 1895–1906 and 1910–
37. Created Lord Quickswood 1941, 185,
231, 232
Cézanne, Paul, 192
Chamberlain, Joseph, 102n.
Charteris, Lady Cynthia, 1887–1960.
Eldest daughter of Hugo, Lord Elcho, and
Mary Elcho. Married in 1910 Herbert
Asquith, second son of H. H. Asquith,
95, 96, 213
Charteris, Hon. Evan, 1864–1940. Son of
tenth Earl of Wemyss. Brother of Hugo,
Lord Elcho. Married 1930 Lady Edward
Grosvenor. Knighted 1932, 15, 17, 54–9,
74–5, 86, 116, 127, 213, 231–2, 245,
262, 266; *et passim*
Charteris, Hugo Francis 'Ego', later Lord
Elcho, 1884–1916. Eldest son of Hugo,
Lord Elcho, later eleventh Earl of
Wemyss. Married in 1911 Lady Violet
'Letty' Manners, 232
Charteris, Ivo Alan, 1896–1915. Second
son of Hugo and Mary Elcho, 232
Chesterton, Gilbert Keith, 213
Churchill, Lady Randolph. Jennie Jerome,
daughter of Leonard Jerome of New York.
Married first 1874, Lord Randolph
Churchill, son of seventh Duke of
Marlborough, 19, 21, 31–2, 41
Churchill, Winston Spencer, 76, 175, 188,
262, 265
Compton, Lord Alwyne Frederick, 1855–
1911. Third son of fourth Marquess
of Northampton. Brother of Douglas
Compton and of Katie Cowper, Ettie
Desborough's aunt by marriage, 25, 98
Compton, Lord Douglas James Cecil, 1865-

1944. Fourth son of fourth Marquess of
Northampton. Brother of Katie Cowper,
Ettie Desborough's aunt by marriage.
Served in South African War 1899–1902,
25–6, 48–50, 81, 98, 109
Compton, Lady Katrine Cecilia, *see* Cowper,
Lady Katrine Cecilia
Cowper, Lady Adine, *see* Fane, Lady Adine
Cowper, Anne Florence 'Pammy', Countess
Cowper. Daughter of second Earl de Grey.
Married 1833 sixth Earl Cowper. Mother
of seventh Earl, and of Adine Fane, Ettie
Desborough's mother. Died 1880, 4
Cowper, Lady Florence Annabel, *see* Herbert,
Lady Florence
Cowper, Francis Thomas de Grey, seventh
Earl Cowper, 1834–1905. Eldest brother
of Adine Fane, Ettie Desborough's
mother. Married in 1870 Katrine Cecilia
'Katie' Compton, daughter of fourth Mar-
quess of Northampton Lord Lieutenant
of Ireland 1880–82, 5, 15, 24, 40, 100
Cowper, Hon. Henry Frederick, 1836–87.
Second son of sixth Earl Cowper and
brother of seventh Earl and of Adine
Fane, Ettie Desborough's mother. M.P.
for Hertfordshire 1865–85, 5, 10, 97
Cowper, Lady Katrine Cecilia, 'Katie'.
Eldest daughter of fourth Marquess of
Northampton. Married 1870 seventh
Earl Cowper, Ettie Desborough's uncle.
Died 1913, 5, 6, 12, 15, 24, 25, 40, 144,
170, 175, 177–8, 218
Crewe, Earl of, 80
Cunard, Nancy, 245
Curzon, George, first Marquess Curzon of
Kedleston, 1859–1925. Eldest son of
fourth Baron Scarsdale. Under-Secretary
of State for Foreign Affairs 1895–98.
Viceroy of India 1899–1905. Lord Presi-
dent of the Council 1916–19. Secretary of
State for Foreign Affairs 1919–24. Mar-
ried 1895 Mary Victoria Leiter of
Washington, U.S.A., 15, 16, 17, 21, 23–
24, 38, 52, 76, 103, 104, 185–6, 224, 262
Cust, Henry, 'Harry', 1861–1917. Great-